Marianne Moore

Marianne Moore at home in Brooklyn, about 1935

Laurence Stapleton

MARIANNE MOORE

The Poet's Advance

PRINCETON UNIVERSITY PRESS

Copyright © 1978 by Laurence Stapleton

Published by Princeton University Press,
Princeton, New Jersey
In the United Kingdom: Princeton University Press,
Guildford, Surrey

All Rights Reserved

Library of Congress Cataloging in Publication Data will
be found on the last printed page of this book

This book has been composed in linotype Baskerville
and designed by Laury A. Egan

Printed in the United States of America
by Princeton University Press, Princeton, New Jersey

Second printing, with corrections, 1979

CONTENTS

LIST OF ILLUSTRATIONS

ACKNOWLEDGMENTS

QUOTATIONS from *Selected Poems* by Marianne Moore, copyright © 1935, by Marianne Moore, renewed 1963 by Marianne Moore and T. S. Eliot. Reprinted with permission of Macmillan Publishing Co., Inc. and Faber and Faber, Ltd.

Quotations from *Collected Poems* by Marianne Moore, copyright © 1941, 1944, 1951; renewed 1969, 1972 by Marianne Moore. Reprinted by permission of Macmillan Publishing Co., Inc. and Faber and Faber, Ltd.

Quotations from *The Fables of La Fontaine* translated by Marianne Moore, copyright © 1952, 1953, 1954, 1964 by Marianne Moore. Reprinted by permission of The Viking Press and Faber and Faber, Ltd.

Quotations from *The Complete Poems* of Marianne Moore, copyright © 1956, 1959, 1966, by Marianne Moore. Reprinted by permission of The Viking Press and Faber and Faber, Ltd.

Quotation from *The Waste Land* by T. S. Eliot, copyright © by T. S. Eliot. Reprinted by permission of Harcourt Brace Jovanovich and Faber and Faber, Ltd.

Quotation from "Peter Quince at the Clavier" in *The Collected Poems of Wallace Stevens*, copyright © Wallace Stevens 1923, 1954. Reprinted by permission of Alfred A. Knopf, Inc.

Quotation from "Still Falls the Rain" in *The Collected Poems of Edith Sitwell*, copyright © Dame Edith Sitwell 1949, 1953, 1954, 1959, 1962, 1963, 1968. Reprinted by permission of The Vanguard Press, Inc.

Quotations from hitherto uncollected poems by Marianne Moore by permission of Clive E. Driver, Literary Executor of the Estate of Marianne C. Moore and of *The New Yorker*: "Mercifully," © 1968 The New Yorker Magazine, Inc.; "Enough," © 1970 The New Yorker Magazine,

ACKNOWLEDGMENTS

Inc.; "The Magician's Retreat," © 1970 The New Yorker Magazine, Inc.

Quotation from letter of T. S. Eliot to Marianne Moore, copyright © by Valerie Eliot. Reprinted by her permission.

I acknowledge here also the aid of a grant from the Penrose Fund of the American Philosophical Society.

The frontispiece and the photographs of the drawings of the Malay Dragon and the Plumet Basilisk are reproduced by courtesy of the Philip H. and A.S.W. Rosenbach Foundation.

PREFACE

My hope is that this study of Marianne Moore's poetry will lead to greater understanding of her work as a whole. There have been a number of searching and intelligent essays about her qualities of imagination. But compared to the attention bestowed upon Pound, Eliot, Stevens, and Williams, inquiries into the whole range and variety of her creative effort have been meager and few.

To take but one example, the first volume of an extensive history of modern poetry treats the early development of her chief contemporaries in some detail, and promises discussion of their later books for the next volume. But Marianne Moore is left behind as a writer whose accomplishment belongs to the first third of this century. This disregards the fact that some of her most memorable poems were written after 1940, and even in the following decades. The changes, and continuing experimentation in her writing, deserve a more accurate view. One reason for the tendency to look upon her poetry as a specialty, rather than a generative power for the future, may be her own "recourse to the mathematics of art," as William Carlos Williams expressed it.

When Marianne Moore referred to her poems as "exercises in composition," she was not underestimating them. Her charm and verve were so remarkable that, when she had become well-known, audiences would listen to a reading of hers without complaining about the lines they let slip past them. She had become a public figure who lent grace to an unrelenting time in American life. Reading her poems in Central Park, in the Boston Public Gardens, in a college auditorium, she captivated her listeners. But that does not mean that many of them returned to her books, and gave new attention to, let us say, "The Octopus," or "Virginia Britannia" or "The Plumet Basilisk." These were not the pieces she would choose for an appearance in the Public Gardens. She was well aware of what could be enjoyed, and comprehended to some degree, on these occasions.

The best of her exercises in composition, like those of great musical composers, or lesser but genuine ones like Purcell or Charles Ives, deserve the kind of study that engages all our faculties. To take part in that and as far as I can to initiate it in others is one of my aims.

I have not attempted to give a biographical account of Marianne Moore. Some day, if a real biographer undertakes it, there may be a Life and Letters of Marianne Moore that could be as gripping as the life of Dr. Johnson. It is to be hoped, in any case, that her complete letters and the principal notebooks will be published. In this book, the study of her poetry is based primarily upon the poems themselves, but relies on the knowledge gained from the notebooks, drafts of poems, and correspondence. The ideas presented here about the poems are set in the context of her life as a writer. To be a writer was for her in the best sense a calling—she could not resist it, and committed to it her mind and heart. But her experience and training made writing a profession, also. To give a true even if incomplete description of a writer at work is the only way to see how life's circumstances made it possible to write particular poems, or sometimes defeated expectations.

Ezra Pound, T. S. Eliot, and William Carlos Williams all had close relationships as writers with Marianne Moore. All of them respected what she wrote and spurred her on. It is only fair to say that she aided their efforts as much as they did hers. Wallace Stevens likewise, although more indirectly, had an effect upon her writing and was the beneficiary of her critical insight. In the course of this book I have kept these literary relationships in view, as they affected her emerging identity. Since plans are under way for the publication of her correspondence with Pound and with

Eliot, I have not drawn upon these letters except in a few instances. Her association with younger writers needs to be described, but should, I feel, be left to those writers themselves.

That she wrote prose as unusual as her poetry has almost escaped general notice. In the third chapter, a consideration of her critical and other prose writing attempts to stimulate wider reading of the prose as soon as an enterprising publisher brings out a more substantial collection. *Predilections*, which includes some but by no means all of her best pieces, has long been out of print.

Marianne Moore's relationship with her mother and with her brother played a major part in her life as a writer. The future biographer will portray this in the round, we shall hope. For the reader of this book, a few things should be set down here. The first is that after her brother became a chaplain in the U. S. Navy, Marianne lived with and looked after her mother until the latter's death in 1947. In fact she rarely was away overnight. They went on vacation together, traveled to England and France in 1911, and again to England in 1927. They also worked together, in that Mrs. Moore cast her sharply critical eye on her daughter's poems and prose, and often assisted in getting material ready for the press.

Warner Moore did everything in his power to aid his mother and sister, to sustain them and divert them, to encourage in every possible way. His long absences on sea duty, or when stationed in distant places like San Francisco or Bremerton or Samoa, account for the many letters that went to and fro. But few families are such ardent letter-writers—the Moores wrote to each other almost daily, and it seems to have been understood that Warner would keep the letters that Marianne wrote to him. Of the thousands now in the Marianne Moore archive at the Rosenbach Foundation, I have read chiefly those having a bearing on her literary work; but no letters are restricted solely to that; and even the portion I have read register a clear impression of their relationship. I believe that Warner Moore was closer to his sister than anyone else was.

The Moores were all of them witty and fanciful people, and shared a fascination with animals. Even in early letters they give each other special names, Mrs. Moore addressing Warner sometimes as "Dear Toady," and signing herself "Turtle," Marianne writing to "Dear Biter" or "Fish" and signing herself "Fangs." A letter from her in 1907 is written to "Dear Mouse, Fish and Beaver from Biter Dog." In that era, it was not uncommon, apparently, for people to adopt these animal names. Virginia Woolf, for example, in early letters signed herself as "Goat" or "Sparroy" and after she married wrote to Leonard as "Dear Mongoose."

After the publication of *The Wind in the Willows* in 1908, the Moores' most frequently used names were "Mole" for Mrs. Moore, "Rat" for Marianne, and "Badger" for Warner. There were many later variations, but these three names indicate the rôles that they chose for themselves. Rat is the poet in *The Wind in the Willows* "singing a little song" and as he "had just composed it himself, so he was very taken up with it, and would not pay proper attention to Mole or anything else." Badger, the strong protector, is the "best of fellows! But you must not only take him *as* you find him, but *when* you find him." And Mole of course was the homebody, starting out on adventures with the others, but "eagerly anticipating the moment he would be at home again among the things he knew and liked." By using these and other animal names, the Moores in their correspondence dramatized their lives; ordinary things like cooking a meal or going shopping are relieved of routine; Rat and Badger are able to reassure one another, to be satirical so as not to be sentimental, to protect themselves by pretending to be minor creatures allied in the face of danger.

Some of Marianne Moore's notebooks extend these reports of day-to-day activities beyond the family circle—the conversation notebooks, especially. There are three kinds of notebooks especially pertinent to the study of her poetry and prose. The first group are reading diaries, as she labeled them, nineteen of them now inventoried, beginning in 1907. The most complete ones go up to 1943, and were indexed by her. After that entries are more sporadic; but the process went on until 1969. One sees in the early reading diaries, where she copied many extracts from book reviews or passages from books of literary history, the shaping of a literary intelligence. More important are entries—sometimes only a few sentences—that found a place in her poems.

The early conversation notebooks contain the sayings of many of her friends in the group of writers she became associated with after 1916—poets and painters and critics, the editors of the *Dial* and others in their circle. "Badger" is often there, Mrs. Moore's comments and Marianne's also are sometimes recorded. After the *Dial* years, the conversation notebooks are mainly the sayings of Mrs. Moore, with interpolations, restatements, and revisions by Marianne.

Of poetry workbooks I have examined five, all that have been inventoried so far. Two are of great value, the others sketchier and containing lines for poems interspersed with other material. In effect the conversation notebooks from 1932 to 1947 are also poetry workbooks.

A problem to be reckoned with—not unfamiliar to anyone who has read the notebooks of Coleridge, Emerson, and Thoreau—is the overlapping of dates and the fact that notebooks intended for one purpose may be at times converted to another. But these are problems for her future editors to analyze. Here, I wish to make only one or two points clear to the reader. The first is that Marianne Moore intended most of her notebooks for professional use. She kept them in a special place in her library. When writing, she had in her writing desk the particular ones needed. The second is that the dates printed on the various kinds of diaries or engagement books that she kept have no bearing on the time when the entries were made. Thus a notebook bearing the date 1864 (long before she was born, of course) contains entries from 1915 to 1919.

In most cases she made entries on the recto and verso of the cover, on preliminary undated pages, and on end pages for cash accounts, etc. Although I have examined all the notebooks I have used, my work with them has been carried on, necessarily, with photocopies. Therefore, the numbering of the pages given in my notes begins with the first page (or the cover) on which anything is written. Likewise, the numbering corresponds to the photocopy page, which is of the verso and recto of the notebook leaves (see Figure 2).

Quotations from the notebooks and correspondence are emended rarely and minimally and only for the sake of intelligibility. That is, incomplete punctuation is completed, when quotation marks in the manuscript are confusing. If a word or letter of a word is supplied by me, it appears in brackets. Words crossed out in either the notebooks or the letters are omitted.

For scholars of this or later generations, and all serious students of this poet's accomplishment, it is fortunate that her many notebooks, the bulk of her correspondence, her manuscripts and library are housed together at the Museum of the Philip H. and A.S.W. Rosenbach Foundation in Philadelphia. I am deeply indebted to the trustees of the Foundation for permission to use material from the archive in their possession. I owe more than thanks to Clive E. Driver, Director of the Foundation and Literary Executor of the Estate of Marianne C. Moore for permission to quote from her letters and other unpublished papers. Mr. Driver has generously granted his own time to discuss questions of many kinds affecting the interpretation and dating of this material. His devotion to Marianne Moore's achievement and desire for a true understanding of it has made these discussions enlightening; and his courtesy has been a constant aid on my visits to the Museum. He has read the entire manuscript of this book with great care, and thereby helped me to eliminate some errors. (For any that remain he is of course not responsible.)

Likewise, I wish to thank and to acknowledge the help of Mrs. Suzanne Bolan, Assistant Director, and of Ann Bolan and Mrs. Patricia C. Willis of the staff.

Copyright on all unpublished material belongs to the Moore Estate, and cannot be quoted without permission of Clive E. Driver, Literary Executor.

For permission to quote from the Scofield Thayer-Marianne Moore correspondence in the *Dial* archive deposited in the Collection of American Literature, Beinecke Rare Book and Manuscript Collection, Yale University, I wish to thank Donald Gallup, Curator of the Collection. Equally, I am indebted to John L. Clark, Esq. and to his predecessor the late Charles P. Williamson, Esq., representatives of Scofield Thayer, for permission to quote from the Thayer-Moore correspondence and to examine other material in the *Dial* collection at Yale.

The chapter on Marianne Moore's translation of *The Fables of La Fontaine* would have been impoverished if I had not been granted the permission of Professor Harry Levin to quote from his correspondence with her. I wish to thank him not only for that, but for his kindness in undertaking to read that chapter.

Many others have been of special assistance to me, among whom I must single out James E. Tanis, Director of Libraries at Bryn Mawr College, and members of the staff of Canaday Library; Emily Wallace Harvey, who was my research associate in work on the *Dial* papers; Kathrin Platt, my research assistant; and several Bryn Mawr College colleagues who answered questions ranging from the habits of the sea unicorn to Platonic philosophy to the early teaching of biology and of the history of art at Bryn Mawr College—Mary S. Gardiner, Myra Uhlfelder, Bruce Saunders, Charles Mitchell, and Willard King. I wish to add special thanks to Hildegarde and Sibley Watson for sharing with me their long friendship with Marianne Moore; Dr. Watson has clarified several questions.

Marianne Moore's niece and namesake, Marianne C. Moore, has generously granted permission to reproduce an early draft of "Propriety" and to quote from one of her aunt's letters to her. And S. E. Moore with equal kindness has allowed me to reproduce her copyright photograph of Ezra Pound and Marianne Moore. I am grateful to them both for help in other ways, as well.

I have saved for the last my thanks to the committee that nominated me for a fellowship from the National Endowment for the Arts, and to the National Council on the Arts for granting the fellowship. It allowed me to take a semester's leave of absence to begin work on this book. More valuable than the grant itself was the encouragement it gave to the whole enterprise.

Note to the Reader

Those who have *The Complete Poems of Marianne Moore* may notice that the lines of her poems quoted in this study sometimes differ from later versions. She called attention to her omissions by stating on a preliminary page that they were "not accidental." There is no indication, however, that she altered the language, and often changed the indentation and line divisions, of some poems. Even these seemingly minor changes affect the rhythm and the relative emphasis of words that rhyme.

The earlier texts of her poems are often superior, I believe. But that is not the principal reason why they are quoted here. Giving the *first finished text*, by which I mean the one she approved in the books beginning with *Observations*, is the only way to show "the poet's advance." The only books of hers that I have not used as sources for quotations are *Poems* (1921), which she did not prepare for publication, and *The Pangolin and Other Poems* (1936), which was privately printed in a specially designed edition.

The fact that my text follows that of *Observations* (1924), *Selected Poems* (1935), *What Are Years* (1941), *Nevertheless* (1944), *Collected Poems* (1951), *Like a Bulwark* (1956), *O To Be A Dragon* (1959), and *Granite, Steel, and Other Topics* (1966) accounts, also, for inconsistency in the spelling of some words, even ones that appear in titles. *Selected Poems* and *Collected Poems* were both printed in England; the sheets were imported for the American edition. Inconsistencies were eliminated in *Complete Poems*. I hope the reader can accept a few, as well as my own preference for the English spelling of certain words.

Laurence Stapleton

Marianne Moore

1

How It All Began

THE time when good writers come to be known by the general company of intelligent readers does not matter so much as the time when they begin to know one another's work. For T. S. Eliot, Wallace Stevens, and Marianne Moore, that beginning was in 1915. In that year Eliot's "The Love Song of J. Alfred Prufrock" and "Portrait of a Lady," Stevens' "Sunday Morning" and "Peter Quince at the Clavier," Marianne Moore's "To a Steam Roller" and "To Statecraft Embalmed" appeared in print. One newly founded "little magazine," *Others*, published all but two of these now-famous poems as well as a few pieces by William Carlos Williams, who had not yet found the right shaping for his way of speech as successfully as the other three. The precursor and dynamo of the modern movement in poetry, Pound, had published his *A Lume Spento* in Venice in 1908 and *Personae* in London in 1911. He, too, contributed several epigrams to the first volume of *Others* and was already beginning to work on the *Cantos*. Simply to name these poems reveals the diversity of talent, as well as the common aims that would develop.

The presence of Marianne Moore in this group needs to be accounted for, more than that of the other four. Pound had already begun to sponsor Eliot's work and had exercised a strong pull on Williams' poetic instincts when they were students at the University of Pennsylvania.[1] Stevens, although not directly in contact with them, was also living in a great city where literary currents can be quickly observed, even by the newcomer. But Marianne Moore had not then corresponded with or met any of them, and her emergence from the obscurity of Carlisle, Pennsylvania, resulted from sheer initiative and determination.

Her correspondence reveals the slow development of professional aims in the six years from 1909 (when she was graduated from Bryn Mawr) to 1915. It is not hard to imagine the restlessness of a gifted woman returning to live in a small provincial city with her mother, and having to learn stenography and typewriting in order to teach "commercial subjects" at the (now defunct) school maintained by the government for the education of American Indians.[2] There were the simple pleasures of neighborhood life, of playing golf and tennis with friends, of journeys to the nearby state capital at Harrisburg, to borrow books from the library and (once) to hear a concert by Paderewski. Fervor implemented her activities in the suffragette movement. "Hall Cowdray [a friend] and I went to the fair to distribute suffrage leaflets and talk to farmers," she reported to her brother. "We found that our Headquarters banner stretched between two maple trees had blown off at one corner. I climbed on a chair and onto the roof of the neighboring 'portable house' and secured it, and then descended with considerably more glibness than I had ascended."[3]

She and her mother and other Carlisle friends were members of the "Woman Suffrage Party of Pennsylvania" and some of her letters describing their efforts are written on the stationery of the "Committee to Organize Cumberland County." Another sphere of action, about which she had conflicting feelings, was attendance at conferences of missionaries—enlivened sometimes by the chance of going to a new place, although she was not absorbed by the subject itself.[4] All the same, the letters radiate the high spirits of youth and dramatize the events of everyday life as they appeared to Mrs. Moore ("Longears" or "Bunny" in these early years), and to Marianne Moore herself, who according to her mood, signs her letters as "Winks," "Ping," or even "Hamlet," but is most often "Rat" when writing to the absent "Badger." He was then studying theology at

Princeton. Letters to him were supplemented by a sort of family newsletter of her creation, the *File*. Through all these descriptions of local life one clear beam of attention shines forward. "I finished a poem yesterday. There is a great deal of work on it and I have been putting it off. I am going to be very harsh with somebody if it—if I do not get it printed sometime."[5] A few weeks later: "I played golf yesterday and wrote a poem and Longears attended to her fox-wood [sic]."[6] Soon thereafter: "I spent yesterday in 'trying out' my bent pin, my pocket of worms, flies, etc. . . . for the netting of Mr. Dell [editor of *Smart Set*]. I wrote one poem fresh. I call it The Embankment. . . ."[7]

As these poems were mailed out, rejection slips came back, from the *Atlantic Monthly, Harper's*, the *New Republic, Smart Set*, the *Yale Review*. She condemned editors' "pigheaded and churlish prejudice against anything new,"[8] aware that her work did not conform to the conventions prevailing in American poetry at that time. Indeed, it was something of a puzzle to find her former neighbor, William Rose Benét, now an assistant editor of the *Century*, more successful in having poems accepted, and that his sister Laura had work published in the *Masses*, which had rejected Marianne Moore's submissions.

But rebuffs and discouragement only produced a determination to write better. After her brother had read one of the rejected poems and offered some comment on it, she replied, "I think your criticisms on my poem are absolutely to the point and the poem hasn't any delicate structure or workmanship to 'carry it' either but I sent Mr. [Floyd] Dell some other things that are more unique and more carefully done."[9] By pursuing every obtainable clue to any new enterprise in the literary world, looking up the ones listed in the *Editor*, she found several "little magazines" that accepted poems of hers in 1915, especially *Poetry*, the *Egoist*, and *Others*.

Poetry, begun in 1912, had the largest circulation and was the only one able to pay its contributors. The *Egoist* had as editors and consultants Richard Aldington, Eliot,

Pound, and H. D., and was identified with the "imagist" movement in poetry.[10] *Others*, a typically American venture, had just come into being, and never obtained a circulation of more than 300. But the real breakthrough for Marianne Moore came when its editor, impecunious and romantically courageous Alfred Kreymborg, took some of her poems and almost demanded that she come to New York. By the charm of luck, two Carlisle friends came to her aid, inviting her and her mother to accompany them on a visit to a session of the YMCA National Training School. Perhaps aware of her daughter's need for freedom at this crucial time, Mrs. Moore declined, and, with the money she saved, ordered a new coat for Marianne.

Thus began what Marianne Moore described to Warner as the "sojourn in the whale."[11] She had made specific plans to meet not only Kreymborg but also J. B. Kerfoot, the literary editor of *Life*, who in one of his recent articles had called attention to *Others* as a harbinger of the new movement in poetry. At that time he was also associate editor of *Camera Work*, where Marianne Moore may have seen the designs of Gordon Craig. In her senior year at Bryn Mawr, she had heard about Alfred Stieglitz from Georgiana Goddard King, then lecturer in comparative literature and the history of art. Miss King was one of the first art historians in America to recognize the importance of Picasso and other modern French painters. She had seen their work at Gertrude Stein's house in Paris, well before the climactic American exhibition, the Armory Show of 1913.[12] In the notebook that Marianne Moore kept for Miss King's course on English prose writers, she wrote down the address of Stieglitz's gallery. To see it on this 1915 visit was one of her first objectives. She wrote to her brother,

> Wednesday morning I went to "291" to see as I thought some of Alfred Stieglitz's photography. Mr. Stieglitz was . . . friendly and . . . said I might come back and look at some of the things standing with their faces

6

to the wall in a back room. . . . He has a magnificent
thing of the sea in dark blue and some paintings of
mountains by a man named Hartley also some Pica-
bias and Picassos. . . . He told me to come back and
he would show me some other things.[13]

That afternoon Kreymborg called upon her, and took her
home to dinner with his wife. Of all the American editors
to whom she had sent manuscripts, Kreymborg was the first
to recognize her distinction. He added a postscript to his
letter accepting the three poems for the December issue of
Others, expressing his belief in her writing as "an amazing
output and absolutely original if with his 'uneddicated
consciousness' [he] might judge."[14] Meeting the Kreym-
borgs' was the central event described in the excited ac-
counts of her "sojourn in the whale." She related in great
detail their appearance, the simplicity of their customs, the
questions and comments she and Kreymborg exchanged on
other writers, magazines, and editors. Then, on her second
visit to "291," as she looked at some copies of *Camera Work*,
she was delighted to find that both Kreymborg and J. B.
Kerfoot were contributors. She told Stieglitz that she had
seen some extraordinary photographs at the Kreymborgs'.
"I said I had not known there was anything in existence
like Steichen's photograph of Gordon Craig. I said at all
events I had never seen anything like it." "Well, there is
nothing like it," Stieglitz answered.[15]

On this second visit Stieglitz introduced Kerfoot, with
whom she had an animated discussion of various literary
figures. Probably to his surprise, she talked to him on equal
terms and had no difficulty in successfully defending her
position when they disagreed. The next enterprise was a
visit to Guido Bruno, of *Bruno's Weekly*, whom she also
impressed by her absolute frankness as well as by her tact.
He gave her copies of magazines and tickets to the Thimble
Theatre, where she and Laura Benét went that evening to
see his "rarefied vaudeville."[16] Bruno also asked her about
her work and suggested that she send further contributions

7

to the *Weekly*. He had published a few of her poems in October.[17] She returned to Carlisle having experienced the stimulation of seeing some great paintings and photographs and meeting people who saw a future for inventive new work in the arts, and who were, furthermore, likely to give a sympathetic response to her own writing. She had made her literary début, so to speak, and had experienced at first hand the cross-fertilization of poetry and painting that was to continue throughout her life as a writer. In her interview with Donald Hall, Marianne Moore said that it was her visit to New York in 1915 that made her want to live there.[18]

Her relationship with the writers whose poems appeared with hers in the 1915 volume of *Others*—Eliot, Pound, Stevens, and Williams—represented a more significant encounter than the exhilarating moments of her "sojourn in the whale." For a long time, that relationship was impersonal and indirect. She did not meet Pound or Eliot until the 1930's, or Stevens until 1942.[19] The idea that her work was "influenced" by Pound and Eliot—as Karl Shapiro[20] scornfully asserted—must be set aside. She could not have read any of Eliot's poems before 1915, for none of them had been published (except in undergraduate magazines). She probably had first read Pound in the *English Review*; there is perhaps one possibility of a technical kind she may have learned from him; little else. In his first letter to her (December 16, 1918) he asked a number of questions—whether she was working in "Greek quantitative measures" or "simply by ear." He says he has not analyzed her metric but thinks it a progress "on something I (. . . so far as English goes) began."[21] He refers to the awareness of quantitative values in meter and to rhythmic patterns replacing the overworked iambic pentameter. To this day no alert reader could possibly confuse any of her poems with a poem by Pound or Eliot. Eliot, in his introduction to her *Selected Poems* of 1935, deliberately states, "So far as my memory extends, which is to the pages of *The Egoist* during the war, and of *The Little Review* and *The Dial* in the years immediately following, Miss Moore has no immediate poetic derivations." In short, neither Pound nor Eliot saw any direct relationship between his work and that of Marianne Moore, constructive and fruitful though their later relationship was to be.

Poems written by Eliot and Stevens while they were still undergraduates show that each practiced conventional forms with skill, and one can detect a certain distinction in a few of these pieces.[22] The verse Marianne Moore published in the Bryn Mawr College undergraduate magazine, *Tipyn O'Bob*, has the economy and concision she always valued. She rarely then attempted more than a set of six or eight lines, always neatly rhymed and natural in tone, free of poeticism and archaism of any kind. After graduating from college, she still occasionally sent in a poem to the *Lantern* (which had succeeded *Tipyn O'Bob*). One of these, "The Talisman," shows a degree of finish and resonance of feeling that represents a move forward.[23]

In his letter to Harriet Monroe recommending T. S. Eliot's "Prufrock" Pound said that Eliot had "modernized" himself.[24] There was no need for Marianne Moore to do precisely that—but like all gifted writers, she had to train and exercise her faculties: to discover what "might lend [her work] impetus."[25] All her life, reading was a special incentive to her own writing; it was never a substitute for experience, but a challenge to her own powers, a test of what she herself might do or connect with subjects she had in mind.[26] One clue to the process by which she turned a leaf from the neat, pleasing, early pieces to a definite signature of her own is worth noting. She said in her Voice of America interview that "Ford Madox Ford's book reviews in the *English Review* (1908 to 1912) [were] of inestimable value to me, as method."[27] She learned something from Ford that Pound had also learned from him—to avoid artificiality and seek the rhythms of speech.

As editor, Ford sponsored Henry James, Conrad, Pound,

9

Yeats, and D. H. Lawrence—among other writers of these years. I am concerned not with influence, but rather with the writer's exposure to possibilities—if to great possibilities, they have to make a difference although they may not be the ones (in her case certainly were not) to be followed directly. What writer could fail to be stirred in his own mind and heart by such an example of genius as Lawrence's "Odour of Chrysanthemums," published in the *English Review* in 1911? Or to hear something different in the cadence of Pound's "The Return" (1910)? And although, as I have indicated, Marianne Moore was never a "disciple" of Pound, she could in her apprentice years have learned one technical possibility from him: a roving over of the rhythm from the end of one line to the beginning of the next that is quite different from what is conventionally called enjambement.

> See, they return. Ah, see the tentative
> Movements, and the slow feet,
> The trouble in the pace and the uncertain
> Wavering.
>
> ("The Return")

This carry-over of the rhythm may entail the division of syllables at the line end, which was to be so marked a feature of some of her early poems. She might, of course, have noticed its occurrence in Ben Jonson, or in Donne's Third Satire.

> . . . but this blind-
> ness too much light breeds.

(Donne's poems observe syllabic correspondences, too).

In any case, while Marianne Moore was alert to changes occurring in the writing of poetry, she was equally aware of her own independence. "The individuality and emotions of the writer should transcend modes. I recall feeling over-solitary occasionally (say in 1912)—in reflecting no 'influences'; to not be able to be called an 'imagist'—but deter-

10

mined to put the emphasis on what mattered most to me, in a manner natural to me," she said in a broadcast on American poetry; earlier having stated, "rhythm was my prime objective. If I succeeded in embodying a rhythm that preoccupied me, I was satisfied."[28]

Her 1915 poems do not have the fluent music sustained by the novel imagery and the play of implicit dialogue, statement, question, and refrain in "Prufrock" and "Portrait of a Lady" or the beautifully subtle development of the four movements, the controlled harmony of "Peter Quince at the Clavier." The first thing we notice in "To a Steam Roller," is its decisiveness and power to surprise:

The illustration
is nothing to you without the application
    You lack half wit. You crush all the particles down
        into close conformity, and then walk back and forth
            on them.

A spark has leapt from the title to the opening lines. And when we read the ending ones, "As for butterflies, I can hardly conceive / of one's attending upon you, but to question / the congruence of the complement is vain, if it exists" we notice the transition from the sting of wit and irony to the ease of humour—and humour is uncommon in poetry. (It was no casual admission years later when Marianne Moore said, "My favorite authors, I think, are Chaucer, Molière, and Montaigne.")[29] "To a Steam Roller" will bear, has often earned, rereading. It creates in poetry a pithy first-hand twentieth-century Theophrastan character; but as we approach the seemingly innocuous ending we can see an individual in the wings.

Skill of an unpredictable kind had appeared, then, but in "To Statecraft Embalmed" a more complex and—at the center of the poem—a more liberating insight finds expression. In a few poems of that time, Marianne Moore had seen in an animal or bird a correlative of the human behavior or trait she would identify ("To an Intramural

11

Rat," "To a Prize Bird," for example). But the symbol of the ibis in "To Statecraft Embalmed" counterpoints a more profound theme; one might describe it as a meditative one, if that term were not in danger of becoming too inclusive.

The opening lines of "To Statecraft Embalmed" ("There is nothing to be said for you. Guard / Your secret, conceal is under your hard / Plumage") resemble "To a Steam Roller" in anatomizing a kind of arrogance or obtuseness; but this poem becomes more concretely visual, and proceeds to a richer internal development, by the second and third stanzas.

> Bird, whose tents were "awnings of Egyptian
> Yarn," shall Justice' faint, zigzag inscription—
>   Leaning like a dancer—
>   Show
> The pulse of its once vivid sovereignty?

The curve of the image, rhythm, and thought suggests something intuitively right as a metaphor, like Shakespeare's "Distinction like a broad and powerful fan / Puffing at all, winnows the light away," where a concept is made luminous by a visible act. "To Statecraft Embalmed" generates a strong climax at its center.

> . . . Ibis, we find
>   No
> Virtue in you—alive and yet so dumb.
> Discreet behavior is not now the sum
>   Of statesmanlike good sense.
>   Though
> It were the incarnation of dead grace?
> As if a death mask ever could replace
>   Life's faulty excellence!

The last short line, expressing a wisdom deeply felt and known, bespeaks a special gift—the power to convey a gen-

erous insight without assuming any mask. This alone sets
her apart from many of her contemporaries.

The delicate but firm structure here becomes evident as
the repeated one-syllable end-rhyme of each brief stanza is
maintained throughout, while the third line of the stanza
is also rhymed to the third line of the next. These two con-
trasting continuities of sound have first a percussive effect,
marking one intent of the poem, and then a dream-like
suspense.

Marianne Moore's accomplishment in these few remark-
able early poems was no doubt aided by the frequent exer-
cise of her technical resources in more transitory pieces
that she never collected in her books.[30] This was (usually)
wise, for, however enjoyable in themselves, the practice-
poems could only have distracted attention from the major
patterns emerging, the growing central strength. Her read-
ers may have noticed that many of the 1915 poems have
similar titles ("To William Butler Yeats on Tagore," "To
a Prize Bird," "To Military Progress," "To a Man Making
His Way Through the Crowd," as well as "To a Steam
Roller" and "To Statecraft Embalmed"). The poems are
witty declarations addressed to a person or creature who is
always addressed as "you" and whose possible reply or re-
action has no seeming relevance to her own observations.
Unlike later poems, these are not dramatic; only one voice
is heard or implied. Beginning in 1916, Marianne Moore
began to permit herself a larger scale of composition and
a more exploratory structure. Unquestionably the New
York visit in the fall of 1915 furnished a powerful stimulus.
But the change in her own circumstances proved to be even
more responsible for the depth of emotion in poems like
"Black Earth" (later called "Melancthon"), "The Fish,"
and "A Grave."

After trying several other possibilities, Warner Moore
had accepted the invitation of the elders to become minis-
ter of the Ogden Memorial Presbyterian Church in Chat-

ham, New Jersey. In the summer of 1916 his mother and Marianne moved there from Carlisle—the family newsletter the *File* noted that in August "two chameleons entered the service of the Rev. J. W. Badger."[31] But not for long. During 1915, Warner Moore had trained as a reserve officer; in 1917 he joined the Navy as Chaplain, the beginning of a long and distinguished professional career. He went immediately on convoy duty in the North Atlantic. Mrs. Moore's first reaction to her son's decision was not a happy one.[32] But for Marianne, the change was momentous. After staying for a time at the manse in Chatham, she and her mother moved to New York, eventually finding the apartment in Greenwich Village where they were to live until 1929. In his interview with her Donald Hall asked if moving to New York led her to write more poems than she otherwise would have written. And she answered, "I'm sure it did—seeing what others wrote, liking this or that. With me it's always some fortuity that traps me."[33] Her emancipation is reflected in the wider scope of feeling, with corresponding experiments of rhythm and a freer line, in the poems of 1916 and the years following.

One that should not have been omitted from *Complete Poems* is "Black Earth." The slow dactylic tempo of its opening lines is unusual:

> Openly, yes,
> with the naturalness
>   of the hippopotamus or the alligator
>   when it climbs out on the bank to experience the
>
> sun, I do these
> things which I do, which please
>   no one but myself.

Although I do not believe in "representative meter" in Pope's sense, the rhythm is oddly similar to an elephant's walking with seemingly soft-jointed ease. Seventeen stanzas, linked by a roving-over of the sense as well as the rhythm, unfold the mysterious progress in animal and man from one phase of experience to another, made convincing by the acknowledgement of forces that we cannot wholly grasp. These glances towards the unknown take the form of an unexpected and self-answering question:

> Now I breathe and now I am sub-
> merged; the blemishes stand up and shout when the
> > object
> in view was a
> renaissance; shall I say
> the contrary?

The "patina of circumstance," the skin "cut into checkers by rut upon rut of unpreventable experience" attest the necessary exposure of everyone to the circumstances of living with other people, be they sustaining, baffling, hostile, or sympathetic.

> Black
> but beautiful, my back
> > is full of the history of power. Of power? What
> > is powerful and what is not? My soul shall never
>
> be cut into
> by a wooden spear. . . .

The reader who knows all Marianne Moore's poems will at once hear a question in a much later one:

> " 'What is love and shall I ever have it?' "
> > ("Logic and 'The Magic Flute' ")

To think that power, or love, is a possession is its undoing. "Black Earth" is a profound poem, the circumference described by the elephant's trunk a symbol of the unity of life and death and the quietly uttered contrast between spiritual pride and spiritual poise formulated simply as a query. The final one offers a test Charles Sanders Peirce might regard as a recognition of the value of "tychism," the unpredictable:

> Will
> depth be depth, thick skin be thick, to one who
> can see no
> beautiful element of unreason under it?

A great deal has been said about Marianne Moore's absorbed interest in animals as central to her poetry; no one has really found terms for this predilection of hers. I have none, except to say that animals are not singular among other phenomena she observes; allegory is not intended, nor, with rare exceptions, the static device of emblem.[34] This problem will be raised again in the discussion of some of her later poems such as "The Jerboa" and "The Pangolin," and of course the *Fables*. For the moment, may it suffice that "Black Earth" and "The Fish" are the two first fully realized studies of this kind. These two poems are notable also for intensity in the use of colour: "The equable sapphire light" that "becomes a nebulous green" in one, and in the other "the turquoise sea" that stirs the "pink rice grains, ink bespattered jelly-fish, crabs like green lilies."

To make the title begin the first line, as in

THE FISH

> Wade
> through black jade

avoids the usual hiatus between the title and the poem and gives an essentially musical momentum, like the one she commented on when quoting a friend's remark that a conductor's signal "begins far back of the beat, so that you don't see when the down beat comes."[35] The rhythm in this poem is quite different from that of "Black Earth." Here the quickly coupled short rhyming lines swiftly reveal the radiant energies in the rock-sheltered pool; and the slowing of the monosyllabic rhymes marks a change in rhythm as the sea brings life into the chasm, which does not itself pos-

sess life but remains its harbour; "the sea grows old in it."
Perhaps only in a few great poems are there similar lines,
that we partly understand because they surpass understand-
ing, and that take us for a moment above the ordinary level
of experience.

Neither "Black Earth" nor "The Fish" can be said to be
complex in the usual sense of that word, although they fuse
image and idea with a fine disregard of open statement.
From "Those Various Scalpels" a more complex pattern
does emerge. T. S. Eliot's comment on it has bearing on a
number of her poems:

> Here the rhythm depends partly upon the transforma-
> tion-changes from one image to another, so that the
> second image is superposed before the first has quite
> faded, and upon the dexterity of change of vocabulary
> from one image to another. "Snow sown by tearing
> winds on the cordage of disabled ships" has that Latin,
> epigrammatic succinctness, laconic austerity, which
> leaps out unexpectedly . . . .[36]

In this respect the poem anticipates later ones like "Vir-
ginia Britannia" or even "Propriety." Nevertheless I am in-
clined to agree with Marianne Moore's own feeling that
"These Various Scalpels" is not wholly successful; even the
epigrammatic ending to which its sometimes stark, some-
times ornamental images lead does not achieve the summa-
tion or inquiry of her other ending lines.

Two other early poems, although in a good sense complex,
attain the unity of feeling that is at the heart of all good
writing (in prose as well as poetry). The title and opening
phrase, "In the Days of Prismatic Color," slip in the ab-
stract word "prismatic" as a subtle announcement of the
primacy of sensation that the whole poem renews. Today,
in critical discourse, even young students resort to "the
green world" and such clichés, and blur the pristine clarity
of a poem like Marvell's "The Garden." But her poem

17

eludes such terms by moving directly from the title to the summons to see how it was,

> not in the days of Adam and Eve but when Adam
>> was alone; when there was no smoke and color was
> fine, not with the fineness of
>> early civilization art but by virtue
> of its originality; with nothing to modify it but the
>
> mist that went up, obliqueness was a varia-
>> tion of the perpendicular, plain to see and
> to account for: it is no
>> longer that; nor did the blue red yellow band
> of incandescence that was color keep its stripe. . . .

Defining obliqueness as a variation of the perpendicular, a geometrical variation not for the sake of deception, but comparable to the pure hue of first-seen colours, achieves a double metaphor. To write a poem about truth with such economy of resource, with no attendant gesture, sets a mark as the waves at high tide imprint the sand.

An early version of the poem was first published in Bryn Mawr's *Lantern*, to which Marianne Moore sent it in 1919, the year of her tenth reunion.[37] When it was published two years later in *Contact*, the "little mag" edited by William Carlos Williams and Robert McAlmon, the author made a decisive alteration in the approach to the final lines. Following the dismissal of sophistication as "principally throat" and the implied comparison of it to a torpid reptile emerging from its lair,[38] the earlier version published in *Lantern* read:

> In the shortlegged, fit-
> ful advance, in the gurglings and all the minutiae, we
>>> have the classic
> multitude of feet—formidable only in the
>> dark. Truth, many legged and formidable also,
> is stationary by choice.
>
> The wave may go over it if it likes; know

that it will be there when it says: I shall be
there when the wave has gone by.

When the poem reappeared in *Contact* two years later, the
revision of these lines showed a master's hand.

In the short legged, fit-
ful advance, the gurgling and all the minutiae—we
have the classic
multitude of feet. To what purpose! Truth is no Apollo
Belvedere, no formal thing, the wave may go over it if
it likes.
Know that it will be there when it says:
"I shall be there when the wave has gone by."

An explanatory statement was omitted ("Truth, many
legged and formidable also, is stationary by choice") to be
replaced by the challenge "To what purpose!" and the se-
verely beautiful image "Truth is no Apollo Belvedere, no
formal thing"—where the negative comparison borrows the
very quality of what is rejected. The consequent rearrange-
ment of the lines frees the rhythm for the calm assurance
of the ending, adapted from something that her brother ac-
tually said in a conversation.[39]
The talent for appropriate informality—in a special
sense—needs to be remembered when we think of the end-
ing of a parallel poem written at this time, "In This Age
of Hard Trying." The last two lines, "The staff, the bag,
the feigned inconsequence / of manner, best bespeak that
weapon, self-protectiveness," recall, perhaps, a painting or
drawing by Dürer,[40] and introduce a theme developed in a
number of later poems ("Armour's Undermining Modesty,"
"The Pangolin," "The Wood Weasel," and others). A num-
ber of critics who have commented on Marianne Moore's
praise of the value of protectiveness have not realized that
her poems explore its meaning not as a defense, or—least
of all—as a shrinking from experience, but rather as a pref-
erence for the incognito, a way to see things in themselves,

19

without modifying them by intrusiveness. Both "In the Days of Prismatic Colour" and "In This Age of Hard Trying," by their quick juxtapositions of the visual and temporal, rub off the accretions of custom.

Marianne Moore's individual perspective had always been there; but the starting-point at first chosen for the poem and its structure had remained impersonal. "A Grave," "New York," and "Is Your Town Nineveh" represent a change. In "A Grave" (originally called "A Graveyard") the poet speaks directly to the "Man looking into the sea / taking the view from those who have as much right to it as you have to it yourself," speaks to the reader, and to herself. This poem exhibits a new experiment with concealed rhyme; and the meter seems wholly right for a sighting taken from land by someone well-acquainted with the sea.

> The firs stand in a procession, each with an emerald
> turkey-foot at the top
> .   .   .   .
> men lower nets, unconscious of the fact that they are
> desecrating a grave,
> and row quickly away—the blades of the oars
> moving together like the feet of water spiders as if
> there were no such thing as death.

An early typescript of this poem shows that it was written in Chatham, New Jersey; that draft is clearly indebted to Poe's "City in the Sea."[41] Her feelings about the first World War and her brother's willing assumption of the dangers inherent in naval service are not absent from the mood of the poem. Observation of a special kind goes on in it—not the satirical notations of human behavior, but that of an eye "with an unusual gift for seeing" (as Marsden Hartley said of Cézanne). The metaphor of "The firs . . . each with an emerald turkey-foot at the top" is atypical; it is, we might imperfectly say, denotative, because the trees are seen immediately in their live exact design, with no interval of comparison. She is one of the few writers who sharpen

20

awareness of the moving or the arrested object, the auditory as well as the kinetic phenomenon, or simultaneously, all of these:

> The wrinkles progress upon themselves in a phalanx—
> beautiful under the networks of foam,
> and fade breathlessly while the sea rustles in and out
> of the seaweed;
> the birds swim through the air at top speed, emitting
> catcalls as heretofore—

Nothing has to be imported for the reader to share the implicit meaning of events that are by most people half-perceived.

The rhythmic measure of the poem advances to a close, reminding the insensitive man addressed that things dropped in the sea are finally bound to sink in it, "in which if they turn and twist, it is neither with volition nor consciousness." This final line connects "A Grave" with "The Fish" and a principal later poem, "What Are Years?" Throughout this early one, a meditation on death in the midst of things, death is not a seeker of revenge, but a rebuke to insensate life. In spite of its sombre mood, "A Grave" also has irrepressible élan.

This was one of the poems that she sent to Pound in 1918, evoking the comment on her meter that has already been quoted. He had mentioned her favorably in writing to editors, but his answer to her letter was obviously his first direct communication with her. It is one of the most striking letters he wrote in those years when he was sponsoring every true talent he encountered; not only that but nurturing the climate of art itself; demanding, but not jealous or competitive, looking for money to keep other writers alive; himself accepting little, meanwhile doing the best work he could in every line he wrote. It is not relevant here to consider Pound's own achievement, but only to show how quickly he recognized Marianne Moore's promise, and sought to know the provenance of her work and her aims.

21

His first response was to state that the poems she sent not only were publishable but should be paid for—but that he had then no expendable funds from the *Little Review*, or hope for space in the *Egoist* (to which he knew she had contributed without being paid). He offered to hold the manuscripts for a new quarterly he planned to launch. The more significant part of his letter deals with the order of words in the last line of "A Graveyard." He queried several words as well as the punctuation in other poems she had submitted. He also asked whether she had been influenced by French poets. Then (as Eliot was to do two years later) Pound offered to get a book of hers into print.

> Dopo tant' anni, I am not yet in the position of a Van Dyke or a Tennyson; but still, I have got Joyce, and [Wyndham] Lewis, and Eliot, and a few other comforting people into print. . . .
>
> For what it is worth, my ten or more years of practice, failure, success, etc. in arranging tables of contents is à votre service. . . .
>
> Your stuff holds my eye. Most verse I merely slide off of. . . . But my held eye goes forward very slowly. . . .
>
> I oughtn't to be too lazy to analyze your metric; . . . but . . . I very often don't analyze my own until years after. . . .
>
> . . . At any rate, it is (yr. metric) a progress on something I (more or less, so far as English goes) began. . . .[42]

He ended the letter by asking if her "stuff" appeared in America.

Marianne Moore's reply is as characteristic as his quick recognition of merit and his inquiries were. If I came across a tattered, unsigned copy of this letter I would know at once that she had written it. Her kind of formality, and use of negative verbs or adjectives or modes of statement is as distinctive as her love of the colloquial—and in her poetry as in her criticism the two reinforce each other. In response

to Pound's natural desire to know something about her, she
answered:

> I am glad to give you personal data and hope that
> the bare facts that I have to offer, may not cause work
> that I may do . . . utterly to fail in interest. Even if they
> should, it is but fair that those who speak out, should
> not lie in ambush.[43]

She then rapidly describes her family background ("Irish
by descent, possibly Scotch also, but purely Celtic"), her
education at Bryn Mawr, the period of teaching in Carlisle,
and the subsequent move to New York. All she says is as
accurate and firm as it is unassuming.

In our time it has become fashionable, especially among
some academic critics, to assume that the "scholar" (that
kind of scholar) knows more about the writer than the
writer knows. I cannot accept this view. No better analysis of
her method of composition—allowing for many variations
and progressions—is likely to be made than her statement
to Pound in this letter.

> Any verse that I have written, has been an arrange-
> ment of stanzas, each stanza being an exact duplicate of
> every other stanza. I have occasionally been at pains to
> make an arrangement of lines and rhymes that I liked,
> repeat itself, but the form of the original stanza of any-
> thing I have written has been a matter of expediency,
> hit upon as being approximately suitable to the sub-
> ject.[44]

Or, as she expresses it in the last line of "The Past is the
Present," "Ecstasy affords the occasion, and expediency de-
termines the form." To unfold a little more of the implica-
tions of these terse statements is to realize a fact that sets
Marianne Moore apart from Pound, Eliot, and Stevens: that
she almost never chose to write in any predetermined meter
or stanza. No sonnets, sestinas, villanelles, heroic couplets,
blank verse, or even, save as an undergraduate, quatrains.

23

(A few of her late poems are in octosyllabic couplets.) To
match the incentive of excitement in an observation or live-
ly stir of expression, she made the original stanza as she
liked it best in rhythm and words. (The original stanza, in
the sense of the one first composed, need not be the first
in the finished poem. Sometimes the last line or last part
of the poem came to her first.)[45]

Replying to Pound's other queries, she disavowed the pos-
sible influence of French poets, whom she had not then
read; by inference she also set aside any direct influence of
Pound himself. Then comes an enlightening acknowledg-
ment: "Gordon Craig, Henry James, Blake, the minor
Prophets and Hardy, are so far as I know, the direct influ-
ences bearing upon my work."[46]

To elucidate and savour this statement would be enough
for a separate chapter, not because "sources" are at stake,
or because sources ever matter taken by themselves, but
rather because she chose her own line of descent.

But our concern is with this poet's advance, not the hand-
grips she found in her reading and her self-won tradition.
As an aside—the minor prophets, Henry James, and Hardy
one might have predicted before reading this letter of hers;
Blake deserves a new kind of attention in this context; Gor-
don Craig's name in this group arouses curiosity. Even be-
fore the time when she could have seen some of his draw-
ings or etchings at Stieglitz's "291" gallery, she had evinced
an interest in his work, and one of her first poems in the
Egoist was addressed to him.[47]

This first letter from Marianne Moore to Pound demon-
strates that she was quite prepared to make her own deci-
sions; and, although still unknown, was not ill at ease with
her peers. The letter also shows that she was willing to
make a concession to an editor (and within limits this will-
ingness continued). Pound had queried the "final cadence
and graphic arrangement of same in "A Graveyard." Her
manuscript read, "it is neither with volition nor conscious-
ness"; he preferred the order "consciousness nor volition."

Answering, she agreed "to end the line as you suggest" and pointed out that for the sake of maintaining symmetry she had subsequently altered the arrangement of lines in the preceding stanzas. She added, "I realize that by writing consciousness and volition, emphasis is obtained . . . and I am willing to make the change, though I prefer the original order."[48] And when she later published this poem in *Observations* she retained her own order in this last line, because, as she inevitably knew, it had more finality of meaning in the context of the poem as a whole.

The term, or more significantly the concept, of volition enters into a number of poems she wrote in this first stage of her advance. "Reinforcements," which appeared both in *Poems* (1921) and *Observations*, is the only piece of hers directly referring to the 1914-1918 war. The last line of this poem expresses not an aphorism but a weighed conviction: "The future of time is determined by the power of volition." Volition, of course, is not necessarily or solely a resolve to act in a given way; it implies a choice of ends, and in turn a choice of means. With this theme in mind, one can see more clearly the interrelationship of a number of poems that present a new phase of the writer's experience. In composing these poems she allowed herself a freer structure, departing from the extreme compression of statement and stricter ways in rhyme that she had earlier followed.

Two pieces from this new period in her writing are best read side by side, or reading either, remembering the other. "Is Your Town Nineveh?" is a poem looking at a horizon from New York; the one called "New York" sees the city from a moral distance. In the latter, New York becomes the horizon of the wilderness. Marianne Moore more than once gave Jonah a place in her compositons; she was evidently as interested in him as Sir Thomas Browne was in Methuselah. A poem to which she gave the title "Sojourn in the Whale" had already lightly presented the theme of the reluctant prophet, and his survival, as an example that could afford encouragement to Ireland in its struggle for independence. But the last lines affirm volition as a power of nature itself. Hearing men say that the feminine temperament, seemingly similar to Ireland, is circumscribed by incompetence and therefore will be forced to give in, "Compelled by experience . . . will turn back; water seeks its own level," the retort comes that

> . . . "Water in motion is far
> from level." You have seen it when obstacles happened
>   to bar
> the path, rise automatically.

"Is Your Town Nineveh?" deserves special notice not only because like other poems it draws imaginatively upon Jonah's initial refusal to prophesy, but because its subdued rhymes represent a change in mode, forecasting her experiments in placing the rhyme on an unaccented syllable. An implicit dialogue questions the prophet who is anxious to escape, and answers sympathetically. After wondering whether personal upheaval in the name of freedom should be subdued, the closing lines acknowledge that this desire cannot be gainsaid.

> Is it Nineveh
>   and are you Jonah
>   in the sweltering east wind of your wishes?
>   I myself, have stood
>   there by the aquarium, looking
>   at the Statue of Liberty.

The reassurance of the last statement is unstressed, yet there is wonder in it. New York stands in the background, implicitly requiring prophecy; the small fish in the aquarium at the Battery betoken the awating whale; escape to the sea, away from the ambiguous Statue of Liberty, may be and may not be freedom.

"New York," in its pungent realism, differs from "Is Your Town Nineveh?" The visible fact of the city's mass "accreted where we need the space for commerce" is realized by New York's having recently become the center even of the fur trade; the pelts and tepees stand for the original savage's romance, and the modern savage's competitiveness. The eighteenth-century elegance of the "beau with the muff" is humorously contrasted with the kind of power now emanating from the conjunction of the Monongahela and the Allegheny, "the scholastic philosophy of the wilderness / to combat which one must stand outside and laugh." The contrast makes clear Marianne Moore's strong awareness of her time, our time, and the intractability of increasing materialism. The poem then rapidly sets up the clay pigeons that are not the true essence of life in New York, rejecting their mechanical side-show effect for the essential thing that retrieves the rest, "the accessibility to experience." The quotation she uses (from Henry James) epitomizes the fascination of life in the city and the need to purify it (as James knew it must be purified), "to stand outside and laugh" in an ironic disavowal of materialism.[49] In her first portrayal of incalculable New York, the sense of place becomes as important in her work as the animal kindom was to be.

Pound's offer to help in the publication of her poems was echoed in many letters from H. D., who returned to America in 1920 with her friend Winifred Ellerman, or Bryher, as she preferred to be called. Bryher made every effort to persuade Marianne Moore to go to England, but met with a refusal each time. I have seen no evidence of any discussion while she was in America of a plan to publish a collection of Marianne's poems.[50] In fact, a similar offer of assistance from T. S. Eliot had been refused.[51] She wrote to him:

Were I to publish verse I should be grateful indeed for the assistance you offer. Your suggestion tempts me beyond my own certain knowledge that I have nothing that ought to appear in book form. For me to be published would merely emphasize the meagerness of my production. Not that I have expressed sentiment that I am unwilling to stand by, but should verse of mine that has been published ever appear again, it ought to be supplementary to something more substantial. But to have friends is the greatest thing. I value more than I am able to say, your approval.[52]

But after Bryher's marriage to the American writer Robert McAlmon, and their subsequent return to England with H. D., they arranged with Harriet Shaw Weaver for the publication by the Egoist Press of *Poems* by Marianne Moore (1921). In July of that year she received a copy of the attractively designed paperbound edition, accompanied by letters from Bryher and Miss Weaver. Her reply to Bryher expressed astonishment:

> . . . it is perhaps well that you even with your hardened gaze, cannot see what it is to be a pterodactyl with no rock in which to hide. . . . You say that I am stubborn. I agree. . . . I had considered the matter from every point and was sure of my decision—that to publish anything now would not be to my literary advantage. I wouldn't have the poems appear now and would not have some of them ever appear and would make certain changes. . . . Despite my consternation, the product is remarkably innocuous. . . .
>
> Your now naked
> Dactyl[53]

The publication of the little book would in time prove to be an advantage. Nevertheless Marianne Moore instinctively felt that her future as a writer was bound up with life in America. That she was still unknown to a larger public was a safeguard rather than a handicap. Luckily her contemporaries did not fail to record some impressions of her in those early years. *The Autobiography of William Carlos Williams* offers not history, but a recollection of his thinking about that time. The association of these two poets was a fruitful one. Two sketches ring with authenticity. In the first,

> Marianne Moore, like a rafter holding up the superstructure of our uncompleted building, a caryatid, her red hair plaited and wound twice about the fine skull, though she was surely one of the main supports of the new order, was no luckier than the rest of us. One night . . . we all met at some Dutch-treat party in a cheap restaurant on West Fifteenth Street or thereabouts. There must have been twenty of us. Marianne, with her sidelong laugh and shake of the head, quite child-like and overt, was in admiration of Mina [Loy's] long-legged charms. Such things were in our best tradition. Marianne was our saint—if we had one—in whom we all instinctively felt our purpose come together to form a stream. Everyone loved her.[54]

On another occasion (perhaps in 1919?) Marsden Hartley "brought a young man with him named Robert McAlmon. Marianne was there and read her 'Those Various Scalpels.' "[55] Alfred Kreymborg's account describes a subsequent evening:

> Reading aloud was soon in order. Even Stevens was inspired to try something. . . . Orrick Johns, Krimmie [Kreymborg] and the rest took their turn and finally Marianne Moore joined them. About two in the morning she read something one could barely hear about "England with its baby rivers and little towns," "Italy with its equal shores. . . ." A beautiful poem which few of the guests could hear distinctly, but which the mystery man from *The Dial* heard so well, he stole over to her and, after a whispered consultation, induced her to part with it. Marianne was the first of "the old guard" to be accepted by the new magazine.[56]

This was a historic event, forecasting a new period in Marianne Moore's work—not discontinuous with the early one, but wider in horizon. She was now at a true center of literary life at a vital moment of growth in American literature and of the establishment of a new liaison with literature in England. Her review of William Carlos Williams' *Kora in Hell* shows how candid she could be about the scope of literature and its necessary, difficult means:

> . . . in his effort to "annihilate half truths," Dr. Williams is hard, discerning, implacable and deft. If he rates audacity too high as an aesthetic asset, there can be no doubt that he has courage of the kind which is a necessity and not merely an admired accessory. Discerning the world's hardness, his reply is the reply of Carl Sandburg's boll weevil to threats of sand, hot ashes and the river: "That'll be ma HOME! That'll be ma HOME!"[57]

This declaration is at once authoritative and open-hearted, consistent with themes that will continue in the path of the poet's advance, exploring "life's faulty excellence."

2

On Her Own

THE "mystery man from the *Dial*" who heard Marianne Moore read her poem "England," and induced her to part with it, was Scofield Thayer. He and his friend James Sibley Watson, Jr., had recently gained control of the fortnightly review, with which they had been associated for some time, and were in the process of metamorphosing it from a journal of liberal opinion and critical discussion into a monthly "journal of arts and letters," reviving for the twentieth century the aims of the transcendentalist *Dial* edited by Emerson and Margaret Fuller.[1] Thayer's name now appeared as editor and Sibley Watson's as president of the Dial Publishing Company. In fact, they shared decisions on the contents of the magazine and set the policy of seeking "aesthetic perfection" without commitment to any one school. As Nicolas Joost, the historian of this enterprise, points out, the *Dial* of the twenties was "a disciplined and ordered artifact." The editors' concern was primarily with "style, structure, texture, technique" and "the content of a story or a poem or a picture was secondary to the art of its execution."[2]

Marianne Moore was one of the first contributors to the *Dial*. "England" and "Picking and Choosing" appeared in the April 1920 issue, and for the next five years, with a few exceptions, she gave the editors her best work. One day perhaps a fuller portrait of and deserved tribute to Scofield Thayer may be achieved, with both the sensitivity and objectivity that he and Sibley Watson expected of their contributors. Their support gave Marianne Moore access to a wider group of readers in this country and in Europe.

Thayer encouraged her ventures in writing poems of greater magnitude than she had hitherto attempted. He provided the opportunity, through his association with Lincoln Mac-Veagh, for the publication of the first book she prepared on her own. And when he decided to resign as editor, he made her his successor. Dr. Watson had returned to Rochester from New York City, but he continued to advise the new editor, and to share decisions with her.[3]

Thayer's friendship, generosity, and belief in her came at a crucial time. Payment for her contributions supplemented the meager income she received as an assistant in the Hudson Park branch of the New York Public Library. But that practical advantage was outmatched by Thayer's encouragement. We can observe this in a letter of July 11, 1921 that he wrote to her from the S. S. Aquitania, apologizing for not having called to say goodbye before he left for Paris. After rapid comments on some *Dial* matters, he spoke of her poem "A Grave," which he said he had read and re-read several times while crossing the Atlantic. "I find (as our friend Mr Pound says) [it] 'stands up' superbly when confronted with the daily and (as our friend Mr Moore says) 'terre à terre' sea." In a postscript he added, "Mr. Cummings who met me here on my arrival agrees with me the Dial has published nothing whatever finer than The Grave."[4]

Thayer's letter evoked from her a rare comment on the poem. Thanking him for not having "repented" of publishing it, she admitted that "to intimate that it bears comparison with actuality is praise that I value profoundly. If you knew of the circumstances under which the poem was written you would know that it would be a reproach to me to have given an impression of anything less than actuality."[5] She was thinking of the difficult time in Chatham described earlier.

Between 1921 and early 1925, the *Dial* accepted twelve poems by Marianne Moore. Some of these, we know, had been written earlier but remained unpublished (like "A Graveyard," which even Ezra Pound could not successfully place for her). A few (such as "New York" and "Is Your Town Nineveh?") have already been discussed, in order to show their difference from related early ones. Many of the *Dial* poems have to do with the zest of defying humbug, blowing away pretense, and sharpening the edge of choice. Among them "Picking and Choosing," "When I buy Pictures," and the less well-known "England" might be singled out. Or "Novices," who are "deaf to satire which like 'the smell of cypress strengthens the nerves of the brain.' " The structure of the new poems is looser, without ever being careless; and some of them are notable for the quiet license taken with syntax. An effort to project strong convictions into the passage of experience supersedes at this time the aim of concision. "The Labors of Hercules," for example, starts off a series of infinitives setting forth the imperatives of the strong, first: "to popularize the mule, its neat exterior / expressing the principle of accommodation reduced to a minimum" and after the repulse of many errors of the meretricious would-be poet or aristocrat, to affirm finally that "one keeps on knowing / 'that the negro is not brutal / that the Jew is not greedy / that the Oriental is not immoral, / that the German is not a Hun.' " The whole poem is an incomplete sentence, deliberately so—the series of infinitives propose something that the reader can complete without being nudged to a conclusion. The four last lines quoted here, when read as we now can read them, anticipate the great war poem "In Distrust of Merits."

Other pieces in the *Dial* group of poems—"Novices" is a good example—derive startling images from quotations and dissolve any sequence of idea or of events in an effect that resembles collage. I do not mean to use that term in a technical sense, nor to imply that Marianne Moore was influenced by painting of this kind. As her sensations on her first visit to "291" reveal, she like other poets responded to the vitality of the modern movement in painting.[6] It is rather that the *principle* of collage casts light on the curious method of assembling images and phrases in these poems.

Harold Rosenberg makes a point that has relevance here. The "revolution of collage," he wrote, "consisted in its incorporating a piece of everyday reality which enters into relationship with every other reality that the spirit has created."[7]

Later in the same article Rosenberg maintains that "as in other twentieth-century creations there is a vein of farce in collage: "its exposure of the duplicity of art. . . ."[8] The irony, wit, the new kind of satire in Marianne Moore's poems never resort to farce as a weapon. Rosenberg's point about the need to expose the duplicity of art has a bearing, however, on "Bowls," "People's Surroundings," "Snakes, Mongooses," and "Novices." For the result of setting unlike things side by side accented by the changing tone of her imported quotations presents a challenge. By implication it fiercely rejects the duplicity of *false* art, and opens a door on the authentic.

In their free treatment of syntax, dispensation with stanzaic form, subordination of rhyme, and particularly in the technique of quotation, these poems are a preparation for the doughty ones placed at the end of *Observations*: "Marriage," "An Octopus," and "Sea Unicorns and Land Unicorns." "Marriage" has a place all by itself in Marianne Moore's endeavour. The other two look forward to the more emancipated compositions that belong to the 1930's. Virginia Woolf in *Granite and Rainbow* speculated on the way the novelist of the future might bring to bear upon tumultuous and conflicting emotions "the generalizing and simplifying power of a strict and logical imagination"—as the poet could.[9] By a route almost opposite to Mrs. Woolf's, Marianne Moore makes an asymptotic approach of the poem to the novella in the tryptich of "Marriage," "An Octopus," and "Sea Unicorns and Land Unicorns." This approach is brought to perfection later in "Part of a Novel, Part of a Poem, Part of a Play."

Letters to Scofield Thayer about her conception of "An Octopus" and "Sea Unicorns and Land Unicorns" are interwoven with discussions of the possible publication of the book *Observations*. The papers of Lincoln MacVeagh, owner of the Dial Press (which had no official connection with the *Dial* magazine), have apparently been lost.[10] Therefore his offer to publish the book and Marianne Moore's initial refusal cannot be reported at first hand. Thayer, who no doubt had prompted the offer, wrote to her on August 19, 1924, expressing his disappointment that she had not seen her way to accept MacVeagh's invitation.

> I can only say that both Mr. MacVeagh and myself would be most sensible of the honour conferred upon us in publishing any work of yours. Nor does it seem to me that the fact that you have been unwilling to allow Mr and Mrs McAlmon to assume further financial risk in reissuing your poems is inexpugnable reason for not permitting a business house like the Dial Press to undertake publishing a book which it would undertake to publish with hope of financial gain. Although, I trust you will believe me, not only with that purpose.[11]

In the spring of that year Bryher and her husband had offered to reissue *Poems* of 1921, presumably with additions, as a publication of the Contact Press, which McAlmon controlled. And Marianne Moore had refused.

Expressing her gratitude to Thayer for renewing MacVeagh's offer, she apologized for not having been explicit in giving McAlmon "the impression that I did not wish my work to be published again; I ought to have said that I am not willing to be published in the company of certain authors." Her brother had pointed out the advantage of being published in America and felt that "choice of The Dial Press would be self-explanatory."[12] Therefore, she would be happy to act on Mr. MacVeagh's suggestion, if he had not changed his mind. To which the encouraging and benevolent Thayer answered, "I am so glad. Never take a woman's no."[13]

Also in the letter accepting the offer of publication, Marianne Moore raised a question important to her:

> If a solution is feasible, I should like to include in any
> further publication, certain pieces that I am working
> on. One of these I intend to offer to The Dial, but the
> other is so long I felt it was rather presumptuous to of-
> fer it since poems are not published serially.[14]

Her next letter refers to her intention to go over the poems in the Egoist Press edition "making changes and rearranging them and adding others that ought to have appeared with them." She welcomed the chance to send Thayer the two unfinished poems, when she had completed them. She remarked again upon their length, and her surprise at their "recalcitrance and undesirable expansiveness, for I am most impetuous and perilously summary in anything which is to me, so vital a matter."[15]

A week later she mailed him a copy of "Sea Unicorns and Land Unicorns," making it evident that the fortune of this poem and of the still uncompleted "An Octopus" mattered so much that she had to see what she could do with these two subjects before selecting the other work for her book.[16]

His reply reassured her, and his query about the sources of her numerous quotations prompted a significant comment: "As for quotations, sometimes I think a triviality gains a little weight by quotation marks; for the most part, however, my quotations have authority."[17] This statement indicates her awareness of a quality in her work already discussed, but needing further application—the way that quotations of varying kinds contribute to the changing tones in her poems, and in some cases to the outcome of the whole. She explained the use of quotations in this poem in some detail, and in the course of the letter expressed a wish that if "Sea Unicorns and Land Unicorns" could be included in her forthcoming collection, she might "append, at the back of the book, notes such as these I am sending you."[18]

Again, Thayer did her a service when he answered, "You and Mr MacVeagh must surely give us these footnotes in full measure."[19] His letter crossed with one from her written on the same day, to accompany "An Octopus":

> I am taking the liberty of sending to you the long poem to which I referred satirically as a serial, feeling that you would be willing to tell me unofficially if you think it unsuited to the book of poems in case it is too lengthy for magazine publication.[20]

But Thayer's good judgment led to the swift publication of both "serial poems" in the *Dial*. In the case of "An Octopus" he offered "felicitations upon the so successful completion of what is—I believe—your longest observation."[21] His praise rallied her self-confidence, for she had not been sure he would think the poem worthy of publication either in the *Dial* or in her book. And she was fortified in her resolve to append notes on her quotations at the back of the book—a decision for which readers, too, must feel a sense of gratitude to Thayer.

"An Octopus" was not, in fact, her "longest observation." The longest of these "serial poems" is "Marriage"; and it was also the first of them to be published, in the brief-lived series *Manikin*, sponsored by Marianne Moore's friend Monroe Wheeler. Her comment on its beginning reveals the kind of effort these three poems exacted. In a letter to her brother she expressed relief that he liked "Novices," and added "I had high hopes of it when writing but much of the nourishment had I thought been punished out of it by the time it came out. I am still worrying over "Marriage" which I am writing for Mr. Wheeler (on Adam and Eve)."[22] By the end of April 1923 she reported that he liked the poem and would publish it.

The drafting of "Marriage" complete, work on "An Octopus" began or was resumed. "Sea Unicorns and Land Unicorns" was the last to be undertaken, after an interval of work on "Peter" and "Silence." Drafts of all of them exist in one poetry workbook, and it is evident that the longer pieces overlap to some extent, in the images involuntarily occurring as the writer balances the motifs selected from her reading and the new impressions of things seen and heard.

The title, "Marriage," is enough to put the reader on guard. We all know some good poems about weddings, whether profound, as Spenser's epithalamium, or light-hearted as Suckling's ballad. The way it feels for two people to be in love, whether married or not—some poems have captured this; on re-reading them one can only be grateful for Donne's or D. H. Lawrence's, or Edwin Muir's. But marriage as a *general* theme is formidable. So is Marianne Moore's poem—formidable, but triumphant. Although the décor is often of a bygone age ("fiddlehead ferns" and "opuntias") the scenes and dialogues of Adam and Eve and the incisive control by the dramatist who presents them will challenge any reader today.

"Marriage," this institution "requiring all one's criminal ingenuity to avoid," was written by a convinced feminist. One of the central lines, "Men have power and sometimes one is made to feel it," is not quoted from another source; it is an outright declaration by the writer herself. Eve, however, is shown no favour. In her various guises she remains "the central flaw / in that first crystal fine experiment." She describes marriage in a way that has an unexpected similarity to a passage in *The Waste Land*:

> 'the heart rising
> in its estate of peace
> as a boat rises
> with the rising of the water.'

(Oddly enough, the quotation that Eve makes her own is from Baxter's *The Saints' Everlasting Rest*). In Book v of *The Waste Land*, after the third of the imperatives *Datta, dayadvham, damyata* (give, sympathise, control), the lines continue:

38

The boat responded
Gaily, to the hand expert with sail and oar
The sea was calm, your heart would have responded
Gaily, when invited, beating obedient
To controlling hands.

(V, 11. 418-22)

Some of the trial lines in Marianne Moore's workbook suggest a different direction for the poem. One rejected passage will show this. It begins "Adam / I have seen him when he was so handsome that he gave me a start / then he went off / appearing in his true colours / the transition fr. Apollo to Apollyon / being swift like Jack before and after the beanstalk."[23] As the thinking about Adam's possessiveness and desire for power continues, a conclusion is made: "this division into masculine and feminine compartments of achievement will not do. . .one feels oneself to be an integer / but one is not one is a particle / in an existence to which Adam and Eve / are incidental to the plot."[24] But this interior dialogue of the writer with herself while drafting the poem was eventually translated into the impersonal irony of the lines that soon appear in the draft, and begin the published poem.[25]

As published in *Manikin* and in all later versions—but not in the workbook drafts—Eve enters the scene immediately after the author's prologue. But more of the action in this dramatic composition is given to Adam. It is he who, "plagued" by the silence of the nightingale that clothes him " 'with a shirt of fire,' " invents marriage. Aided by a selection of phrases from the most unlikely sources, a portrait emerges of several characters who might have adorned a Shakespearian comedy or a story by Henry James (even of Adam Verver in some moments that James does not describe). Eve, although sometimes silent like the nightingale, has in fact destroyed "the ease of the philosopher / unfathered by a woman," and is "constrained in speaking of the serpent / that invaluable accident / exonerating Adam."

Any physical relationship between Adam and Eve is sug-
gested in the poem only by the imagery—marriage as "fire-
gilt steel," Adam's "shirt of fire," "the strange experience of
beauty" that "tears one to pieces," Eve's knowledge of " 'that
strange paradise' " where the heart rises " 'in its estate of
peace / as a boat rises / with the rising of the water.' "

A line in the *Manikin* version[26] that was drastically pared
down when the poem appeared in *Observations* is really a
subtitle—"one's self love labors lost." In the final speeches
of Adam and Eve they are not talking to one another. Each
is speaking to an unknown auditor—about the nature of
woman as man sees her, and of man as woman sees him.
The portrait of his self-love, so great that he can permit no
rival, and of hers, "who cannot see herself enough," and is
incapable of generosity in her relationship with Adam,
brings out a resemblance to Molière's *Misanthrope* that is
tacit throughout the poem. The admission that " 'Every-
thing that has to do with love is a mystery' " looks down a
similar avenue; it is a quotation from a book on La Fon-
taine's Fables, roughly translating a line from the fable
"Love and Folly," that Marianne Moore was to translate
quite differently many years later.

Taken as a whole, "Marriage" is unlike any other piece
by her. Its brilliance is set off by a faceting that prevents the
reader from looking at the center of poetic energy. One ven-
tures the guess that "Marriage" comes close to a roman à
cléf in verse, and had special meanings for particular read-
ers that can only be more abstractly glimpsed by later ones.
Both the reading and conversation notebooks show a pre-
occupation with this subject in the early New York years.
One conversation with Stieglitz is set down in some detail.
He spoke of the lack of understanding between him and his
first wife; that he married her because he was told that she
expected him to. "So one day I woke up and found that
I was married. . . . Now she blames me for the very thing
that she married me for. . . . She said to me you are only
fit to be a lover. Well why shouldn't I be a lover? If a mar-

ried man must stop being a lover the moment he is married
there is something wrong w[ith] the institution."[27] The
poem begins "This institution"—a rare example of Mari-
anne Moore's placing the object of a sentence first—and it
is likely that the term stayed in her mind after these touch-
ingly frank disclosures by Stieglitz.

More immediately in the background of the poem was
the widespread discussion of Bryher's marriage to Robert
McAlmon in 1921. Mrs. Moore and Marianne had invited
them to tea in February with Scofield Thayer and Sibley
Watson. A letter to "Badger" described the occasion. "The
girls arrived at about twenty past. Hilda had just had time
before the men came, to say that W. had been married to
'Robert' a little while before and that that had made them
late. The girls looked lovely and the men were graciousness
and responsiveness itself but what an earthquake."[28]

Two months later, when Marianne Moore was having
dinner with Thayer, he gave her a clipping from the *New
York Times* about the wedding. The headline was " 'Heir-
ess' Writer Weds Village Poet" and the account stressed
Greenwich Village gossip about the reported proposal of
the wealthy Miss Winifred Ellerman, who had taken the
nom de plume, Bryher, to the impecunious bohemian Robert
McAlmon. Marianne refused to see anything humorous in
the newspaper story, and said that she found the marriage
anything but romantic. Whereupon Thayer asked if it was
unromantic to be married on Valentine's Day.[29] A number of
their friends believed that he wished to marry Marianne;[30]
doubtless he was not alone in this hope. Circumstances like
these account for the turbulence of the early drafts of the
poem and the current of emotion that sustains its high com-
edy when perfected. No one seems to me to have read it
with better understanding than William Carlos Williams.
"Of marriage there is no solution in the poem and no at-
tempt at a solution; nor is there an attempt to shirk thought
about it," he wrote in 1924.[31] In the same article he arrived
at the principle that I believe a modern reader can only

41

endorse: "The interstices for the light and not the intersti-
tial web of thought concerned her. . . . Thus the material
is as the handling: the thought, the word, the rhythm—all
in the style. The effect is in the penetration of the light it-
self; how much how little; the appearance of the luminous
background.[32]

Williams' statement could equally well have been made
about "An Octopus." In writing this poem Marianne Moore
continued to weave quotations into the fabric of her design.
But the ironic tone of the dramatic dialogue in "Marriage"
is provided by bits tidily borrowed from literary sources
ranging from Amos and Ecclesiasticus to Trollope and Ezra
Pound. "An Octopus" dispenses with narrative and dia-
logue. This documentary in verse proceeds by intent de-
scriptive passages that build from romantic or humorous
phrases of travel books and matter-of-fact details given in
government pamphlets on the national parks. Some of the
most powerful effects are again achieved by combining
phrases from other writers in a totally new and unexpected
context. The glass mountain "hovers forward 'spider fash-
ion / on its arms' misleading like lace; / its 'ghostly pallor
changing / to the green metallic tinge of an anemone
starred pool' " [*Illustrated London News*]. The fir trees in
" 'the magnitude of their root systems,' [John Muir] / rise
aloof from these manœvers 'creepy to behold,' [*Illustrated
London News*] / austere specimens of our American royal
families, / 'each like the shadow of the one beside it. / The
rock seems frail compared with their dark energy of life,'
[Ruskin] / its vermillion and onyx and manganese blue
interior expensiveness / left at the mercy of the weather."
The metaphor requiring an adjustment of one's own per-
ception (the moving arms of the octopus "misleading like
lace")[33] is Marianne Moore's invention, and so are the
images that take us up onto the mountain. It is a unique
procedure.

Throughout, the composition sustains a contrast between
the unusual surface colours (as in these introductory lines)

and the whiteness of the omnipresent height. The bear's
den is composed of "topaz . . . and amethyst quartz" and is
hidden in blue forests. There are "miniature cavalcades of
chlorophylless fungi / magnified in profile on the mossbeds
like moonstones in the water" and "white flowers of the
rhododendron surmounting rigid leaves / upon which mois-
ture works its alchemy / transmuting verdure into onyx,"
and other flowers "like pink sapphires in the pavement of
the glistening plateau." Among the many animals whose
ancestors preempted the mountain as their property—the
"exacting porcupine," the rat pausing to smell the heather,
the thoughtful bears, the elk, deer, or marmot—one emerges
in a dramatic moment:

> . . . farther up, in stag-at-bay position
> stands the goat,
> its eye fixed on the waterfall which never seems to fall—
> an endless skein swayed by the wind,
> immune to force of gravity in the perspective of the
>   peaks.
> .   .   .   .
> it stands its ground   .   .   .   .   .   .
> black feet, eyes, nose, and horns engraved on dazzling ice-
>   fields,
> the ermine body on the crystal peak;
> the sun kindling its shoulders to maximum
>   heat like acetylene, dyeing them white—
> upon this antique pedestal   .   .   .   .

This passage is in high relief in the overall composition
of "An Octopus." The reminder of vast age ("antique ped-
estal") is quickly followed by a sense of change on the moun-
tain. "Maintaining many minds," it is "the home of a diver-
sity of creatures," among whom the tourist climbers and
their guides are transients.

Who but Marianne Moore would think of the Greek
character and of Henry James as essential to the conclusion
of "An Octopus?" The association prompting this is easier

to follow in the longer text printed in *Observations*. For in later collections she deleted thirty-two lines about the mountain flowers. Supreme among them was the greenish orchid named Calypso, "anomalously nourished upon glacial ledges." A passage of great fascination and beauty was sacrificed, in order to move more quickly to the final realization of the mountain's antiquity in its historical past and in an ideal time essential to the central meaning of this poem. Calypso's only neighbour on her rocky ledge is a noisy bluejay who "knows no Greek." The Greeks enter the poem as symbols of clarity, able to resolve complex questions, and ascribing "what we clumsily call happiness" to a spiritual substance or power—"such power as Adam had and we are still devoid of." The maneuvering arms of the octopus reach out here to the poem "Marriage," and from the glassy essence of the mountain we see as "In the Days of Prismatic Color," her concept of Adam in Paradise.

To restore this vision is the spell of Mount Tacoma, "this fossil flower concise without a shiver, / intact when it is cut, / damned for its sacrosanct remoteness— / like Henry James 'damned by the public for decorum'; / not decorum, but restraint. . . ." The fossil flower, Tacoma, stands for the art of nature, as Henry James becomes a symbol of man's capacity for art. The integrity of the mountain, the kinds of life it nurtures, manifest the "love of doing hard things" necessary to art. The summary statement, "Relentless accuracy is the nature of this octopus / with its capacity for fact," makes the physical reality of nature comparable to mind. The end is a cinematic long shot of the unconquerable mountain in its totality of action:

> the lightning flashing at its base,
> rain falling in the valleys, and snow falling on the peak—
> the glassy octopus symmetrically pointed,
> its claw cut by the avalanche
> "with a sound like the crack of a rifle,
> in a curtain of powdered snow launched by a waterfall."

In a curious way, "An Octopus" belongs in the company of Yeats's "Sailing to Byzantium"; the octopus of ice stands for eternity in contrast to the finite ways of human beings. And like Marvell's "Nymph Complaining," Marianne Moore's "An Octopus," after all the richness of colour and violent action, presents a transcendent image of stillness and whiteness: "this fossil flower concise without a shiver."

But unlike Yeats's hammered gold, "An Octopus" is not an artifice; and unlike the statue of the fawn, the mountain with lightning flashing at its base, and sounding avalanche, and waterfall, is a living phenomenon. The resemblance to "Upon Appleton House" (different as these two poems are) is closer, in that "An Octopus" is a poem about a particular place, opening vistas of time into other spaces, a poem about the findings that can occur there, as unpredictable life, seeking its own unity, continues at the end.

"An Octopus" also poses a question that has been more fully explored in discussions of Pound, or Eliot, or Stevens: —that is, of course, the means pursued by these various writers in creating a longer poem, at a time when narrative had for the most part been rejected. Although Marianne Moore never attempted any composition in verse as long as "The Waste Land" or "The Cantos" or "Notes towards a Supreme Fiction," both "Marriage" and "An Octopus" are longer than anything she had hitherto written, or was to write in the future. They would have to be considered in a category of "longer" poems, which she had moved toward as early as 1916 in "Critics and Connoisseurs." Without major dependence upon myth, or myth interlarded with history, or the use of "personae" for aspects of the poet's mind, in "An Octopus" she had invented something different from the forms evolved by Pound or Eliot or Stevens. The reader who has pondered this question wonders why I have not mentioned *Paterson*. The reason is not merely that *Paterson* is a much later work, or that, to my way of reading it or thinking about it, Williams' poem is very uneven, but rather that "An Octopus" is more like *Paterson* at its best, especially, of course, Book I, than it is like anything written by the others.

The more we read her poetry, the clearer it will be that her work derives its strength from something profoundly American in the "raw material" from which these compositions are made. In discussing the books that were to follow *Observations* it should be possible to bring out more fully what this implies, how in the long run a fresh response to the changing resources of the English language and a strong awareness of "the American grain" interact to the benefit of both, as had of course been true from the time of Emerson.

"Sea Unicorns and Land Unicorns," the third of these "serial poems," experiments further with shadings of expression by the use of phrases imported from other writers, *inter alia* Spenser, Henry James, J. A. Symonds, Leigh Hunt, Pliny, and Charles Cotton, and the narratives of Elizabethan voyagers. Here, old British pair, the lion and the unicorn, are woven into a storied tapestry in which one commander (Cavendish) brings back the horn of a sea unicorn to Queen Elizabeth and another (Sir John Hawkins) describes an abundance in Florida of " 'land unicorns and lions, / since where the one is, / its arch enemy cannot be missing.' "[34] The sea unicorn is the narwhal, native to Arctic or Antarctic waters. Like Queen Elizabeth, Marianne Moore had received a precious narwhal's tusk from an expert voyager—her brother Warner. A wholly original theme in this poem is that the traditional opponents, lion and unicorn, link the old world to the new and Eastern America to the far West.

> Britannia's sea unicorn with its rebellious child
> now ostentatiously indigenous of the new English coast
> and its land lion oddly tolerant of those pacific counter-
>   parts to it,
> the water lions of the west.

No doubt, while writing a draft of this poem on one of her visits to her brother's family in Bremerton, she had seen the sea lions. Having reminded the reader of the combination of these strange animals in tapestries, the poem develops the myth stemming from Pliny, that the unicorn when hunted can elude its pursuers

by an unmatched device
wrought like the work of expert blacksmiths,
with which nothing can compare—
this animal of that one horn
throwing itself upon which head foremost from a cliff,
it walks away unharmed,
proficient in this feat, which like Herodotus,
I have not seen except in pictures.

The difficulty of taking the unicorn alive opens into the medieval myth that it can be tamed only by a virgin. Nothing explicit links the poem to "Marriage"; but the relationship between them is suggested by an earlier passage: "Thus personalities by nature much opposed, / can be combined in such a way / that when they do agree, their unanimity is great." The cadence of the final lines is beautifully controlled and the way that the quotations are absorbed by the unique diction of the writer has much to do with the musical effect. So has the shift to a simple narrative mode, as

. . . unfearful of deceit
etched like an equine monster on an old celestial map,
beside a cloud or dress of Virgin-Mary blue,

. . . .

the unicorn "with pavon high," approaches eagerly;
until engrossed by what appears of this strange enemy,
upon the map, "upon her lap,"
its "mild wild head doth lie."

The words in quotation marks are from an anonymous medieval poem; as Marianne Moore pointed out to Scofield

47

Thayer, she substituted "its" for "his" in the last line. There can be no doubt of the improvement in the cadence obtained by this minute *ritardando*.

An amusing section of *Comment* in the *Dial* of March 1925 rallied the "authoress" for using the myth of the unicorn's being tamed by a virgin. "Why," the writer inquires, if the taking of a unicorn is so easy, "do we find relatively so few examples of this interesting species in captivity?" With assumed indignation he inquires whether she "would attribute the sad lacuna in, for example, our Bronx [zoo] to some reticence in the shapely beast itself which should remove it, as by a compulsion of its own inward nature, from all female society," or would she "refer this fact, more cynically (and, it does seem to me, much less acceptably), to a standing paucity of virgins?" It is evident that the writer was animated by a desire to arouse interest in Marianne Moore's new book, and likewise that he was aware of some of the nuances of meaning that connect "Marriage," "An Octopus," and "Sea Unicorns and Land Unicorns." In fact, the author of this unsigned article was Scofield Thayer.[35]

These three poems and a few others completed between 1919 and 1924 may be looked upon as a landing-stage, a culmination of Marianne Moore's early writing. Without sacrificing the aptitude for concision, she had given greater freedom to her power of observation, and directed it to a wider range of human experience. In "Marriage" and "An Octopus" she invented a sustained poetic discourse without stanzaic arrangement. She knew of course that some readers would misapprehend her increasing use of quotation. Her later demure apology in *Collected Poems* could be misleading. The need to acknowledge indebtedness, and the seeming disclaimer of her own invention in the statement that there are "lines in which the chief interest is borrowed," are not the real point at all. Shakespeare and Milton wrote lines in which the source of vitality came from other writers, whether Plutarch or Virgil or the Old Testament or the New. They did not need to put the words absorbed in quotation marks, and thus have given many scholars harmless and delightful work to do. Ezra Pound and Eliot usually but not always indicate that they are quoting, or half-quoting, or misquoting other writers. But the purpose of their quotations is to evoke memory, to juxtapose past and present, or to maintain what Pound called the "subject rhyme."[36] Marianne Moore's incorporation of phrases or sentences from a widely varied list of authors has an essentially different purpose, for which the quotation marks are essential. A "hybrid method of composition," as she terms it, may produce something as unique as a hybrid plant. By this method she could avail herself of intersecting perspectives and changing tones of speech; the typographical device makes this clear to the reader and allows one kind of modulation at her command. Sometimes, too, the quotations are introduced for a dramatic effect, or a satiric one. If the reader looks carefully at the change in phrasing from the quoted source to the line in the poem, the purpose becomes more evident. There are some borrowed phrases not enclosed in quotation marks, as well as some where the punctuation indicates that her expressions are quoted, when in fact they are not.

Another development in the newer poems is the greater latitude taken with rhyme. As soon as she began to publish beyond the audience reached by the Bryn Mawr undergraduate magazines, she carefully arranged the typography to indicate the pattern of rhyme. Some readers probably miss this clue, since like other versatile poets of this century she adeptly combines unrhymed and rhymed lines.

In the earliest poems rhythm and the way of rhyming simply correspond; in the poems of greater freedom in structure and depth of intent, rhyme is integral to rhythm —they cannot be separately heard. This is true even of relatively simple (which does not mean easy) poems like "To a Chameleon" and "The Talisman." But in the complex poems at the end of *Observations*, especially in "An Octopus," only a careful reader will be aware of the rhyme.

Even T. S. Eliot thought it was written in free verse. Actually, rhyme is a strong element in the poem; but it belongs wholly to the texture of language. Further, every resource of off-rhyme or partial rhyme, and internal rhyme, becomes appropriate. One cannot tell whether Marianne Moore had read Wilfred Owen or Gerard Hopkins at this time, although it is possible that she had. But her adoption of these new variations on rhyme is quite different from the harmonies brought over from the Welsh *cynghanedd* by Hopkins, or the dissonant chords of Owen's war poems.[37]

A surprising fact should be entered here as a tracer of her evolving style. She had been able to convert certain kinds of strength that belong to prose to the different structures of poetry. It is not hard to see this in short poems like "To an Intramural Rat" or "To a Steam Roller," and in "Critics and Connoisseurs" the possibilities are still more evident. But one resource of this kind she did not call upon: the chance to poise the sentence in a noticeable lively relation to the line or stanza.

This will be evident if we think of poets who like to make syntax support or vary the rhythm in accord with changes in the mood or emotion of the person speaking. Wyatt is one of the best. Minute alterations in the refrains of his lyrics are a pleasure to hear. The changing parallels in Ben Jonson's "Charis: Her Triumph" give another example. Dylan Thomas had the temerity to add a word to a sentence in one of St. Paul's epistles to create the strong affirmations of "And death shall have no dominion." None of these patterns would have been natural to Marianne Moore. Her preference was for a conversational tone, for informality and hidden music. Yet she admired the elusive rhetorical patterns in Wallace Stevens. In discussing "Certain Phenomena of Sound," she remarks on "the art of velvet emphasis, suspended till scarcely detectable."[38] And although she did not refer, in her essays on Eliot, to the rhythm of *Ash Wednesday* or *The Four Quartets* she was quite aware of his syntactic parallels. But at this time, as she achieved the

richness, the magnitude of "An Octopus," the effect of en-
semble rather than of a solo instrument, or a soliloquy or
song or invocation, was needed. To have made a more con-
trolled syntax dominate the conversational fragments or in-
terpolated details from quotations would have destroyed
"the concealment of the subject within a continuous tex-
ture,"[39] that she was practicing at that time.

But we can rightly see these experiments and conquests
in rhythm or rhyme or matrix of language only as the out-
ward counterpart of inner feeling. It was from the strong
value attached to actuality that she could ascend to imagina-
tion's higher attention. The distinction between the false
coin and the mint, between humbug and the testimony
truthfully spoken, is not blurred by the illusion poets al-
low. The poems in *Observations* benefit from the unde-
ceived mind of a master of satire, but are not limited to the
satirist's purpose. The writer who in her early thirties spoke
of "the inevitable attrition of experience" also believed that
"the poet watches life with affection."[40]

3

"Some of Her Prose"

IF she could have managed it, Marianne Moore would have begun her professional life as a reviewer. Before the move to Chatham, New Jersey, in 1916, she made a fierce attempt to get work of this kind on one of the Philadelphia newspapers, being willing to write other pieces for them if asked. "Rats need room to experiment and grow that is the main thing and *they need pay*,"[1] she wrote Warner. She and her mother soon set out for Philadelphia "with belts and pistols" to see a Mr. Lion of the *Evening Ledger,* "Mole" being prepared to "roar at him through a keyhole" and then to let "Rat . . . roar at him and squirrel at him."[2] But nothing came of this campaign.

To be sure, the immediate point was the practical one. Yet she had submitted prose to the *Egoist,* and in a letter to H. D. expressed an almost wistful interest in the novel as a form. She did, later, begin a piece of fiction that she referred to as "my story"; it is really a fictionalized version of scenes and people she knew, and remains unpublished. Toward the end of her life she began to write a memoir, but was unable to complete it. Her published prose, therefore, consists of essays and reviews, edited interviews, and statements about herself and her beliefs. A full account of her prose will be possible only when her manuscripts and her voluminous correspondence have been published.

The reason for initiating a discussion of her prose here is that it drew upon energies active in her poetry, but needing a different outlet. Her essays and reviews set up an imaginative discourse with the reader different from that maintained in her poetry. And a dialogue is going on there,

too, with Pound and with Eliot, with Williams and with
Stevens (who was the only one not to enter that dialogue
openly). Later, the dialogue includes writers of a younger
generation.

Although the *Egoist* did accept her brief essay, "The Ac-
cented Syllable," a more ambitious piece dealing with Poe
and Byron was returned. Soon after her poems had begun
to appear in the *Dial*, Ezra Pound urged Scofield Thayer
to get "some of her prose."[3] Thayer responded by giving
her important books to review at some length[4] and he (or
Sibley Watson) accepted essays of hers as well, particularly
the strong one on Sir Francis Bacon.[5] There were also the
many "Briefer Mention" notices—for the January 1925 *Dial*,
for example, she wrote eleven. One would hardly single them
out as a significant part of her criticism. But anyone who has
ever undertaken similar chores will understand the hard
work required to review eleven books for one issue of a
monthly journal. After Marianne Moore assumed the chief
responsibility for editing the *Dial*, she wrote the unsigned
"Comment" sections and provided a great many of the
"Briefer Mention" notices, for which the editors were not
paid, although other contributors were. After the *Dial*
ceased publication, her principal reviews were done for
Poetry or the *Nation* or *New Republic*, and a major essay
or essay-review might appear in the *Hound and Horn* or
the *Criterion*.

This pattern of professional activity partly accounts for
the fact that she wrote a substantial body of criticism about
her own contemporaries. Eliot was reluctant to do this, as
he explained:

> It has been only under peculiar conditions that I
> have ever been able to interest myself in criticizing—
> except in the currents of conversation—contemporary
> writers. In the case of authors whose work one considers
> pernicious . . . one figures to oneself occasionally an ob-
> ligation to denounce or ridicule. In the case of authors

whose merits have been ignored or misunderstood, there is sometimes a particular obligation of championship.[6]

But for better-known or widely recognized authors, he believed that the task of criticism must be left to the succeeding generation. A thoroughly understandable point of view, and one which in any case we would never question, as a writer's decision about what he is *not* going to write. Yet we may be glad that neither Coleridge nor Dr. Johnson shared it. Anything more than casual and abbreviated criticism of writers by their contemporaries is, in English at least, relatively recent. Had Ben Jonson's dialogue between himself and Donne survived the fire, it would be the first important discourse of this kind.

The effort of a good writer to describe what he finds most compellingly good in the work of his contemporaries has a value different from that of any other kind of criticism. There is no substitute for the artistic energy you either find, or against all odds keep looking for, in the writing of your own time. If we cannot experience excitement in it, somewhere—the excitement of pleasure—we are not likely to connect as strongly with the writing of the past. We shall miss the surprise it has. Inevitably, we derive an irreplaceable enlightenment from the notations of the best writers of our own time about the present conditions of their craft, and its new requirements.

Besides review-articles or essays on Eliot, Pound, Williams, and Stevens (of which only a few are included in *Predilections*), Marianne Moore wrote on George Moore, Shaw, E. A. Robinson, Vachel Lindsay, Hardy, Yeats, Gertrude Stein, E. E. Cummings, and some poets of the generation following hers—Elizabeth Bishop, for example. Unlike Pound and Eliot, she never adopted any special province of the past, and she had not the same kind of historical sense as either of them, or the polemic sense, or the power of abstract formulation. Yet there are unifying principles in

these essays of hers; she is always measuring by a plumb
line of moral conviction and technical insight, and her be-
lief that charity is inherent in imagination. Then, she has
a detective instinct for the symbols that reveal a writer's
"logic of preferences."

Eliot's, she found (when reviewing his *Collected Poems*
[1936]) were for "stillness, intellectual beauty, spiritual exal-
tation . . . 'the glory of the hummingbird,' childhood, and
wholeness of personality—in contrast with noise, evasive-
ness, aimlessness, fog, scattered bones, broken pride. . . ."[7]
But perhaps in *Sweeney Agonistes* the contrast is blurred,
or clumsy?

> In *Sweeney Agonistes* Mr. Eliot comes to us as the
> men of the neighboring tribes came to Joshua under a
> camouflage of frayed garments, with mouldy bread in
> the wallet. But the point is not camouflaged. Mortal
> and sardonic victims though we are in this conflict
> called experience, we may regard our victimage with
> calmness, the book says; not because we don't know
> that our limitations of correctness are tedious to a soci-
> ety which has its funny side to us, . . . but because there
> is a moment for Orestes, for Ophelia, for Everyman,
> when the ego and the figure it cuts, . . . the good cheer
> and the customary encomium, are as the insulting wig-
> waggery of the music-halls.
>
> . . . There is, as the author intended, an effect of
> Aristophanic melodrama about this London flat in
> which the visitors play with the idea of South Sea lan-
> guor and luxury—work annihilated, personality nega-
> tived and conscience suppressed: a monkey at hand to
> milk the goat and pass the cocktails—woman in the
> cannibal pot or at hand to serve.[8]

Here is no theorizing or abstract analysis; instead we are
prodded to think about the play by a quick-witted specta-
tor-reader, by her rhythmic answer to the human ambience
it creates. Marianne Moore had, in life, an astonishing abil-

ity to understand the needs and resources of other human beings; as a reader of literature, this absolved her from commonplace expectations. New juxtapositions arise from the unusual freedom of perception: "the sense of mortality" in Hardy, "not divided from immortality," Bunyan also knew, and Bunyan, like Hardy, in guiding us "through the pleasing agonies and painful delights' of an imagined world has caused ordinariness to be clothed with extraordinariness."[9]

For a critic to praise justly, and without exaggeration, is hard; it may be harder still, when praise is due, to make it relevant—to make it mean anything specific in reference, and specifically alive in statement. This difficult art goes to the root of criticism. For praise that counts is not encomium, is certainly not compliment, but attempts identification. It no longer adds a mere *plus* (or when not bestowed, a *minus* sign); it ceases to refer primarily to the writer, and becomes the predicate attaching itself to the work in question. Because Marianne Moore exemplifies the reserve and the "immunity to fear"[10] of the true writer, her praise of the work she admires suggests the outline of her poetics.

Ultimately, the strength of her criticism derives from the fact that so much has been thought through beforehand, about many things at a distance from the immediate subject. This forehandedness—human, literary, moral—gives critical writing a tone one finds lacking in many of the set-pieces of modern exegesis, which sometimes exhaust the air needed for the reader and the book to breathe in. Because she respects the writer's or artist's reserve, and feels at home with it, there is incorruptible counsel in a sentence of hers that encloses Blake's own counsel: "As for labour, 'the hard wiry line of rectitude and certainty in the actions and intentions' of Blake teaches one to dispel all hope—and fear —that great art is 'the fruit of facility.' "[11] It is worthy of reflection that "Many sagacities seem in Dürer not to starve one another."[12] This, like many another sentence or phrase, exemplifies a characteristic use of negative verbs or adjectives as an aid to accuracy; she is not *saying* something negative, of course. She suggests a different reconciling and reinforcing of "sagacities" when she finds that

> hostile though specific theories may be and riotous as the artist may sometimes seem in his attitude toward the existing body of art, in so far as a thing is really a work of art it confirms other works of art.[13]

One reason why Marianne Moore's prose is enlivening is that it grows out of deep feeling—which cannot be separated from her deliberate effort to understand the life of form. This intention appears at least as early as 1909, when she took Miss King's course in "Imitative Prose Writing" at Bryn Mawr. The title of the course is abominable, but probably misleading. Her notes show that she then read Bacon, Hooker, Fulke Greville, Raleigh, Jeremy Taylor, Burton, Milton, and Clarendon. Discussions ranged up to Pater, Swinburne, and Henry James, and apparently there was emphasis upon—or perhaps the student singled out—the nature of irony and satire. One of the instructor's principles about this went into her student's notebook: "in Irony the pt. is to keep your temper and not fall into invective. Em. Dickinson Hooker Swinburne James observers of civility and decency of order they accused of being carnally minded and earthly minded."[14] The attention paid to Bacon at this time surfaced later in one of her best essays.

The text as published in the *Dial* is more rewarding than the one in *Predilections*,[15] which is condensed and slightly watered-down. I restore part of this sentence as helpful evidence: "The explicit technical view which Sir Francis Bacon takes of writing at once denotes the expert: his admiration for Machiavelli's suiting of form to matter."[16] Marianne Moore did not trust a writer of either prose or poetry who did not take an "explicit technical view" of his work (whether or not that was communicated to the reader other than *implicitly* being at the writer's discretion). Another point about Bacon set down with terse authority also has a bearing upon her prose as well as her poetry; that is, "In Sir Francis Bacon conclusiveness and contempt for tact are always at variance with the known necessity for caution."[17] Setting aside the relevance of this to the political dangers of his own era, we may look upon it more generally as a polarity evident in Marianne Moore's writing—her "burning desire to be explicit" balanced by "wariness" with words and respect for the imaginative reserve necessary to magnetic expression.[18] We may follow her own thinking on such matters in "Feeling and Precision," "Humility, Concentration, and Gusto," and "Idiosyncrasy and Technique."[19] That being the case, we may prefer to look a little further into the individuality of accent in her prose.

When we do, we become aware of her responsiveness to the cadence and inventiveness of those seventeenth-century writers she liked. In more than one of her sentences we hear a reverberation of rhythm, or a tone, characteristic of Browne:

> The opinion of the sceptic that the artist can thrive only under the most favorable conditions is often shared by the artist; but discipline under provocation, an integrity of confident expectation, the refusal to be warped by misadventure, are not infirm refutations.[20]

This rhythm, this tone, cannot be imitated; it can be renewed only by writers who similarly move from keenly apprehended thing or event or underlying trust in unifying forms. Marianne Moore has brought this account forward into the twentieth century as Emerson and Thoreau did in the nineteenth—and they too are ancestors of hers. As she once stated, Emerson's *Representative Men*, "fearless in appraisal and comparisons, aids one in being affirmative yet not invariably encomiastic."[21]

The idiosyncrasies of style in her prose revive certain eighteenth-century exactitudes as well, and these too she would acknowledge. "Dr. Johnson's critical observations and didacticisms throw light, or stimulate resistance," she said.[22] (Some of today's poets whose carelessness or insensitivity she intended to rebuke must relish the occasional Johnsonian effect in her reviews, since they admire her nonetheless.[23]) Her way of expressing admiration or approval of a writer's work may be to admit that it "detains attention," or "commends itself." A sentence may begin "Appreciation which is truly votive and not gapingly inquisitive. . . ."[24] Were one to read no further in the same sentence, the temptation would be to believe oneself listening to an author of the late eighteenth or early nineteenth century. But no, it is not solely Jane Austen's example that provides a prefiguration of these mannerly salutations. Personal conviction moves through more rapidly; there are no safe, however valid or intelligible, assumptions. We may be as often reminded of the more romantically independent affirmations of Charlotte Brontë.

In fact, Charlotte Brontë could at need write with the celerity, the successful passing shot we may also admire in Marianne Moore.

> The Misses Sympson and the Misses Nunnely looked upon her, as quiet poultry might look upon an egret, an ibis, or any other strange fowl. What made her sing so?

So Charlotte Brontë describes Shirley, as she "impressed all, and charmed one." It is accident, but amusing, that in defending Emily Dickinson against thoughtless detractors Marianne Moore declares, "Unless it is conceited for the hummingbird or the osprey to not behave like a chicken, one does not find her conceited."[25]

But the tempo of Marianne Moore's thinking is of our own time. The pleasing reminders of seventeenth- or eighteenth-century prose writing result from similarly rooted faith and courtesy; but they do not overlay the economy and irreverence congenial to us. In its figures of sound and sense, her prose speaks in the accent of her own time.

Often a metaphor or comparison gains its chief effect through her more than casual acquaintance with particular sports: sailing, dancing, or horsemanship. Praising the bravura of Wallace Stevens, she matches it when she says, "Upon the general marine volume of statement is set a parachute spinnaker of verbiage which looms out like half a cantaloupe and gives the body of the theme the air of a fabled argosy advancing."[26] At this point it does not matter whether or not you know the poems she refers to; but it is all the more amusing if you do. Stravinsky's characteristic way of ending a composition is like "the recoil of a good ski-jumper accepting a spill."[27] The rhythm of Ezra Pound's *Cantos* "is a firm piloting of rebellious fluency; the quality of sustained emphasis, as of a cargo being shrewdly steered to the edge of the quai."[28] These prose metaphors have the kinetic aptitude of similar ones in her poetry. In a different review of *The Cantos*, she describes them as having "the effect sometimes, as in the medieval dance, of a wheel spun one way and then the other; there is the sense of a horse rushing towards one and turning, unexpectedly rampant; one has stepped back but need not have moved."[29]

Visually, too, the metaphors of her prose waken attention as do the ones in the poems, observations of the same mind and eye. Pondering the theme of "The Comedian as the Letter C," she compares the composition itself to a metaphor, "which becomes as one contemplates it, hypnotically incandescent like the rose-tinged fringe of the night-blooming cereus."[30] Again writing of *The Cantos*, she sees Pound's *materia poetica*, "the usual subjects of conversation between intelligent men," as "arranged in the style of the grasshopper wing for contrast, half the fold against the other half, the rarefied effect against a greyer one."[31] She has defined a principle of poetic composition in her statement that "poetic virtuosities are allied—especially those of diction, imagery, and cadence."[32] In her prose, diction alone may do the work of metaphor ("the swarming madness of excellence stays with one"[33] should furnish an example).

The rhythm of the prose is marked by the same instinct for the weight and configuration of syllable with syllable that is noticeable in her verse. A net effect of spontaneity overcomes one's sense of how much disciplined skill is at command. Her ways of using quotations in her essays and of introducing them in the poetry differ. In prose they provide unexpected diversions, and swift changes of impression that avoid the mechanics of transition, like different flowers in a border. By cannily borrowing words from others, she is able not only to season her wit with kindness, but to formulate some major propositions she is not going to be assertive about. And often the quotations are unexpectedly a reprieve, since what we genuinely laugh at is at best impersonal, and frees us from the strictures of the occasion. In this manner she corrects a potentially snobbish remark made by E. F. Benson in a book on Charlotte Brontë:

> Charlotte Brontë's father, Patrick Brunty, peasant schoolmaster, was a person of easy conscience when he usurped "the noble surname" Brontë, Mr. Benson thinks: though to the dull conscience of some it is like the kiss requested of Anna by the circuit-rider in Hardy's story. It would do her no harm and would do him a great deal of good.[34]

Quotation alone may be the springboard of metaphor; for example, in the finding that "imagination of the finest type involves an energy which results in order 'as the motion of a snake's body goes through all parts at once, and its volition acts at the same instant in coils that go contrary ways.' "[35] Or quotation may build an otherwise unobtainable extension of experience from one activity of life to another; this happens when it is suggested that "The riot of gorgeousness" in which a particular poet's imagination takes refuge, "recalls Balzac's reputed attitude to money, to which he was indifferent unless he could have it 'in heaps or by the ton.' "[36]

To mortice quotation into her own text with such dex-

61

terity is one secret of her rapid execution. Her quotations always quicken reflection. Likewise, the aphoristic quality of the single sentence reinforces it enough to carry the current of ideas through the piece as a whole. Bacon recommended aphorisms as the way to represent thought in growth. Marianne Moore's defining phrases also ask the reader to complete a proposition for himself: "the dominance without protest, of humility,"[37] or "hope, which in being frustrated becomes fortitude."[38] Such essential telescoping is sometimes produced by antithesis or (as partly noted earlier) by the uncommon double negative. A phrase alone may powerfully express antithesis: the "frugally unified opulence"[39] of Wallace Stevens, for example. In describing the "Corpus Christi" as sung by the English singers, she referred to "the buried fire and almost tuneless murmur of the tune with its slow fast according tongues of discord";[40] and the antithetic metaphor searches the essence of the music, yet seems involuntary.

Few but poets are likely to learn from the technical notations in some of her essays and reviews, but it is for poets that these suggestions were put there. Her notes on this subject have to do with language, with possibilities of rhythm, and with kinds of rhyme. She likes adjectives, if at all, that have the force of verbs. She tends in her prose as well as her poetry to dispense with connectives, whenever she can. One is aware that she is sensitive to the slightest implication of words and even to the heft of syllables. In questioning a weak but not incorrect choice of tense by a younger writer, she asks, "Has every phrase the feel of the rest of the words?"[41] She finds "instinct for words . . . well-determined by the nature of the liberties taken with them."[42]

But it is in response to the possibilities of rhythm, of kinds of rhyme, that her technical comments will evoke continuing interest. She is one of the few writers who has paid special attention to accelerations of tempo: in discussing one poem, she admires "brilliance gained by acceler-

ated tempo in accordance with a fixed melodic design."[43]
Acceleration affects rhyme as well: "the accelerated light
final rhyme, . . . the delayed long syllable."[44] She thinks that
"the better the artist, . . . the more determined he will be
to set down words in such a way as to admit of no inter-
pretation of the accent but the one intended."[45] Surely an
admirable, an assisting principle, if it were possible to as-
sure another generation of the music in poetry—so many
harmonies of Donne were so long neglected, and more re-
cently of Milton.

Her concern with technical skill is never subordinated to
or seen in isolation from insight into experience. For per-
ception of style extends to the work as a whole, where style
is the strong or shaky trestle for the writer's intention to
travel. She regards it as virtually a moral strength for a
writer to labor at his craft; "a severely intentional method
of procedure" is a worthy attribute and "the literary reader
tends not to be compensated by moral fervour for technical
misapprehensions."[46] But at a higher point, she held that
skill in presentation confirms whatever fundamental under-
standing of ourselves a poem may capture. In translation,
quite as in original work, character ultimately tests style:
"Translation requires that one put at the service of some-
thing not one's own, the most sharpened and excellent tools
in one's armoury: that is to say, there is character rather
than good fortune in translation of finish."[47]

For her the "detachment of faith" gives unanalyzable
veracity to works of art; and it appears in her concept of
sagesse as a moral rather than intellectual quality. "We owe
life our sagesse," she once said.[48] But admiration of a writer
may need to be qualified on behalf of a truth that is un-
represented. When a particular writer evinced "an interest
in retaliation," this seemed "at variance with creative pow-
er."[49] Cynicism implies "a grudging view, a lack of breadth,
of noble reverie, of the detachment of faith."[50] The latter
phrase makes a speculative distinction. Yet her affirmations
do not ally themselves with any limited perspective.

63

In making works of art, the only legitimate warfare is the inevitable warfare between imagination and medium and one finds it impossible to convince oneself that the part of the artist's nature which is "rash and combustible" has not been tamed by the imagination, in those instances in which the result achieved is especially harmonious.[51]

Therefore she finds Edward Arlington Robinson's "persistently tentative credulity" and Hardy's "tenacious incredulity" "obversely helpful."[52] Her respect for Hardy is firmly stated. "If one must go to extremes it should be . . . in avowing the obverse of the statement that Mr. Hardy is a 'pessimist.' . . . Discouragement, Premonitions, Questionings, are very essential parts of answers."[53] Recognition of the sense of wonder in Hardy is well-weighed by one whose faith in human nature is undismayed by knowledge of its limits.

Her later essays, some of the brief ones reprinted in the *Reader*, share the informality and ease of some of the later poems. Invisible logic supplies an invisible muscular strength in pieces like "A Burning Desire to be Explicit" and "Profit is a Dead Weight."[54] But because she is never self-righteous, cheerfulness breaks in, and an impression of wit and verve propels us through the sequence of ideas more easily than we could move if they were not so disarmingly arranged, dressed to a serpentine design of helpful diversions. Readiness to move along, optimism about endeavour, stimulate the reader to novel endeavours of his own, the only tolerable kind of imitation.

There are perhaps too few concessions to the reader in other respects: an almost relentless compression sometimes, the reserve she rightly values as a principle of criticism and of art being occasionally too finely operative. This may be inevitable where the matrix of criticism and poetry appears to be the same: the "observations" in prose scanning another sector of experience. But the unpublished letters will make up for all seeming lacunae.

Her family correspondence comes closest, probably, to being a self-portrait. The tone of her letters as editor of the *Dial* is vastly different. They are all written as from a spokesman, saying what "we" will accept, or wish to have reviewed, or would like to have contributed. But in spite of scrupulous editorial responsibility and care to indicate what might be the expectations of Scofield Thayer or Dr. Watson, the young editor did not hesitate to use her own initiative and to proffer encouragement, praise, or sometimes admonition. In his interview with her, Donald Hall got her to admit her tendency to rewrite or demand revision on various occasions, and this sometimes evoked the anger even of friends like William Carlos Williams or E. E. Cummings.

One hopes that all her *Dial* correspondence will be published in full—letters from other writers to her as well as her replies and her initiatory requests. She was active—trying to get for the *Dial* Yeats's preface to *A Vision*, some of Williams' *Paterson* in an early stage, an essay from Eliot on the criticism of poetry, and accepting some of Joyce's *Finnegans Wake* ["Work in Progress," at that stage]. For legal reasons this acceptance was qualified; Joyce (represented by Sylvia Beach) naturally refused to make excisions and demanded return of the manuscript.

The *Dial* correspondence reflects critical principles like those of her reviews; the phrases she quickly set down never seem merely utilitarian, but are, nevertheless, a kind of intellectual shorthand. But the warmth, the tact, and considerate attention often impressed the recipients of her requests (even when she had necessarily to emphasize the time when material had to be in, or the impossibility of accepting it if it was to be published elsewhere before its appearance in the *Dial*). Thus we find Thomas Mann, to whom such reminders were sometimes sent, progressing from early replies signed "Ihr sehr ergebener Thomas

Mann" to "Mit freundlichtsten Grüssen." Her correspondence with another older writer, George Saintsbury, evoked sprightly and amusing anecdotal letters from him; she and her mother felt a personal concern about his well-being.

One notices her sure instinct in proposing books that Eliot might particularly like to discuss, editions or critical analyses of writers like Crashaw, Henry Vaughn, Andrew Marvell, Baudelaire, von Hügel. She exercised the same effort to provide stimulating and financially helpful opportunities for many less well-known writers—Conrad Aiken and Witter Bynner, for example. She had some difficulty in overcoming Pound's reluctance to send poetry to the *Dial*; as editor she was finally successful in obtaining some of the *Cantos*; she also persuaded him to do a critique of the work of William Carlos Williams, as well as various other critical pieces. The nature of these letters—diplomatic, appreciative, yet fundamentally impersonal—is different from her later correspondence with the same people when she was writing as an individual.

The best part of her correspondence with writers—Pound, Eliot, Williams, Auden, Elizabeth Bishop, and others—awaits publication. The main importance of the *Dial* correspondence consists in the evidence of a sensibility at work affecting the main stream of artistic life in the nineteen-twenties, in Europe as well as America. Through her work as editor she acquired a hidden strength that lends power and zest to her later prose. The collaboration with Thayer, Dr. Watson, and Kenneth Burke had been a fruitful one, suggestively portrayed in the two essays contributed to *Life and Letters Today* in 1940-1941 (later included in *Predilections*, somewhat abridged).

Only when we can read the main body of her letters, as well as the essays and reviews not yet collected, will it be possible to perceive the skills of the essayist and the critical energies present in another form. Then, Marianne Moore's gifts as a prose writer will emerge more clearly, and she will

66

take her place in the long tradition of poets who are also enlightening as critics.

Of these poet-critics, we find two principal kinds: those whose criticism is built out of questions which could not be used in their poetry, but which only writers can propose, and those whose critcism is, on the contrary, closer to sketching or drawing, exercises of a skill similar to that of the poetry, but directed to a different object. To the first class would belong Dryden, Dr. Johnson, Poe, Arnold, Eliot; to the second, Sidney, Ben Jonson, Coleridge, Hopkins, Yeats, and Marianne Moore. But, as Eliot said in another way, and on another subject, the several voices of criticism will at times be heard simultaneously.

The difference remains a noticeable one. From the prose of Hopkins or Marianne Moore, we might be able to imagine what the poetry is like; from the critical essays of Eliot, we might infer what he thinks about some poets he has never discussed, but we could hardly imagine the kind of verse he has written.

In either case we cannot easily do without the prose of a good poet. For the structure of a poem and the unique vantage-point of experience from which that structure emerges do not afford occasion for all the kinds of observation that a given writer is prepared to make. The more scrupulous the writer, the more then will be lacking if we cannot read the writer's prose as well as poetry, essays as well as novels. Fortunately, and let us hope before too long, we shall have many volumes of the Moore letters to read, some rounding out her criticism, others vernacular explorations of her own life and of "love in America"—to borrow a phrase from one of her last poems.[55] Something she said of William Carlos Williams is at the heart of her best prose, especially in the letters: "That's the beauty of it; he is willing to be reckless; if you can't be that, what's the point of the whole thing?"[56] But not to worry; that kind of recklessness has its own decorum.

4

Arrivals and Departures

REFERRING to the decision to end publication of the *Dial*, Marianne Moore said that some of her friends felt that she ought not to continue as its editor because that task left her no time for writing poetry. She did not publish any of her own poems during these five years; and from the extant notebooks one cannot judge whether she had completed any new ones.

A number of poets have refrained from writing verse for a considerable period of time—Hopkins after entering the Jesuit order until the composition of "The Wreck of the Deutschland" seven years later, Valéry's self-imposed silence for a longer period. For Marianne Moore, the span of years when she gave most of her time to the *Dial* was not a willed or dramatic interruption. She continued to take notes in her reading diary and conversation notebooks, storing up facts and images that were later to be converted into poetry. The new poems she sent out between 1930 and 1934 were proof that she not only held the ground won by "Marriage" and "An Octopus," but could see into a more open country, and find paths to enter it. From examining the poetry workbook she used between 1922 and 1931, it seems to me that this development, particularly as it is reflected in "The Hero," overlaps the major poems at the end of *Observations*. Some of the new poems were germinating in her mind.

The result of this further and perhaps more simply confident development is presented in *Selected Poems* of 1935. Opening the volume one begins to read "Part of a Novel, Part of a Poem, Part of a Play," and immediately receives the pleasure of a differently composed rhythm and a more spontaneous sense of the way people live, giving character to and taking character from the places where we see them to be most naturally at home.

Postponing for the moment the chance to understand more fully why this tripartite composition stands at the gateway of a terrain not entered on before, either by the poet or by the reader, I prefer to discuss others which look both forward and backward in their tracings of imagination. "The Jerboa" and "Camellia Sabina" are related poems because both assemble with minute care evidence of the obsession with luxury, particularly when it provides the opportunity for devoted craftsmanship. The final summing up appears in the contrast between this passion for luxury and the ways of two innocuous, seemingly insignificant creatures, the desert rat and the meadow mouse. But these two poems bring places alive, as well as animals; and "Camellia Sabina" reflects the writer's life-long interest in flowers, their appropriateness or lack of it to particular occasions or moods.

Preparatory work on "The Jerboa" exemplifies Marianne Moore's self-discipline and initiative. We cannot say, of any of her poems, when the ignition began. But the fact that the Moore library contained five volumes of Gibbon's *Decline and Fall of the Roman Empire* and that the reading diary of 1916-21 includes pages of notes on the taste for luxury does not lack significance.[1] Her studies for "The Jerboa" prompted many visits to the American Museum of Natural History and correspondence with the curator, Dr. Raymond Ditmars.[2] This combination of themes selected from the notebooks, and forays into the places where unusual things could be seen, or heard, or touched, characterize her life as a poet. And she could be as startlingly attentive in a museum as she was at a circus. The movies, another favorite resort, she valued highly, especially the movies shown at the Pratt Institute.

"The Jerboa" sets side by side an imperial world of brilliant artifice and the crafty devices of adaptation to a hostile environment shown by an innocuous animal. The subtitles given to the two distinct parts of the poem underline the ironic contrast between "Too Much," the opulence and insatiate desire for luxury of imperial Rome, and "Abundance," the freedom and economy observable in the behavior of the jerboa, a small rat thriving in the desert sands.

In form, "The Jerboa" exemplifies a musical structure in its presentation of the first subject ("Too Much") by exposition and development of the theme, then introduction of the counter-subject. No approximation or lack of vigour dims the account of avid pleasure-seeking expressed by a passion for artful inventions. The colossal bronze fir-cone with holes for a fountain that pleased the Pompeys and later came to be known as the Pope's, "passed for art." In this world artisans made colossi and people "understood how to use slaves"; the wealthy gave children "little paired playthings such as / nests of eggs, ichneumon and snake," or put goose-grease paint in boxes "with pivoting / lid incised with the duck-wing," or kept "locust oil in stone locusts."[3] A careful eye has observed these determined self-temptations, and seen through

> . . . an evident
> poetry of frog grays,
>> duck-egg greens, and egg-plant blues, a fantasy
>> and a versimilitude that were
>> right to those with, everywhere,
>
> power over the poor.

Here is the triumphal arch of meaning. The first part of the poem skillfully moves from Rome to the luxuries of Egypt and the objets d'art named for the king who feared snakes and tamed "Pharoah's rat, the rust- / backed mongoose . . . [whose] restlessness was / its excellence; . . ." The mongoose, even if tame, belongs to another world, however,

> and the jerboa, like it,

> a small desert rat,
> and not famous, that
>   lives without water, has
>   happiness. Abroad seeking food, or at home
>   in its burrow, the Sahara field-mouse
>   has a shining silver house

> of sand . . . .

The counter-subject, then, the jerboa whose desert life tells us that "one would not be he / who has nothing but plenty," emerges at the end of the first part of this poem. We are now ready for the exposition and development of the counter-subject in the second part, "Abundance."[4]

The six-line stanza of "Too Much" is continued, but the movement is faster; exhilaration marks the tempo of this part. The title of Africanus, the conqueror sent from Rome, more truly belongs to the

> untouched: the sand-brown jumping rat—free-born; and
>   the blacks, that choice race with an elegance
>   ignored by one's ignorance.

A swift change brings into the company of true conquerors of the desert the biblical Jacob, whose experience was part terrestrial and part celestial. His vision of steps of air and air angels proves that "the translucent mistake / of the desert"

> does not make

> hardship for one who
> can rest and then do
>   the opposite—launching
>   as if on wings, from its match-thin hindlegs, in
>   daytime or at night. . . .

The rapid development of the counterpart theme, the instinctiveness of the jerboa's habits, the attractiveness of its coat, shapely ear and tail, all for protection, lead to a cre-

71

scendo and the final resolution. The effect of modulation by different intervals and a different rhythm from the pampered ease of luxury is written into the poem itself.

> By fifths and sevenths,
> in leaps of two lengths,
> > like the uneven notes
> > of the Bedouin flute, it stops its gleaning
> > > on little wheel castors, and makes fern-seed
> > > foot-prints with kangaroo speed.

And in the final stanza, introduced by an accelerated rhythm and characteristic light rhyme ("Its leaps should be set / to the flageolet"), the jerboa's[5] perfection supersedes the elegance of the Roman craftsmen:

> > pillar body erect
> > on a three-cornered smooth-working Chippendale
> > claw—propped on hindlegs, and tail as third toe,
> > between leaps to its burrow.

However much we may admire the "serial" poems "Octopus" and "Marriage," we cannot deny that they do not afford the clarity of structure evident in "The Jerboa," nor the possibilities of variation and experiment in the solution of both subject and counter-subject, with appropriate adaptation of the stanzaic pattern.

Two of the other new poems in this book parallel "The Jerboa" in theme—the bankruptcy of spontaneous life that results from luxury and pomp. Both differ from "The Jerboa" in form: "Camellia Sabina" because of its more casual tone and procedure, "No Swan So Fine" by its succinctness and compact authority.

Using an eight-line stanza rhyming the first to the last line (although fortified by some light internal rhymes and echoes of rhyme between stanzas), "Camellia Sabina" begins in an aside about the Bordeaux plum, in its foil-sealed, glass-blown jar signed with the craftsman's name. Then this bit of enjoyableness is dismissed with the offhand comment

"Appropriate custom." But these opening lines lead to an enlargement of the initial suggestion that luxurious items require special care. The wealthy merchants of Bordeaux grow camellias "catalogued by / lines across the leaf," some with proud names like "Gloria mundi," that must be kept under glass. Among the many others described by Abbé Berlèse, in his monograph on them, is "the smaller, Camellia Sabina / with amanita white petals . . . / pale pinwheels, and pale / stripe that looks as if on a mushroom the / sliver from a beet-root carved into a rose were laid." (This intricate metaphor results from a poet's eye looking at an illustration in a book.)

The same Bordeaux connoisseurs who grow the greenhouse camellias also take pains to select the vintage wines of their district. Their connoisseurship has a mild resemblance to the hedonism of imperial Rome. The sudden introduction of the counter-subject converts a seemingly minor observation into a poem. In contrast to Bordeaux we are transported to a different territory where the field mouse, relishing the seed of the wild parsnip, the sunflower, or the morning glory, may stroll under the vines of the Bolzano grape. The field mouse, like the jerboa, symbolizes "abundance" rather than "too much."

> . . . . . Does yonder mouse with a grape in its hand
> and its child in its mouth, not portray
> the Spanish fleece suspended by the neck? . . .

A photograph the Moores had liked gave rise to this handsome flourish. In a letter to her brother (November 6, 1932) Marianne Moore reported that she had got for "Mouse" a second-hand copy of the *National Geographic* with "the original of the Mouse with the Grape . . . the original reproduction of the Californian's photograph. . . ."[6] The final stanzas proceed quickly to the last one where we read that "the gleaning is more than the vintage." This moral climax allows the poet to dismiss the first subject with an ironically rhymed parenthesis "(Close / the window,

73

says the Abbé Berlèse / for Sabina born under glass.)"; and the poem ends with a salute to the grape chosen by the meadow mouse, "O generous Bolzano!"

"The Jerboa" had been accepted by *Hound and Horn*, but although encouraged by Lincoln Kirstein's inquiry about an additional poem, Marianne Moore gave priority to Pound's request for something new to include in *The Active Anthology*. "I have been finishing a poem on the camellia and the prune for him," she wrote to Warner. "Sounds something like Will Rogers but is serious" (February 6, 1933). A poem that can delight and teach the reader, and that obviously gave pleasure to the writer, "Camellia Sabina" has neither the amplitude of treatment nor the originality of contrast that we find in "The Jerboa." T. S. Eliot's arrangement of the poems in this 1935 volume shows inherent skill in placing "No Swan So Fine" immediately after "Camellia Sabina." An incisive study on a related theme, it started from a newspaper quotation ("No water so still as the / dead fountains of Versailles"). The poet's sharp eye on the swan "with swart blind look askance / and gondoliering legs" gives contrasting reality to the artificial one, the objet d'art that must be someone's property:

> the chintz china one with fawn-
> brown eyes and toothed gold
> collar on to show whose bird it was.

In the reading diary of 1930-43, one may see the sketch drawn by the observer-poet of the candelabrum tree of Louis XV in which this artificial swan was lodged.[7] The apt description of it in the poem gives proof, as do the precious artifacts described in "The Jerboa," of her own liking for the craftsman's excellence. Perched on the sculptured flowers, the swan is "at ease and tall." But their one-time owner? Like the fountains of Versailles, "The king is dead." In fourteen incisive lines the case stands without appeal. There is no place here for romantic faith in the happiness of the jerboa ("O rest and joy, the boundless sand") where the animal's leaps are worthy of musical accompaniment. For precision and finish, "No Swan So Fine" might be compared to the earlier "To Statecraft Embalmed"; but, again, its elegant censure allows no room for the insight afforded by "life's faulty excellence." Exhilaration in this poem arises from the conclusive rejection of an attractive temptation.

In various ways these new poems may be seen as connected, while at the same time the metrical effects and the sources of feeling and experience drawn upon exemplify the writer's ability to summon untried powers. If "The Jerboa," "Camellia Sabina," and "No Swan So Fine" exhibit differences in the manner of advancing upon related themes, "The Buffalo" and "Nine Nectarines" invite another kind of attention from the reader. These two poems appeared in the same issue of *Poetry* (Chicago) in November 1934. In "The Buffalo," the writer relied on earlier associations, whereas in "Nine Nectarines" she proceeded from more recent observation.

An entry made in 1920 (reading diary 1916-21, p. 144) quotes a passage about the Indian water buffalo (who is the real hero of this poem), with emphasis on its "jet-black" horns and on the skeleton adapted to the kind of service it gave. Twelve years later the poet began clipping pictures of buffalos, one from the *Arts Weekly*, one from the *New York Times* (of the water buffalo from Eastern Asia), and added others in 1933, including one of an article referring to "The Over-Drove Ox" print at the Metropolitan Museum and a picture of oxen used on the Coolidge farm in Vermont.[8] But it must be stressed that no such items would find a future context in a poem unless the poet's mind and sensibility could afford them meaning, and the skill needed to place them in a visual mosaic.

On this poem both Marianne Moore and her brother placed special value. She wrote him when she had begun it, and ironically said it might not be as good as Bayard Taylor, "but will be the most I can produce—in quality . . . ." (August 6, 1933). A month later she wrote, "I am in love with my buffalo (Indian Buffalo) half done. . . ." By the fall of 1934 she could report that her buffalo "the same which took your fancy" had been accepted by Morton Dauwen Zabel for *Poetry* (Chicago).[9]

"The Buffalo" is a poem that resulted from an admiration for animals capable of service under hardship. The wild ox tamed to help in plowing the land was noble in its alliance with the extinct aurox or the bison. The reason why Marianne Moore loved "her buffalo" comes alive in the poem. In élan and interior shapeliness it must give way to a later poem meditating a similar theme, "The Arctic Ox," and does not bear comparison with "Elephants." Yet we may not set aside her own regard for this poem. At the back of her mind in this tribute to the aid to man given by the buffalo, the Indian water buffalo especially,[10] there may well have been the metaphor used when Saul on the road to Damascus was told "it is hard for thee to kick against the pricks"—prick meaning a goad for oxen, or sometimes a word used for yoke. For Saul it was to be a merit to accept this goad. As an admirer of Hardy, too, she must have known his poem, "The Oxen"—quite unlike her own, but symbolizing something responsive to good in the nature of this animal.

When considering the relationship to each other of this whole group of poems, it should be borne in mind that Marianne Moore was working on some of them simultaneously, or was making preliminary studies for a future composition while concentrating on the perfection of one already begun. Likewise, she was planning for their publication in an entirely professional way. She wrote to Warner that "The Buffalo is 'accepted of course' Mr. Zabel says, "and he wants another thing to pair with it . . . but my paws are so full of the book I am not sure I can do one; but maybe. The *Pelican* for the Criterion—if it *is* for the Criterion—got finished only now—this evening."[11] Part of the remarkable distinction of her poems arises from the fact that ardent labor was the midwife. Marianne Moore would have completely understood Eudora Welty's principle: "You have to have an idea so strong it compels you to write. Only a strong idea has vitality and you give it all you've got."[12]

When an editor asked for a poem, the poem, even if it hadn't yet been written, was not far away. Something that had stirred her consciousness would prompt this poet to verify, to explore its import. The nature of the initial datum (donné) was discovered in the poem itself, in the act of writing it. The notebooks show the "feeling and precision" that went into the preparation for that vital act. Just as a tennis champion has to practice, or a racing yachtsman to qualify in trial races, Marianne Moore had to read, or go to a movie, or a museum, or make sketches of treasures seen in an art dealer's window, to open the latent meaning in her own sensations.

Some months later she told Warner, "I am writing like a demon with canton-flannel horns on my Nectarines poem."[13] When she sent it to Zabel to be paired with "The Buffalo," she furnished the title "Imperious Ox, Imperial Dish" for the two pieces, but they are not really connected.

"Nine Nectarines" can be more intelligently read as an advance upon "Camellia Sabina," or, best of all, for its singular rhythm and tonal scale. Speculating on the incentive for this poem, one perceives that the rapt attention to the nectarine and peach arose from seeing them in a beautiful design on a rare piece of Chinese porcelain. Then, consulting the *Encyclopedia Britannica*, she made notes upon the wild and the cultivated nectarine and peach, as related varieties. This would have been of no avail if the semblance of the poem were not already in her mind, but she found clues that she needed. The *Encyclopedia* informs us that the French botanist de Candolles considered the peach to be of Chinese origin, although no wild specimens had been noticed in modern times. Among other references on this subject the *Encyclopedia* included Darwin's *Variation of Animals and Plants under Cultivation*, with which the poet was already familiar. Luckily the Pratt Institute had a copy of

Candolles' book. Notes were quickly taken, with emphasis on the pattern of growth in twigs, leaves, and fruit, in comparison with the nectarine.[14] She skilfully transposed this accurate botanical description into another key for the opening movement of the poem.

> Arranged by two's as peaches are,
> at intervals that all may live—
>   eight and a single one, on twigs that
>   grew the year before—they look like
> a derivative;
>   although not uncommonly
> the opposite is seen—
> nine peaches on a nectarine.

This is a truly metaphysical beginning: a major theme presents itself in the seemingly innocuous observation that the nectarines grow on the branch in groups of two—in order "that all may live." For, in the next stanza, we read that the peach *Yu*, if eaten in time, prevents death; hence the group of nine becomes an emblematic group, flawless as the art of the Chinese who made the much-mended porcelain plate.

Readers who have followed Marianne Moore's poetry in the separate volumes become aware of her practice in revising. Some of the pieces in *Complete Poems* have the same text as the one first published, others have been slightly revised, and a few show major changes, usually for the sake of compression. This is a subject we can consider usefully only when all her writing can be brought into one framework. Only a new variorum edition would show why, as readers, some of us may prefer the earlier, or an earlier, version. In *Selected Poems* (1935), "Nine Nectarines and Other Porcelain" contained eight stanzas of eleven lines each. In revising the text for *Collected Poems*, she left the first three stanzas and four lines of the next stanza intact and the one word at the beginning of the next line that completes the sentence. She omitted the rest of the fourth

78

stanza, and all of the three following ones. Fortunately the concluding stanza was unchanged. The title now became simply "Nine Nectarines"—for what has been taken out is, so to speak, chiefly the "other porcelain" made in China with designs to please the European importers. In the writing of the first published version these designs had evoked the poet's interest as well, but she saw that they were not essential to the theme.

Since Marianne Moore, to my best knowledge, never wrote anything at all that failed to stimulate, or charm, or divert the mind, it will always be worthwhile to read the deleted lines in this poem and in others. But—in comparison with the costly omissions in "Part of a Novel, Part of a Poem, Part of a Play" (to be discussed at the end of this chapter)—the more compressed version of "Nine Nectarines" is a distinct improvement. The poem has a unity that it lacked in the 1935 text. The swifter development sets free a living concept that the somewhat digressive middle section of the earlier version tended to blur. We can see now that the "wild spontaneous fruit," the nectarine, intimates immortality like the peach from which it may be a derivative. These meditations are protected with a tentativeness and a questioning like Sir Thomas Browne's in *Pseudoxia Epidemica*.

> Like the peach *Yu* . . .
>
> . . . .
>
> the Italian peach-
> nut, Persian plum, Ispahan
>
> secluded wall-grown nectarine,
> as wild spontaneous fruit was
> found in China first. But was it wild?
> Prudent de Candolle would not say.

She incorporates in the poem the query of the prudent botanist whose comments she had entered in her reading diary. But the note sounded here is quickly resumed in the final stanza, to be directly linked with another symbol of immortality:

> ... the nectarine-loving kylin
> of pony appearance—the long-
> tailed or the tailless
> small cinnamon-brown, common
> camel-haired unicorn
> with antelope feet and no horn,
> here enamelled on porcelain.
> It was a Chinese who
> imagined this masterpiece.

Nectar, from which the term nectarine comes, is food for the gods; the kylin is the mythical creature, the oriental counterpart of the European unicorn, on whose back were written magic signs copied by the emperor Fu Hsi when the kylin emerged from the Yellow River. The legend is that from these signs the emperor provided China with its first written language. A much later appearance of the kylin heralded the birth of Confucius.[15]

"Nine Nectarines" concentrates a high imaginative potency in this shorter text—a power that is recaptured when one reads primarily to enjoy the rhythmic variations and the faultlessly pitched sound, as well as the liveliness of colour and clean craftsmanship in the designs presented to the eye. The quick opening rhythm (unusually iambic, for her) gives way to variations leading the first sentence to the indefinable musical phrase "nine peaches on a nectarine." The slender crescent leaves of the tree are "green or blue—or both, / in the Chinese style," the fruit is a colour we can't mistake, of "puce-American-beauty pink." And there is an almost Dürer-like studiousness and affection in the few lines retained from the original fourth stanza, introducing the

> unantlered moose, or Iceland horse,
> or ass, asleep against the old

> thick, low-leaning nectarines that is the
> colour of the shrub-tree's brownish
> flower.

T. S. Eliot's editorial skill on behalf of other writers was again put to advantage when, in arranging the order of *Selected Poems*, he placed "The Fish," written years earlier, right after "Nine Nectarines."[16] Contrasted they may be in a number of good ways, but in the rhythmical skill that guides the sequences of colour and shape they go well together.

"The Plumet Basilisk" experiments with composition differently. I have applied the term "complex" to some earlier poems, such as "An Octopus" and "Marriage," in a favorable, somewhat Aristotelian sense.[17] "The Plumet Basilisk" is, however, not only complex but complicated; one can therefore select only certain aspects of this quadripartite poem, to suggest the special virtues (and the very characteristic kind of imagining) that inhere in it.

Marianne Moore knew Shakespeare well, in her own unhackneyed way of reading, and might have said of herself "Sometimes / we see a cloud that's dragonish." For dragons and their minor kin, chameleons and other lizards, tortoises and tuateras, are at home in her poetry, especially in "The Plumet Basilisk." In "The Jerboa," a perfectly natural step was taken from the life implied by some remarkable objects designed by man to an art worthier of imitation, the economy and style of the desert-dwelling rat. "The Plumet Basilisk" achieves another kind of equilibrium, by a counterpoint of the legendary and the real. Literature, whether of the Far East, or Greece, or the Anglo-Saxon and British world, is replete with dragons. The literary origin of Marianne Moore's dragons joins company with her knowledge of biology;[18] both are fortified by her exact eye for the movement and appearance of animal, insect, bird, or man.

Preparation for writing "The Plumet Basilisk" began in the summer of 1932 and went on simultaneously with the finishing of "The Jerboa." In mid-July she wrote "Dear Pago-Pago" (for Warner Moore was now stationed in American Samoa) that she was just beginning to concentrate on "The Plumet Basilisk." A visit to the Natural History Museum two weeks earlier had afforded numerous observations, including a sight of a live scorpion. There were kangaroo rats and pocket mice but no jerboas. In the reptile section she saw the "diving feather basilisks in which I am interested." They

> "come from Costa Rica and are different from frilled lizards and from Flying dragons of Malay. [The] latter have at each side of the body a wing supported by six ribs and they are like medium-sized butterflies. They plane down through the air, lighting on orchids or on spotted leaves . . . are exhibited at the Museum on a nutmeg tree—one in air, suspended by a wire, and two on the orchid blossoms with the wings folded . . . like a half-closed umbrella. The basilisk, however, is the prince of lizards in my estimation—bright green with 8 bands on the tail and three plumes— . . . can run a little way on the water before diving. . . ."[19]

Warner Moore had offered the term "feather basilisk" for plumet (plumiferous) and Marianne's next letter to him is signed "Yr. affectionate Basilisk"; this became a frequent signature, the most amusing version being a drawing of the creature with "Feather B." typed below it (November 19, 1932). Her forays to the Natural History Museum or to movies shown at the "Rat Academy" (Pratt Institute) resemble a painter's working outdoors rather than in the light of his studio. Two final necessary experiences for "The Plumet Basilisk" were at hand. Fortunately, Captain Stanley Osborne was lecturing on Australia and New Zealand at the Pratt Institute. A film of the tuatera, shown "because I had asked for it," afforded clear images of this lizard. "The tail has [a] saw-tooth crest like an alligator's, but the breast bone is a bird's, and the head is turtle like . . . it is the one surviving reptile from the great age of reptiles. These lizards

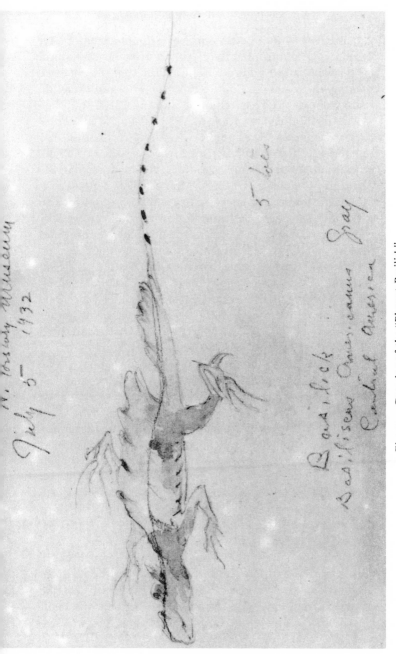

Figure 1: Drawing of the "Plumet Basilisk"

. . . usually live in a petrel's hole or accommodate a petrel in theirs." And on a final visit to the Museum of Natural History she talked with a man who had seen plumet basilisks on the water in Costa Rica, and who said "they do jump from 50 to 60 feet off a tree into the water."[20]

A letter written by "Rat" to "Pago Pago" in the latter part of December, when she was "pushing my basilisk to a conclusion," described other researches as well as a "Folk Exhibition," and modern paintings and sculpture at the Museum of Modern Art. Mrs. Moore added a postscript: "If a person wanted a measure of comparison by which to describe Rat, is there anything or anybody on the earth or elsewhere known to man, whereby some ideer of 'im could be got?" On Christmas Eve Marianne wrote that "December 22, round five oclock Samoan time, Feather hatched, and I hastened to send a picture to The Criterion. I don't care if it gets refused. If it does I am going to send it to The Yale Review, and then to Scribner's, and one or two other places. . . ." Eight months later Lincoln Kirstein accepted "The Plumet Basilisk" for the *Hound and Horn.*[21]

For a reader, the challenging question about "The Plumet Basilisk" asks, "How well do I hold the complete poem in my mind, and why do I read it less often than some of her other poems—yet am oddly moved by it when I do?" Part of the answer depends upon the structure of the poem itself; another part stems from one's own unfamiliarity with the places frequented by these lizards, their dragon cousins, and the living, not mythical, plumet basilisk. In effect, most readers bring less to this poem than is needed. The structure of the poem does not in itself aid us; we must study the complete text and read it a number of times before we become aware of its plenitude of meaning.

Here are four sections, varying in length, about three lizards. The first and last sections, each bearing the title "In Costa Rica," present the plumet basilisk, a native of the American continent. The second section introduces a small newt found in Malay, the only living dragon that seems to fly, as the wide membranes of its extended ribs act like a parachute when it planes down in swift descent from a tree. The third member of the cast, the tuatera, is an inhabitant of New Zealand.

To embark upon the poem we must accept the writer's predilection—evident long before she published a book with the title *O to Be a Dragon*—for the saurian tribe. Of the many entries in her notebooks having a bearing upon this subject, I find most enlightening a passage she copied from *The Expositor's Bible*:

> Upon a warm spring day in Palestine to sit upon the grass, beside some old dyke or ruin . . . is indeed to obtain a rapturous view of the wealth of life. How the lizards come and go among the grey stones & flash like jewels in the dust! And the timid snake rippling quickly through the grass & the leisurely tortoise with his shiny back, and the chameleon shivering into new color as he passes from twig to stone & stone to straw. . . . What a loss of colour, the lizards alone would imply. . . . But as Isaiah declares—whom we may imagine walking with his children up the steep vineyard paths, to watch the creatures come and go upon the dry dykes on either hand—the ideal is to bring them into sympathy with ourselves. . . ."[22]

This last sentence offers us the clue, if it be needed, to "The Plumet Basilisk" in particular, as well as, obviously, to other poems, where "the ideal is to bring them into sympathy with ourselves."

Dragons find an honorable place elsewhere in the Bible; Marianne Moore had read *Beowulf*, too. Yet no matter what a writer may have read or revolved in his mind, some direct experience generates the current of feeling needed to make the poem live by itself. To visit her brother when he was stationed on the west coast in 1920, Marianne Moore and her mother embarked on the U.S.S. *Mercy*, sailed through the Panama Canal and northward, passing the coast of Costa Rica. I do not know if any stop was made there; it is my impression that there may have been. A beach, a fire of driftwood and the green colour in the flame; here we are outdoors, not in a museum or library where life has been stored up only to emerge as events make space for it. The poem begins and ends "In Costa Rica," home of the extant, not extinct, miniature dragon, the real not mythical *basilicus americanus*. The attributes and story of this still living creature make it a cousin to dragons that defend treasure, and symbolize the power of metamorphosis in living forms.

What keeps the reader's attention and evokes his wonder (even if, like this reader, not a dragon-fan) is the high style of visual design, the humorous rearrangement of traditional dragon attributes, and the variations in rhythm corresponding to these patterns. The basilisk of the new world appears where "In blazing driftwood / the green keeps showing at the same place," like the colours of the fire-opal. He is himself a "living firework," but amphibious. The poet, trained in the study of biology, knew that the extinct pterodactyls were a half-way stage from fish to bird, and ultimately, because they were among the earliest saurian land-dwellers, represented a stage in the ascent of man. When the plumet basilisk dives to the stream bed, he hides

> . . . as the chieftain with gold body hid in
>
> Guatavita lake.
> He runs, he flies, he swims, to get to
> his basilica—'the ruler of Rivers, Lakes, and Seas
> invisible or visible,' . . .
> —and can be 'long or short, and also coarse or
> fine at pleasure.'

The poem plays on the origin of this lizard's name in the Greek term *basilica* or royal dwelling-place. Recalling the dragons who guarded the Hesperides, the plumet basilisk differs from them by taking refuge in the water, just as the Aztec chief hid his treasure from marauding Spaniards.

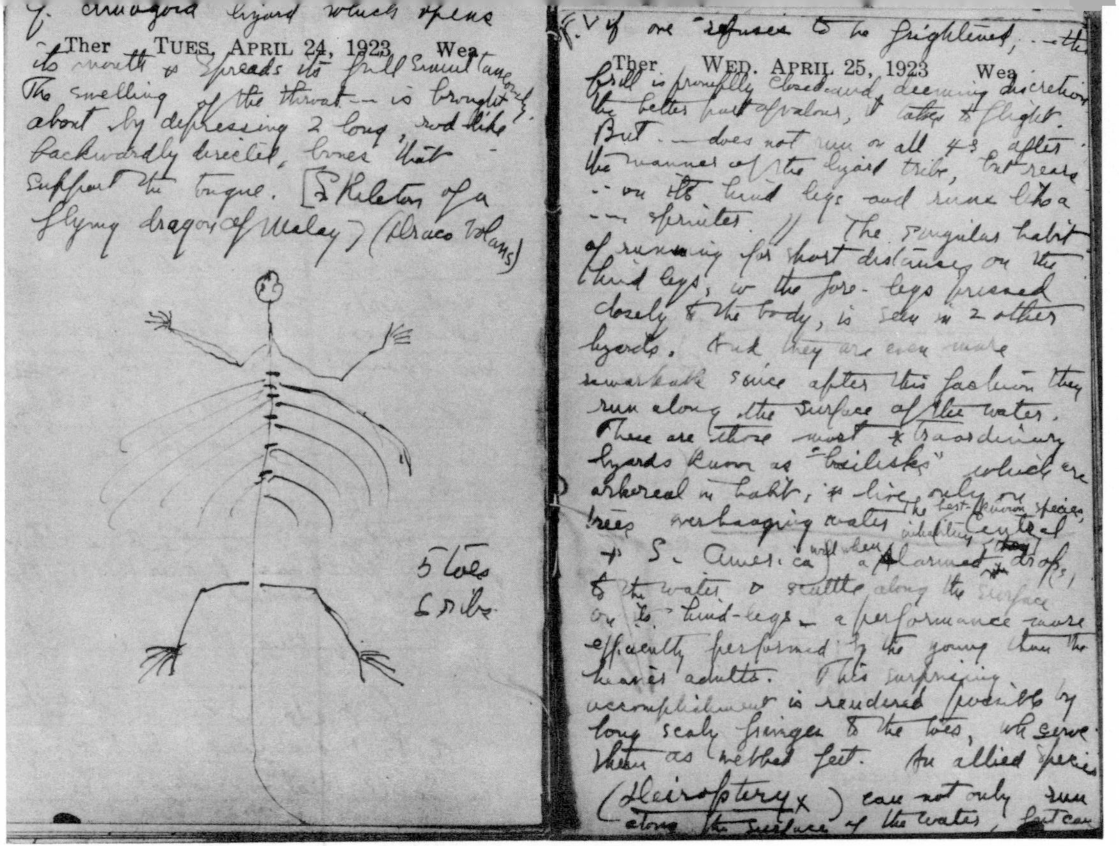

Figure 2: Facsimile of Notebook Page with Drawing of the Malay Dragon

The transition from this bold opening movement to the Malay dragon's continent is disarming: "We have ours; and they / have theirs." The careful drawing of the anatomy of the Malay dragon and the notes of her observations at the Museum of Natural History[23] come alive in the language of the poem:

> Floating on spread ribs,
>> the boat-like body settles on the
> clamshell-tinted spray sprung from the
>> nutmeg-tree—minute legs
>> trailing half-akimbo . . . .

Yet this accurately described lizard is "the true divinity of Malay," a "harmless god," a "serpent-dove peculiar / to the East."

We leave him there, to ponder briefly on another sea lizard, the tuatera of New Zealand, willing neighbour or even host to the birds who evolved from reptiles. One phrase lightly accentuates this motif: "Bird-reptile social life is pleasing." The nesting of birds among tortoises can be observed today in the Galapagos Islands, not far from Costa Rica. When the tuatera has been placed among his dragon kind, we are again recalled to the tradition of dragons guarding treasure by a novel version of it in today's world of business:

> In
>> Copenhagen the principal door
> of the bourse is roofed by two pairs of dragons standing on
>> their heads—twirled by the architect—so that the four
> green tails conspiring upright, symbolize four-fold
>>> security . . . .

These images were provided by a drawing in one of the notebooks.[24]

In the last section of the poem a surprising change of structure takes place. Each of the first three sections contains three stanzas of five lines. When the final section circles back to Costa Rica, to the basilisk, "one of the quickest lizards in the world," the pattern is enlarged to six five-line stanzas, followed by a coda varying in meter and line length. We reach the moral center of the poem in this final section, rediscovering the "extraordinary" basilisk whose external traits and markings, although "a faulty decorum," hide him "till night-fall, which is for man the basilisk whose look will kill; but is / for lizards men can / kill, the welcome dark." These lines reverse the traditional myth of the death-dealing basilisk's eyes. The dangerous eyes are those of predatory humans from whose sight the dark delivers him.

When the meter shifts, the shorter stanzas can incorporate a slight revision of lines written many years earlier in a poem published in the Bryn Mawr College magazine. "He once expressed a curious wish / to be interchangeably man and fish" now becomes "the plumet portrays / mythology's wish / to be interchangeably man and fish." The amphibious nature of man had its place in her writing even when she was a student. The place of the saurians on the chain of being symbolizes man's place.

The emerald opal and black opal colour motif signifies not only the day- and night-time appearance of the basilisk, but the invisibility of phenomena we may visually sense. We may audibly sense, too, "the noiseless music that hangs about / the serpent when it stirs or springs." These attended to, unexpected signs and sounds betoken (as the rhythmical pattern again opens out in a longer stanza)

>   our Tower-of-London
> jewel that the Spaniards failed to see, among the feather
>   capes and hawk's-
>
> head moths and black-chinned
>   humming-birds; the innocent, rare, gold-
> defending dragon that as you look begins to be a
>   nervous naked sword on little feet . . . .

89

He is innocent, a creature that will not kill but instead epitomizes life ("white fire eating into air" . . . a "look of whetted fierceness"). Only when he dives down to the world of treasure his "quicksilver ferocity" is "quenched in the rustle of the fall into the sheath / which is the shattering sudden splash that marks his temporary loss."

The ending of "The Plumet Basilisk" provides one further instance of absolute individuality. No one else could have written or would have attempted to write this poem, and the last line is its signature. When the visible becomes invisible, the loss is temporary—but nevertheless a loss. We may, and should, compare this final line with the last line of "Black Earth" ["Melancthon"] of "The Fish," and of "A Grave."

"The Frigate Pelican," a native of our Southern coast, also flies over the Pacific waters where the basilisk may dive, but the frigate bird doesn't alight on the water as some other sea birds do. The frigate bird is not a predator but a pirate; accurately portrayed in the facts and metaphors fused in the poem: "The toe / with slight web, air-boned body, and very long wings / . . . duplicating a / bow-string as he flies overhead." The design of this poem is intricate. The visual pattern of the bird's flight is the dominant one, in the beginning, the middle and the end of the poem:

> the unconfiding frigate-bird hides
> in the height and in the majestic
> display of his art. He glides
> a hundred feet or quivers about
> as charred paper behaves—full
> of feints; and an eagle
>
> of vigilance . . . .

This theme is paralleled by two others, oddly linked, a musical and a social one. The fundamental structure of the poem can be better understood in the *Selected Poems* text than in the later ones, from which almost six stanzas were omitted, removing a section introducing the curious creatures that the frigate bird can see from its great height: the tame armadillo, the fer de lance near the "spattered blood" orchid, a jaguar and small cats, which "like the literal / merry-go-round, come wandering within the circular view / of the high bird." Only by going back to this section can one grasp why the exclusive frigate bird has been compared to Handel; for both are solitary, in contrast to the company of creatures seen in the jungle. Then, too, one can understand why the "be gay civilly" motif is resumed, contrasting the pleasure of people watching the moon rise on the Susquehanna, and the artfulness of the bird sleeping in the mangrove swamp, who "wastes the moon."

All three themes or motifs are brought into a true relationship in the last two stanzas of the earlier text, the "tune's illiterate footsteps of the carousel" and the frigate birds flying in a

> reticent lugubrious ragged immense minuet
> descending to leeward, ascending to windward
>
> .   .   .   .
>   Theirs are sombre
> quills for so wide and lightboned a bird
>   as the frigate pelican
>   of the Caribbean.

The lines from the passage quoted above connect the musical movement of the bird's flight with the "impassioned Handel" of stanzas three and four, then provide an apt, unexpected rhyme, whereas the revised version lacks a final rhyme.

The only conclusion to be drawn from contemplating some of these revisions is that the student of Marianne Moore's poetry—and all good readers of whatever age are necessarily students—must own or gain access to the successive editions of her work. For the enjoyment and understanding of "Part of a Novel, Part of a Poem, Part of a Play," we must acquaint ourselves with the fact that there exist in book form three different versions of the poem that originally bore that title—the one in *Selected Poems*, the briefer one in *Collected Poems*, and the expanded text in *Complete Poems*. These texts originate in the version published in the June 1932 issue of *Poetry: A Magazine of Verse*.

This poem comes first in *Selected Poems* (1935), in *Collected Poems* (1951) and *Complete Poems* (1967), where it bears the explanatory subtitle "Revised, 1961." Regardless of the variations in the texts presented by these three major editions of her work, beginning here will stir the imagination of any reader for whom there is hope. Marianne Moore in her long life wrote many poems that will be read in times to come, yet none—in however new a strain, however irreplaceable—none, I think, to excel this one. "Part of a Novel, Part of a Poem, Part of a Play" conferred a new life on the poet's own power, giving it the kind of profundity we observe in *What Are Years* and *Nevertheless* as well as in other poems in the books that followed.

To simplify a complicated matter, may I state that to me the text in *Selected Poems* of 1935 remains the best, and then try to explain. A great deal hinges upon the title, and on the fact that the poem as a whole creates living people, not relying on the more oblique approach to human qualities evident in the aphoristic early poems or in compositions like "The Jerboa," "Camellia Sabina," "The Plumet Basilisk" or "The Frigate Pelican."

As early as 1916, in a letter to H. D., Marianne Moore expressed her fascination with the possibilities of the novel as a form. Her reading diaries contain many excerpts that would be somewhat baffling as evidence of a poet's interests, yet seem entirely relevant to the awareness a novelist must have: of places, occasions, and of behavior in the outward man that reflect inner constitution and feeling. The early reading diaries contain lengthy extracts from Saintsbury's the *English Novel*, from the verdicts on other novelists in George Moore's *Avowals*, from Conrad, Henry James,

Joyce's *Dubliners*. These notes as well as early recognition of vital power in the fiction of D. H. Lawrence show her attraction to the novel as a form.

More telling are other entries in her notebooks, of actual conversations that, like her letters, incorporate a living idiom. She recorded conversations by her friends, her neighbours, by dilettantes who sought her attention, by solemn college professors, by athletes. The striking phrases of southern negroes heard when she visited her brother Warner were set down, and the equally vivid expressions of the caretaker, Homer, at the summer camp of the Eustis family on Black Lake, New York. Comic descriptions of people and their houses, their furniture, the food served to guests at parties abound in her letters. All these accounts show alertness to the goings-on that are grist to the novelist's mill, or appear in the dialogue of a play. It was pointed out in the chapter on her prose that she worked off and on writing a partly autobiographical novel that she referred to as "my story."[25]

We have less evidence of any early attempt in the direction of dramatic form. But admiration for Shaw, awareness of the Noh plays evoked by Pound, recognition of Yeats's triumphant struggles in the Abbey Theatre, and her animated descriptions of plays that she saw bespeak the fascination that eventually led Marianne Moore to dramatize Maria Edgeworth's *The Absentee*. She hoped that it might be performed and had some discussion about this possibility with Lincoln Kirstein.[26]

Her strong response to these other literary modes has something to do with the originality, the articulate ease and serene mastery of "Part of a Novel, Part of a Poem, Part of a Play" as published in *Selected Poems* of 1935. To understand why this is the best of the three versions published in her books one must pause briefly over the text as it first appeared in *Poetry* (Chicago) in June of 1932.

Here the reader encounters three sections, seeming to parallel the three terms of the collective title. The first section, then and subsequently called "The Steeple-Jack," was

followed by "The Student" and "The Hero." Each of these
has its own structure, the first one of thirteen six-line stan-
zas, the second of fifteen four-line stanzas, and the last of
six nine-line stanzas, all with correspondingly different pat-
terns of rhyme and syllabic arrangement. When Marianne
Moore reconsidered and revised the text for inclusion in her
Selected Poems of 1935 she kept the first and final sections
essentially the same (save for shortening a part about the
flowers and plants that grow in the seaside town), but
omitted entirely the middle section, "The Student." It was
not abandoned but spun off, to reappear in a more concise
form in *What Are Years* (1940).[27] But in *Selected Poems*
the theme of the student as belonging to an honorable and
congenial world (where "there is nothing that / ambition
can buy or take away") was not sacrificed, for there, as in
the original version

> . . . The college student
> named Ambrose sits on the hill-side
> with his not-native books and hat
> and sees boats
>
> at sea progress white and rigid as if in
> a groove. . . .

The student named Ambrose occupies an essential place in
"Part of a Poem, Part of a Novel, Part of a Play." He likes
"an elegance of which the source is not bravado." His is the
point of view that unifies the whole, for he knows by heart
the sugar-bowl shaped summer house and the pitch of the
church spire

> . . . not true, from which a man in scarlet lets
> down a rope as a spider spins a thread;
> he might be part of a novel, but on the sidewalk a
> sign says C. J. Poole, Steeple Jack,
> in black and white, and one in red
> and white says
>
> Danger.

Here the momentum begins that verifies the title of the poem, and leads to the observation in the twelfth stanza that "The hero, the student, / the steeple-jack, each in his way, / is at home." The natural development was to continue directly to the section called "The Hero," without pausing to amplify the content of the student's experience.

"The Steeple-Jack" section deserves to be thought of as part of a novel, and "The Hero" as part of a play. The last stanza in the first section prepares for the more dramatic movement that follows:

> It could not be dangerous to be living
> in a town like this, of simple people,
> who have a steeple-jack placing danger signs by
> the church
> while he is gilding the solid-
> pointed star, which on a steeple
> stands for hope.

The star has its ineffable meaning, hope; but danger is real, too, not the danger of something falling down upon you, but the danger of unreality—in the church itself the banal or ignorant sermon, in any one of us unwillingness to reject what we know to be untrue, or the pretense that we feel at home where we are not at home.

The hero won't do this: that section, where the first and last lines of every stanza rhyme with "hero," opens with a stage set that doesn't obtrude and needs no props. We don't find ourselves in a different place from the town where Dürer could have lived; but we move away from the locale of "weeds of beanstalk height," away from the neglected yew inhabited by the owl of "scarebabe voice." With cryptic speed we are translated to a universal company, of Jacob, Joseph, Cincinnatus, and Regulus, and then of Bunyan's Pilgrim. He has to "go slow"

> to find his roll; tired but hopeful—
> hope not being hope
> until all ground for hope has

>   vanished; and lenient, looking
>   upon a fellow-creature's error with the
>   feelings of a mother—a
>   woman or a cat.

The theme of hope so quietly stated at the end of the first
section of this composition, a contrast to and counterpart
of danger in the continuing novel of the seaside village, re-
turns as a preliminary to the final dialogue. The speech we
hear in the last stanza of "The Hero" is good enough for
any play. The unnamed hero enters at the end of the stanza
just quoted, and takes the spectator-listener to a scene at
Mt. Vernon, where the "decorous frock-coated Negro"

>   answers the fearless sightseeing hobo
>   who asks the man she's with, what's this,
>   what's that, where's Martha
>   buried, "Gen-ral Washington
>   there; his lady, here"; speaking
>   as if in a play—not seeing her; with a
>   sense of human dignity
>   and reverence for mystery, standing like the shadow
>   of the willow.

The climax of "The Hero" is not an action, it is in the
lines that celebrate a purity of attention. The hero is not
"out / seeing a sight but the rock / crystal thing to see . . . .
that covets nothing that it has let go." We have come to this
brim of revelation from the quiet village where there is
nothing that ambition can buy or take away, as pilgrims
lured by the poem, the novel, the play, to the startling evi-
dence of things unseen. "Part of a Novel, Part of a Poem,
Part of a Play" achieves a portrait of American life, the
good of it, the threat to its inherent promise, the liberation
of what is ultimately not local (the "startling El Greco")
but has it generation here. ("The rock crystal thing to
see" came surprisingly to my mind when first seeing a major

96

painting by Bierstadt.) This must be what W. C. Williams valued in this poem when he first read it in *Poetry* (Chicago), and wrote, "Your words have an immediate quality which only comes when the intelligence matches the acuteness of the perception to which you add an aimed heat of the emotions. . . . And to me especially you give besides a sense of triumph in that it is my own scene, without mistaking the local for the parochial."[28]

Williams' expression "my own scene," an American scene but not a "parochial" one, accurately denotes the sense of place in this poem. The town that "Dürer would have seen a reason for living in" is not one to be found on a road map. In the nineteen-sixties, a reader wrote asking about the "eight stranded whales" and about the steeple-jack, C. J. Poole's, identity. Marianne Moore replied that eight whales had been stranded either in Sheepshead Bay or Brooklyn Harbor, and that the steeple-jack C. J. Poole, with his red sign warning of danger, had been engaged in repairing the steeple of the Lafayette Street Presbyterian Church in Brooklyn. But she said that in writing the poem, she had in mind various New England seacoast towns where she had stayed. The town, that is, was one seen by "the eye of the mind," primarily New England in character as other parts of the physical description show, where steeple-jacks do the same work and whales (the small ones known as pilot fish) do get stranded, and might attract the anatomical eye of a Dürer. Here again what counts is the landscape and seascape with people in it; to create this a writer can lay his hand on anything in agreement with the intrinsic design.

The title "Part of a Novel, Part of a Poem, Part of a Play" indicates a kind of writing Marianne Moore had not hitherto attempted, although observations of a similar kind were present in "New York" or in passages of "An Octopus." In her *Complete Poems* she again included the college student named Ambrose, without whom neither the whole composition nor its structure has full meaning.[29] But she did not use the collective title. That is the chief reason why I think that the text as printed in *Selected Poems* is the best one.

T. S. Eliot was the person chiefly responsible for the publication of that volume. From time to time in 1933 there had been talk of re-issuing *Observations*. Robert Frost met Marianne Moore after reading his poems at the Pratt Institute in 1933 (an occasion described by her as "the best thing we've had in the way of contagious sincerity"). Frost told her he had admired her first book, had even attempted to see her when she was at the *Dial*. "I wish I could do something for you and help you and I think I could. Is your book being republished?" Learning that it was not, he offered to see Lincoln MacVeagh on her behalf. But she said no, she would not wish that, and in fact had just recovered the copyright.[30] A few months later she was approached by "a Mr. Martin Jay" who proposed re-issuing the book. After briefly considering this possibility, she decided against it.[31]

Eliot, whom she had for so long admired and as far as she could befriended, met her at an opportune time on his return to America in 1933.[32] Not at this meeting, which was brief, but in letters to her, he slowly overcame her reluctance to republish *Observations* with the addition of a small number of new poems.

Her reluctance stemmed first from a sense that she did not have enough significant new work. In a letter of January 31, 1934, Eliot offered a firm guideline:

> The point at which one has "enough" for a book (of verse) is not a quantitative matter alone: it comes at the end of a paragraph, or chapter, however short; it's a question of form. One only has not enough, when one feels that the poems written require the cooperation of certain poems not yet written, in order to be themselves quite. I mean that on the one hand I don't want to badger you, and on the other hand I think you have enough.[33]

This assurance would have overcome the doubt of most writers, but it took Marianne Moore a month to decide to give her new work together with a copy of *Observations* to Mr. Frank Morley of Harcourt Brace, Eliot's friend and American publisher. Her second scruple—that she had refused an offer to republish by McAlmon's Contact Press, and had some kind of commitment to Macmillan, was more quickly overcome. In March she wrote to "Dear Badger—Volcanologist" who was now on his way home after two years in Samoa. She said that Mr. Morley and Eliot and Mr. [Harold] Latham, vice-president of Macmillan's, were "my first experience of real publishers." She had "demurred" about agreeing to the publication of the proposed new book, "whereon I had a terrific shove from the rear from Ezra Pound."[34]

While plans were made for the joint publication in England and America of *Selected Poems*, she was still working on some that would be included in that book. "The Frigate Pelican" was not finished until April, and "Nine Nectarines" was still to be written. One can feel nothing less than a sense of awe when reading her spontaneous comment to her brother (newly arrived in America) about the latest stage of her endeavours—all that she had done since beginning to write poetry after ceasing to be editor of the *Dial*. "*The Pelican* for the Criterion—if it *is* for The Criterion—got finished only now—this evening. Mouse has 'puzzled her puppy-brains' over it, now admits it excellent, & likes very much: 'the true knight in his jointed coat, with stiff pig gait—the tame armadillo.' . . . Everything I do is clumsy but may get more felicitous if I keep on working."[35]

In June she had the contract from Faber and Faber, and by-passed her twenty-fifth reunion at Bryn Mawr to keep on with "Nine Nectarines" and to complete the notes for *Selected Poems*. But a friend of 1909, Fannie Barber, invited her to dinner with two other classmates on June 6th. "The news of reunion was very relishable." And one of the three friends there, Nellie Shippen, who was on the staff at Macmillan's, remarked, "Today I saw a memorandum, 'Selected Poems by Marianne Moore with introduction by T. S. Eliot.' Tell us about this Marianna, what happened?" The news was out, and Fannie Barber "motioned the other three to lift up their glasses. They were drinking sherry wine." After questions about Mr. Morley and the arrangements he had made for joint publication, "Fannie raised her glass again in a very businesslike way of satisfaction and said 'Faber and Faber.' The health was drunk."[36]

With work still to do on *Selected Poems*, Marianne Moore and her mother went to Virginia in August 1934, to visit Warner, now stationed in Norfolk. And the live impressions stored up on this short vacation resulted in a major group of poems published a year later, in *The Pangolin*. Once again the enterprising and generous Bryher arranged for the publication of her friend's work in a small, beautifully designed edition. Marianne's correspondence with the illustrator, George Plank, reflects the pleasure she took in the drawings he made, in the choice of paper, in the selection of the Curwen Press to print the book. George Plank felt as much admiration for the new poems as Bryher and her husband did. He wrote on receiving "Virginia Britannia," "Your poem makes me a bit drunk. I think a government ought to subsidize you to go to all sorts of exciting places where you would use that eye of yours for your delight and ours."[37]

In *The Pangolin* the Virginia poems are grouped together under the title "The Old Dominion," with "Virginia Britannia" standing first. And this gives the right place to a composition that in many respects renews and develops the possibilities explored in "Part of a Novel, Part of a Poem, Part of a Play." For "Virginia Britannia" is a poem about a place and its people, this time people seen in a perspective that allows the contrarieties implicit in the colonial settlement of the Old Dominion to counterpoint the events and customs of a later day. "Virginia Britannia" also builds on the imminence of danger and the presence of hope that "Part of a Novel" weighs in the balance; but the adversary dangers and the rescuing hope emanate from different sources here.

To compare the notations of Virginia and Virginians made before the actual writing of the poem, and their incorporation into the poem itself, gives an illumination something like the X-ray of a painting. The collection of the Moore manuscripts at the Rosenbach Museum includes "The Gray Linen Travel Notebook" (her own title for it). Setting out from Norfolk, she crossed the James River on a ferry appropriately named Captain John Smith. Noting the swallows collected on the wire over the ferry entrance, the wide brown river, the emerald mounds of the old fort on the Jamestown side, she walked to the enclosure of the church built in 1617, now partly restored. Approaching it, she saw a magnolia tree with one bloom, and like other tourists was struck by the great sycamore growing out of the tomb of an early minister, Dr. James Blair, and his wife Sarah. This was a sight to rival the hackberry tree with a trunk three feet in diameter, covered with ivy, and higher than the church tower.

For anyone first coming to one of the earliest settlements on the American coast there is a sensation of awe; the immediate impressions collected in the Gray Linen Travel Notebook were to illuminate a universal theme. But few visitors would have looked so carefully at the facsimile of Captain John Smith's coat of arms (of special interest to her because of the ostrich with a horseshoe in its beak), or would have so deeply felt the meaning of the inscription commemorating "a great sinner waiting for a joyful Resurrection" (a tomb with a sword fern growing out of the stone). Outside the church (where she had sketched the altar rail), a fritillary and a large black butterfly flew in and out of the cemetery. Proceeding to the museum, she saw a few old

101

bricks found in unearthing the foundations of the original church. One bore a dog's footprint, one a deer's, and one the imprint of a woman's shoe.

Without now attending further to the notations on Jamestown in "The Gray Linen Travel Notebook," let the poem announce itself by its trumpet voluntary opening.

> Pale sand edges England's Old
> Dominion. The air is soft, warm, hot,
>   above the cedar-dotted emerald shore
> known to the redbird,
>   the red-coated musketeer,
>   the trumpet-flower, the cavalier,
> the parson, and the
>   wild parishioner. A deer-
>   track in a church-floor
> brick, and a fine pavement-
> tomb with engraved top, remain.
> The now tremendous vine-en-
> compassed hackberry
>   starred with the ivy-flower,
>   shades the church tower.
> And "a great sinner lyeth here" under
>   the sycamore.

Notes from the travel notebook fade in comparison. The landfall in the Old Dominion attracts the eye and mind instantaneously; we sense the welcoming present and the vivid past without pausing to compare; the syncopated rhymes speed us from musketeer to wild parishioner and cavalier, the deer-track in the church yard is below the starred tree that *shades* the church tower—a different thing from being merely higher than the tower. "Virginia Britannia" progresses by fascinating transitions, both spatial and temporal, from the graveyard where a sinner waits in joyful hope of resurrection, to the Indian headquarters of Powhatan, to the elegance of the one-brick-thick serpentine wall designed by Jefferson for the University of Virginia. Vistas open into the world of the rare Indian—Powhatan, on whom the early settler Christopher Newport placed a fur crown, a symbol quite as absurd as the coat of arms of Captain John Smith, "with ostrich, Latin motto, / and small gold horse-shoe, / as arms for an able / sting-ray-hampered pioneer." Like the Indian, more than equal to the white man is the negro, "inadvertent ally and best enemy of tyranny." His idiom allows us to see the world of racing and hunting as part of what has come about by " 'advancin' backwards in a circle.' "

The final movement of the poem is an exposition of "stark luxury" contrasted with innocence. Marianne Moore, as all who knew her would agree, herself enjoyed "an elegance of which the source is not bravado." But as her letters, her conversations with her mother and close friends, and many entries in her notebooks attest, she looked upon artificiality of manner and deliberate display of wealth with a kind of fascinated horror. She at first relied on satire and then developed a more Jamesian irony to epitomize the vanities of human choices. In "Virginia Britannia," she observes that some flowers there have an "anaesthetic scent / as inconsiderate as / the gardenia's" and that "Terrapin / meat and crested spoon / feed the mistress of French / plum-and-turquoise-piped / chaise-longue"; it is a region "not noted for humility." Present day civilities—the "stone- / topped table with lead cupids grouped to form the pedestal," or "the French mull dress with the Madei/ra- vine-accompanied edge"—are but "stark luxuries." The central insight cannot be evaded: that "not one / of us, / in taking what we / pleased—in colonizing as the / saying is—has been / a synonym for mercy." Recognizing these opposites frees the mind to relish the true Virginia, Jefferson's university with its serpentine wall, the rattlesnake emblem of liberty, "don't tread on me," or the small hedge sparrow that "even in the dark / flutes his ecstatic burst / of joy."

The concluding stanzas round out the time, until at sun-

103

down we see beyond the distinguished milieu of the Old Dominion. The live oak, the cypress, the aged English hackberry become part of the foreground, the sunset flames against the darkening ridge of trees,

> while clouds, expanding above
> the town's assertiveness, dwarf
> it, dwarf arrogance
>   that can misunderstand
>   importance; and
> are to the child an intimation of
>   what glory is.

The evocation of Wordsworth's "Ode on Intimations of Immortality" is deliberate, and the more successful because the resonance of the last lines in "Virginia Britannia" leads to a different kind of resolution. Having approached the Virginian coast from the outside, where the sea and pale sand set limits to dominion, having then seen into the past and present of Virginia, its victories and defeats, the mind may emancipate itself again. Looking up at the clouds belonging to no one, the child's wonder surpasses mundane glory.

Of the four Virginia poems, this one is the most fully orchestrated and was rightly placed first at the beginning of *Pangolin*. "Smooth Gnarled Crape Myrtle" varies the theme of the socially elegant world "unfortunate" in its pastiche of art, where it is but a step from being "a blameless bachelor" to the self-seeking men in the world of Congreve. This well-composed piece strikes me as a storing up of something for the poet's own later reckoning. Of the two other poems in the group, "Bird-Witted" has deservedly found many admirers and "Half Deity" should acquire them if readers are willing to go back to it as it appears in revised form in *What Are Years* (to be mistakenly, in my belief, excluded from *Collected Poems* of 1957 and *Complete Poems* of 1967).

104

If we take "Virginia Britannia" and "Bird-Witted" as guides to this poet's new resources, two points become clear. First, it would be false to look upon Marianne Moore's poetic achievement as a kind of twentieth-century bestiary (although this is the chief emphasis of several critics).[38] Second, whatever she may have derived from omnivorous reading, visits to museums, movie-viewing, and like activities, her own expert innocent eye, trained on real not legendary creatures, actual happenings, the American city or town, a bit of landscape in England or Italy, is the source of her best work. Every line of "Bird-Witted" reflects the amusement and pleasure more briefly set down in notebook entries, stimulating the excitement of finding the appropriate meter and rhymes for this experience. The accordion-shaped verse paragraphs accord with the opening and shutting wings and spread tails of the fledgling mockingbirds; the contrast between their "high-keyed intermittent squeak" that sounds like broken carriage springs and the note "with rapid unexpected flute- / sounds leaping from the throat / of the astute / grown bird" turns into an expert dissonance at the end, to repel the "intellectual cautious- / ly creeping cat." "Bird-Witted" demonstrates a skill comparable to that of a small master-drawing in its selectiveness and decisive execution.

"Half Deity" has a rightful place beside the other Virginia poems; it creates the setting for an appropriate myth. Perhaps, reading the poem in the revised version printed in *What Are Years*, one may see that the writer did not quite succeed in working through the parallel between the child's approach to the butterfly and its rebuff when the butterfly succumbs to Zephyr's enchantment. The minutely described yellow swallow-tail, flying on its migration "with droverlike tenacity" lights on an elm, and is approached by a nymph dressed in Wedgwood blue, who tries to touch it, and unsuccessfully follows as it flutters from tree to tree or settles on a flower:

> . . . then pawing
> like a horse, turns round,—apostrophe-
> tipped brown antennae porcupining out as
> it arranges nervous
> wings. Aware that curiosity has
> been pursuing it, it cannot now be calm.

The nymph's large eyes that with agitated glance explore the insect's face are compared to Goya's crouching cats facing a tame magpie. No wonder that the butterfly "springs away . . . trampling the air as it trampled the flowers" and "indifferent to her." The enigmatic conclusion follows:

> . . . It was not Oberon, but
> this quietest wind with piano replies,
>
> the zephyr, whose detachment was enough
> to tempt the fiery tiger horse to stand,
> eyes staring skyward and chest arching
> bravely out—historic metamorphoser
> and saintly animal
> in India, in Egypt, anywhere.
> Their talk was as strange as my grandmother's muff.

"Half Deity" suspends itself from a miniature narrative of another episode the writer had witnessed in Virginia. Its meaning touches only lightly on the symbol of immortality; the metamorphosis from worm to half deity gives Psyche a right to escape, even from child-like marauders, and be borne away once more by Zephyr.[39] In the last line these connotations are dismissed in the odd, matter-of-fact comment: "Their talk was as strange as my grandmother's muff." The effect resembles that of a last line in an earlier, quite different poem where the butterfly will not stay, and "to question the congruence of the complement is vain, if it exists." Fancy is modified by a swift descent of the curtain.

"The Pangolin" is the final poem in the little volume bearing that title, and represents a noticeable change in

Marianne Moore's handling of resemblances between the human and the animal worlds. The opening stanzas tersely describe the ant-eater almost as a scientist might, if scientists availed themselves of metaphor. The scientist would see "the closing ear- / ridge . . . and similarly safe / contracting nose and eye apertures." But he would not make *us* see "the artichoke set leg- and body-plates," and the tail, "graceful tool, as prop or hand or broom or axe." Description leads into motion, as the pangolin ant-eater cautiously works down the tree with the "form and / frictionless creep of a thing / made graceful by adversities, con- / versities." Suddenly the poem delivers a twentieth-century aphorism, Baconian only in its concision: "To explain grace requires a curious hand." And then it introduces another context of thought, to justify the symbolism of animals, their meaning as objects for contemplation. Why would monks have graced the spires of churches and cathedrals with animals, why would sculptors have "slaved to confuse / grace with a kindly / manner, time in which to pay a debt, / a graceful use / of . . . stone / mullions branching out across / the perpendiculars"? The recurrence of the term *grace* is woven into the poem as the antidote to obversity.[40]

Swiftly the affectionately accurate anatomy of the pangolin as the model of exactness "with certain postures of a man," makes way for the entry of man himself.

> . . . Bedizened or stark
> naked, man, the self, the being
> we call human, writing-
> master to the world, griffons a dark
> 'Like does not like like that is
> obnoxious'. . . .
>
> Not afraid of anything is he
> and then goes cowering forth, tread paced
> to meet an obstacle
> at every step.

The poem has turned around to bring man out of a moral seclusion suggested in the earlier lines, "Sun and moon and day and night and man and beast / each with a splend- / or which man / in all his vileness cannot / set aside, each with an excellence!" Man, as the poem progresses, has various animal skills and traits; he is a paper-maker like the wasp and, "strong-shod" like the ant-eater, he lives in his own habitat and slaves between sun and moon. But he is capable of learning that humour saves a few steps, can even save years. Like the armoured animal, he may be the prey of fear, be thwarted by the work undone. But he can redeem his errors, and

> [say] to the alternating blaze,
> "Again the sun!
> anew each
> day; and new and new and new,
> that comes into and steadies my soul."

Marianne Moore's poetry has many puns; and, like the seventeenth-century poets, here she allows the full meaning of sun as the Son to conclude "The Pangolin." From the point of view of form, it is particularly worthwhile to read this poem after the earlier "Black Earth" and the later "Elephants." "Black Earth" may seem more like a tale in a bestiary, where animals suggest or symbolize human traits. But even in "Black Earth" the appearance and behavior of the elephant invite contemplation of "the patina of circumstance [that] can but enrich what was / there to begin with," as well as of the "beautiful element of unreason under it." We have transcended the unvarying point of view of the bestiary or of allegorical parallels here, and even more so in "The Pangolin" and "Elephants."

The group of poems in *The Pangolin*, building upon the new work in *Selected Poems*, prepares the way for two of the most memorable books of poetry to appear in the fifth decade of this century—*What Are Years* and *Nevertheless*. First in "Part of a Novel, Part of a Poem, Part of a Play," then in "Virginia Britannia" and "The Pangolin," innovations in structure had continued. In discussing the serial poems "Octopus" and "Marriage," I suggested, cautiously I hope, the nature of collage. A musical pattern is more evident in these later poems. "The Jerboa," as has been shown, has some resemblance to the development of subject and countersubject in the fugue. But "Part of a Novel, Part of a Poem, Part of a Play" introduces and harmonizes its themes with greater simplicity and economy. "Virginia Britannia" keeps time to changes in human time corrresponding to different intentions and motives in our history and eventual future. "The Pangolin," Leonardo's "replica" as "artist engineer," anticipates poems like "Four Quartz Crystal Clocks" and "The Icosasphere." But in its haunting sequence of the struggle for life of the animal stepping in the moonlight, on the moonlight, and of the "serge-clad" mammal, man, renewed by the sun's alternation with the dark, there is expert presentation of major themes varied by subordinate ones. In such poems, unfailing musical inventiveness accompanies a moral confidence that can abide its own questionings.

5

The Poet's Advance

THE publication of *Pangolin* proved a good transition for Marianne Moore. When she had finished new work that could be added to this little private edition, she for the first time took the initiative in arranging for the publication of a book, with *What Are Years* in 1941, then the book that followed it, *Nevertheless* (1944).[1] Her skill and, one might say, hardihood in these negotiations resulted in her maintaining essential control of the manner and timing of publication.

When she learned accidentally, in 1940, that Macmillan had remaindered the unsold copies of *Selected Poems*, she might have felt discouraged. But not so. After attending service at the Lafayette Street Presbyterian Church on November 21, 1940, she wrote to her brother. The letter is a study in detachment as a makeweight for potentially bad news. She described how the "Bear," disappointed in the sermon, left for home "emitting low growls." On the way they bought "a small 10-cent tub of German icecream at the Oxford Delicatessen," to round out their lunch of romaine lettuce, eggplant, stewed tomato, baked potato and "grass juice." Praising her brother for his endurance and courage, she reminded him of his belief that "having surmounted bad things many times over, means that there is not going to be any collapse of power now." She continued:

> Bear and I were somewhat roused the other day to hear from James Laughlin that my *Selected Poems* had been remaindered by Macmillan. I . . . learned by phoning Macmillan (learned confidentially) (!) that 496 copies . . . are being sold to the Gotham Book Mart for 30

110

cents a copy. Bear thought we should pounce on some copies for ourselves so ordered 2 and then 4 and finally 20 @ 30 cents a piece. It's a compliment that a shop which is a judge of standard modern work bought the book. . . . James Laughlin wrote as if a foul assassin had sneaked up upon me. But housekeeping is housekeeping. To have had the book printed is the main thing, & all will be well if I can manage to produce some first-rate stuff. To dominate the situation is for me, antelope, to do, in a conclusive way.

Mild as she might appear to be, unassuming as she certainly was, she was not naive, not indifferent to seeking the best result. The new poems to be grouped with those in *Pangolin* would make a volume too small for Faber and Faber to publish under wartime controls,[2] and she now dealt directly with Macmillan. Within a few months of the remaindering of *Selected Poems* she had an agreement for the publication of *What Are Years*.[3]

Soon thereafter (in 1943) she determined to make another book out of the four poems she had written since *What Are Years* and two that she planned to write. Tactfully, she informed Mr. Latham that the Cummington Press would bring out a small edition, and asked permission to do this. At once he replied: "Of course we want to do anything that Miss Moore wants us to do. At the same time, I am a little unhappy that Macmillan can't be publishing a book for you. Are these six poems which you say you might include in the Cummington Press book of any length at all? Could they, taken together make a small book for us to do?"[4]

All due honour to Harold Latham and the Macmillan Company in those days of wartime restrictions! Within two months Mr. Latham had made a favorable decision. "We shall be very happy indeed if we may publish the little book of poems. It promises to be a smaller book than we usually do, but it will certainly be a distinguished addition—no matter what its size—to our list."[5] In such fashion was the agreement made (with the manuscript still incomplete) for the second of the two "slim volumes," *What Are Years* and *Nevertheless*, written when Marianne Moore was at the height of her power. The contract offered her a straight royalty of ten percent. Replying, in Mr. Latham's absence, to his secretary, Marianne Moore accepted the offer with her usual courtesy. She did, however, add in the last paragraph that she had received the day before an offer from Contemporary Poetry of Baltimore to issue this book at a royalty of twenty-five percent and had informed them that her contract with Macmillan Company "would preclude such an undertaking."[6] The matter now settled, she went ahead to finish the poems still to be added to the others. For each of these books, she used the title of one poem that epitomized the spirit of the whole.

The grave and beautiful poem "What Are Years?" has no predecessor in Marianne Moore's writing. Its utter simplicity of language is quite different from the intricate variations of a poem like "The Jerboa," and the form resembles the plainsong rather than the sonata or fugue. The musical structure verifies in modern speech the underlying parallel rhythms, the antithetical questions and resolutions, found in the Bible. The opening lines present parallels and contrasts. The question "What is our innocence, / what is our guilt?" is, like the subsequent "whence is courage," unanswerable, but affirmative. The antiphonal response, "All are naked, none is safe" brings the meaning into the sphere of charity, of love that is greater than hope. Courage is the heart of hope, and by means of the opposites "dumbly calling, deafly listening" stirs the soul to be strong in defeat, even in death.

At this turn in the poem (the movement from the first stanza to the second), one becomes aware of soundings being taken in a simpler but not less powerful spirit, like some in the book of Job. Several verses in Job come to mind in the reading of "What Are Years?", for example Job's response to the initial calamities he suffers: "Naked came I out of my mother's womb, and naked shall I return thither: the Lord gave, and the Lord hath taken away; blessed be the name of the Lord. Is there not an appointed time to man upon earth?" (7:1). When the Lord speaks to Job out of the whirlwind, his declarative questions (by which all Job's lesser ones are answered) resemble the meditative queries that link "What Are Years?" with "In Distrust of Merits."

The second stanza returns to the metaphor of the sea imprisoned in a chasm at the end of the earlier poem, "The Fish." There, too, the counterpoint was between the animation of creatures kept alive in the rock pools by the entering sea, and the fact that "the chasm side is dead."

> The water drives a wedge
> of iron through the iron edge
> of the cliff; whereupon the stars
>
> pink
> rice-grains, . . .
> crabs like green
> lilies, and submarine
> toadstools, slide each on the other.

But if the chasm side is dead, nevertheless "Repeated / evidence proves that it can live / on what can not revive / its youth. The sea grows old in it." The chasm is a real fissure in the rock, and the time of what lives in it and of the returning tide, is world time, geological time. In "What Are Years?", the same phenomenon becomes the metaphorical equivalent of man who acknowledges mortality, and in so doing emancipates himself from it. He who accedes to mortality

> rises
> upon himself as
> the sea in a chasm, struggling to be
> free and unable to be,
> in its surrendering
> finds its continuing.

Resolve, not acquiescence, marks the choice of one who "strongly feels." His "resolute doubt" leads to the origin of courage, as

> The very bird,
> grown taller as he sings, steels
> his form straight up. Though he is captive,
> his mighty singing
> says, satisfaction is a lowly
> thing, how pure a thing is joy.

Like that earlier moral insight, "life's faulty excellence," the affirmation does not stem from a naive or uncritical sense of how things are. The central lines, "satisfaction is a lowly / thing, how pure a thing is joy," create the knowledge they embody, and justify the balanced antiphonal ending of the poem: "This is mortality, / this is eternity."

From early drafts, it appears that the death of an individual, probably a child, summoned an effort to understand why the unanalyzable loss then felt was translated into belief in the meaning of that person's, and potentially of everyone's, life. The will to live with the knowledge of man's mortality becomes, against all odds, an act of courage equivalent to faith.

The first worksheets for the poem reveal a memory of Chaucer's "Prioress's Tale," where even after his death the child, "the clergeon," continued to sing "Alma redemptoris mater." Tentative early lines refer to "the little clergeon full of glory," and "the clergeon / in Chaucer's dirge." The drafts soon begin to introduce comparisons with a bird, first a seemingly actual one, "lost young bird," glum "at being found, heart heard," then resort to a more symbolic visual image: "This is the loss taught by that song / and silver-fabriced wing / there must be that with which to match the soul." Some of these drafts[7] are essentially efforts to state the theme in general terms; others search for concrete equivalents of the perplexities, and possible transcendence, of suffering and death. They bear little resemblance to the finished poem—with one exception.

From the beginning some of the profound simplicities were present, surrounded by lines either lacking in inherent relevance or somewhat inert because of their vagueness. While we cannot accurately discern the sequence of the early drafts, one, bearing the date July 1931 in Marianne Moore's handwriting, shows this combination of vagueness and somewhat uncertain groping for the image to offset it —yet, miraculously, there are the lines, "What is our innocence? / and what is our guilt?" In others, that for similar reasons I should place very early, she had found the final parallel of the finished poem: "This is mortality, / this is eternity." These drafts confirm her statement that sometimes the final lines of a poem occurred to her first, or if not always first, soon enough so that she knew the whole composition must move towards these lines.[8]

It is evident that over a long period Marianne Moore had worked on "What Are Years?" The poem we now have is distilled from emotions for which she had to find, and ultimately did find, an impersonal order, when all minor traces of feeling or temporary association had been cut away. Even after the revision dated April 5, 1940, read for a Radio America broadcast,[9] small improvements were made to achieve the poem finally published in 1941 in the book bearing its name.

Of the eleven other poems in that book, all are worthy to bear company with the title poem, although differing from it in the depth of experience sounded as well as in the patterns of rhyme set off by the rhythm. The successive drafts of "What Are Years?" result in an economy that underscores the inevitability of every word in the finished text. In eight sentences forming three stanzas of nine lines each, only twelve lines are rhymed, with only moderate emphasis on the rhyme. "Light is Speech," in contrast, has an animated, even syncopated pattern of rhyme appropriate to its fervour, its generous tribute to a then prone ally in the war.

Perhaps on her visit to Brittany, in 1911, Marianne Moore heard the Breton word *Creach'h* (in "the Creach'h d'Ouessant lighthouse,") pronounced to rhyme with *speech*). The iteration of the central word arrives at another original proverb: "Yes light is speech. Free frank / impartial sunlight, moonlight, / starlight, lighthouse light / are language." That being so, the lighthouse may be extravagantly regarded as the descendant of Voltaire and of Montaigne. And the "frankness" of light is a timely pun, leading to the final theme, " 'The word France means enfranchisement.' "

"He 'Digesteth Harde Yron' " is a divertimento of variations upon the theme of "The Jerboa." Her letters show a long-standing admiration of the ostrich. With clever indignation she refutes the legend of its inability to distinguish between seeing and being seen. On the contrary, the real ostrich of the poem is "never known to hide his / head in sand," but "feigns flight / to save his chicks," and is "a symbol of justice." The rhymes in this poem accentuate particular facts, and are natural and unforced as well as surprising. The ostrich watches his chicks with a maternal concentration, after

> he has set on the eggs
> at night six weeks, his legs
> their only weapon of defense
>
> . . . .
>
> he has a foot hard
> as a hoof; the leopard
> is not more suspicious.

We see him flying "on feet not wings—his moth-silk / plumage wilted by his speed; / mobile wings and tail / behaving as a sail." With similar controlled speed the poem moves to its climax.

> The power of the visible
> is the invisible, as even where
> no tree of freedom grows
> so-called brute courage knows.

116

Heroism is exhausting, yet
it contradicts a greed that
did not wisely spare
the harmless solitaire

or great auk in its grandeur. . . .

The ostrich, only remaining giant bird, contradicts the greed of men who try to decoy and kill it, and like the jerboa, refutes man's luxury as "too much." The poem has a romantic ending. Xenophon's metaphor, with which the text opens, reappears: "This one / remaining rebel / is the sparrow camel." In a letter of January 15, 1941, addressed to "Dearest Pigeon-wings," then in New London, Marianne Moore had remarked "I rather favor as a title for my ostrich The One Remaining Rebel as making a nice echo for the conclusion."[10] Although she chose instead a phrase from Lyly's *Euphues* for the title "He 'Digesteth Harde Yron,' " the twofold emphasis is clear, the superlative adaptability of the rebel as an antidote to greed.

All the poems in *What Are Years* can be seen as studies in the equation between obstacles and endurance, exile and return, resistance to what is hostile to life, fortified by trust. It is appropriate therefore that a place was found in this book for "The Student," a poem that, as we have seen, was originally intended to be the second section of "Part of a Novel, Part of a Poem, Part of a Play,"[11] and was omitted from that composition in *Selected Poems* (1935). There, the independent development of its theme would have disturbed the unity of the whole. Yet its value lies in the active testimony—not undermined by sentiment—of the firm reality in a student's life. Set apart, the poem keeps its consanguinity with "The Steeple-Jack" and "The Hero." For the student's life can be heroic only when he bypasses dangers more threatening, since not as evident, as those the man of action meets—the dangers of "bookworms, mildews, and complaisancies." Although not named in the later version,

117

Einstein and Emerson have a place in the poem, and Burke defines the student's necessary stubbornness:

> ... Wolf's wool is the best of wool,
>   but it cannot be sheared because
>   the wolf will not comply.[12]

A student must be warier of temptation than Samson, and he must also refuse the services of a courtier:

> he renders service when there is
> no reward, and is too reclusive for
>   some things to seem to touch
> him, not because he
>   has no feeling, but because he has so much.

Perhaps, like many things the student attempts, this poem gets off to a slow start and the first stanzas are too expository, but the last half allies itself with and reinforces many of her stronger compositions. It is the clue to what insensitive readers do not understand about her poetry.

Imagination seeking and instinctively finding a new field lends surprise to "Spenser's Ireland." Wholly different in tone and tenor from the title poem of *What Are Years?*, and different too from anything Marianne Moore had previously written, "Spenser's Ireland" sets a new mark in the poet's advance. "Virginia Britannia" and "New York" celebrate places that she knew at first hand. "Spenser's Ireland" is a place seen wholly by the eye of imagination. A phrase or sentence from a book, an article, a lecture had lighted on fertile ground, in the receptive heart of someone who felt an affinity for this land of her ancestors.

The opening lines (as originally published) invite the reader to follow on a journey more enticing than the actual traveller's: if Spenser's Ireland "has not altered" it follows that in "the kindest place I've never been, / the greenest place I've never seen" the stranger is welcome. If "every name is a tune," so, too, the swiftly woven lines of the poem shape a musical dialogue. Relatively few of her poems begin and end with the writer speaking in her own person, but the romantic spell of this one depends upon the word of the teller. A rapid question fortifies the declaration of belief:

> Outwitting
> the fairies, befriending the furies,
> whoever again
> and again says, "I'll never
> give in," never sees
>
> that you're not free
> until you've been made captive by
> supreme belief,—credulity
> you say?

The cunning harmonies of this poem light up every facet of the art, the skills, the resources of the Irish people. The fingers that divide the wings of the fly and wrap it with peacock tail feathers for the fisherman, the "concurring hands" weaving flax into damask show a pride in their care equal to enchantment. The glow of the "purple coral fuchsia tree" excels the gold torcs and lunulae made by ancient islanders. These musical examples speed along by aptly spaced rhymes, with confirming melodies of pitch. Another skeptical question is followed by a dramatic avowal of identity. From a rather diffuse article by Donn Byrne she lifted one of its lively statements, and added her own question mark: "The Irish say your trouble is their / trouble and your / joy their joy?" then the comic refusal:

> I wish
> I could believe it;
> I am troubled, I'm dissat-
> isfied, I'm Irish.

It is a poem written to be read aloud, and gave scope to her dramatic talent. "Spenser's Ireland" is as much about the people who live there as it is about "the greenest place I've never been," but the people inhabit a special

119

landscape where you find "the guillemot / so neat and the hen / of the heath and the / linnet spinet-sweet." This last sequence of phrases bespeaks not "relentlessness" but the singing power of the poem.

T. S. Eliot had reason to say, in his introduction to *Selected Poems* of 1935, that Marianne Moore was not a writer of "lyric" verse. We all know how difficult it is to specify what lyric means; but it has traditionally implied both simplicity and brevity as well as intensity in the development of a theme, and musicality of tone. All Marianne Moore's poems show musicianly skills, but in "Spenser's Ireland," the composition itself seems to have a tune or melody and anticipates later poems like "The Mind is an Enchanting Thing," "Propriety," or "Logic and the Magic Flute."

Placed at the end of *What Are Years* is a curious poem, "The Paper Nautilus." It begins oddly, with a disclaimer, a seemingly irrelevant one.

> For authorities whose hopes
> are shaped by mercenaries?
> Writers entrapped by
> teatime fame and by
> commuters' comforts? Not for these
> the paper nautilus
> constructs her thin glass shell.

To begin this poem apparently required a taking-off point of some kind—as some ducks must patter a few steps on the water before flying. The ensuing description of the convoluted shell concentrates on the maker's watchful care of the eggs concealed in it, the shell itself a "perishable souvenir of hope." The central paradox reveals itself as analogous to Hercules, who had been "hindered to succeed"; thus the intensively guarded eggs "coming from / the shell free it when they are freed." A beautiful visual image plays on the double meaning of chiton as both a garment and the outer covering of crustaceans. The abandoned shell has:

120

> . . . wasp-nest flaws
> of white on white, and close-
>
> laid Ionic chiton-folds
> like the lines in the mane of
> a Parthenon horse,
> round which the arms had
> wound themselves as if they knew love
> is the only fortress
> strong enough to trust to.

Love, a word that Marianne Moore rarely wrote into a poem, has the more force thereby. By this aphorism, comparable to some in her early poems, but one that depends on intuition more than observation, Marianne Moore ends *What Are Years* with a metaphor for faith as finely tempered as the transcendent questions and prophetic rejoinders of the opening poem.

Perhaps one of the most moving things about her life as a writer is the combination of modesty and determination, of respect for the inner sources of experience and sheer hard work, willingness to do her utmost once she had embarked on a theme, and, in accord with her modesty, by no means conflicting with it, a confidence in what could be done. Having successfully arranged for the publication of *What Are Years*, she naturally felt an interest in its reception— not hungry for the praise no one can accord true poetry, but anxious that it be read, that it be reviewed by a few capable of understanding. Humorously deprecating the likelihood that the book would be assigned to reviewers from whom the commonplace verdict might be expected.[13] she was pleased that W. H. Auden's piece in the *New York Times Book Review* brought a fresh point of view about her accomplishment. It was all the more welcome from a writer of a younger generation whose own poetry stemmed from quite different concerns and was distinguished by other skills. Auden admitted that five years earlier he could not comprehend the merits of *Selected Poems*, and had not been aware of her originality. Now, he confessed that he had learned new ways of writing from her.[14] Other reviews helped to give the book the chance it deserved. She forwarded a few of them to her brother.

Meanwhile, as before, while one book was being printed she had started on the poems that were to appear, three years later, in *Nevertheless*. And she was simultaneously preparing some lectures and articles or reviews that she proposed to include in that book. But publishers did not like the plan of combining some new poems with prose.[15] None of her criticism, therefore, was collected until *Predilections* came out in 1956.

Of this new group of poems the earliest to be published was "The Wood Weasel," obtained by the *Harvard Advocate* for its April 1942 issue. Given the fact that the thrifty and frugal—but equally generous—poet conscientiously reported to her brother the small sums paid her by magazines,[16] one cannot fail to notice her generosity in yielding to the requests of relatively little-known publications, which usually pay nothing to contributors. "The Wood Weasel" became a favorite of those who heard her read it; she herself so obviously enjoyed its wit and the conviction inherent in its self-protective irony. Probably few recognized the extra pleasure of the acrostic formed by the initial letters of each line, which spell backward from last line to first the name of her friend Hildegarde Watson. "The Wood Weasel," like the vulnerable poet, is "his own protection from the moth," but an emblem of grace as well, who "emerges daintily" and wears a "sweet face" above his powerful feet. That all the lines are rhymed gives a different accent to this flourish of praise for the "wood-warden."

This poem and "Elephants" are the only ones about animals in *Nevertheless*—a point worth making because studies that emphasize Marianne Moore's animal kingdom often fail to recognize the equal strength of poems in which the "transfiguration experienced"[17] does not arise from our non-human human fellow-creatures. But "Elephants" creates a study comparable to "Black Earth," although different in structure and set in a different key.

Everyone who knew Marianne Moore soon learned of her predilection for elephants. This poem includes the phrase "magic hairs"—and on a visit to the circus or the zoo she herself collected them, seizing an opportune moment to snip some from the tail or the trunk, using a small scissors that she carried with her for this purpose. Her elephant-hair bracelet, she would explain, brought good luck, and had the added virtue of being warm.[18]

But when her brother sent her a different bracelet, a metal one from which small elephants dangled, she wrote enthusiastically and began with perhaps her most comprehensive statement about their meaning:

> The nine, the sacred nine, are here . . . and what a sight 9 two-tails, every one a little different from the others. Nine is a sacred number in the far east, you know, and the white or sacred elephant of Kandy is called the *Lord Elephant*. Well—in Africa, the elephant hairs and ivory can only be worn by the wives of hunters that have killed or captured lions, & anything = elephant that is creative—a symbol of fertility, I believe. As applied to me, that would mean poems & book reviews & a *wiser head*. [Then she describes the "amulet" at some length.]
>
> These two tails are more and more to me as I dwell upon them. I can't make out what they are standing on —a lotus leaf, or a sacred pearl or the globe. I gotta determine this. Well Bible as I said to Cub, Badger has imagination, that's why he lights on these singular and lovable things. . . . This here bracelet is not "cold" to my skin nor do I feel it when on, it is so light, so I figure I am gonna wear it pretty much all the time.[19]

This letter helps to identify the difference between her first major elephant poem, "Black Earth," and "Elephants" of 1943 (which had been written and published a short time before her brother sent her the bracelet for which she thanks him here). The later poem presents a series of scenes: of elephants fighting, of one in a dry stream-bed cradling the sleeping mahout in the hollow of its body, of a procession following the white elephant that carries "the cushion that carries the casket that carries [Buddha's] Tooth." She had abstracted the most telling facts from the lecture-film "Ceylon, the Wondrous Isle," to which she acknowledges her indebtedness.[20] But the concrete events typical of the captive elephants' life are arranged to suggest and confirm virtues worthy of man's imitation. Their procession is a pattern of "revery not reverence." For even the august white elephant

> Though white is
> the color of worship and of mourning, . . .

> is not here to worship and he is too wise
> to mourn,—a life-prisoner but reconciled.
> With trunk tucked up compactly—the elephant's
> sign of defeat—he resisted, but is the child

> of reason now. His straight trunk seems to say: when
> what we hoped for came to nothing, we revived.

His acceptance resembles Socrates' equanimity in confronting injustice. The elephant is not only allied to man, his gentleness in offering bent foreleg and an ear to grip for his "gnat-sized trustees" to climb aboard, "expounds the brotherhood / of creatures to man the encroacher." He can do this because he remembers what he has experienced; he proves the sense of the verb *büd*, to know. It is fortunate that he can't do some of the things that Buddha, or man the encroacher, is all too prone to do, like turning heat, when "exasperated," "to earthquake-fire."

Anyone who has read the poem even once will remember some of the new aphorisms it progresses to, especially the last two lines ("Who rides on a tiger can never dismount; / asleep on an elephant, that is repose"). But built into the poem as a whole are the powerful themes of acceptance of

124

service, of the beauty of gentleness, the willingness to admit uncertainty and ignorance, to test the unknown. The poem certainly also has a bearing upon war, on the nature of peace, and can be read as a gloss upon "In Distrust of Merits." "Hardship makes the soldier; then teachableness / makes him the philosopher"—not a Philosopher-King, but a soldierly philosopher. We understand then why the elephants "can change roles with their trustees." But one aphorism leaps beyond the context of the poem. The elephant-rider sleeps as soundly in the hollow of the elephant's body as if he too were an elephant,

> incised with hard wrinkles, embossed with wide ears,
> invincibly tusked, made safe by magic hairs!
> As if, as if, it is all as ifs; we are at
> much unease. . . .

The inescapable uncertainty of life, of creative life as well as every other, remains. The elephants have "magic's masterpiece . . . / Houdini's serenity quelling his fears," hence they are a pattern of the modern pilgrim's revery, not reverence—"a / religious procession without any priests." The analogy prepares us for the "as if" that must remain incomplete.

This unfinished "as if" parallels certain passages in the earlier poem, "Black Earth":

>   my back
> is full of the history of power. Of power? What
> is powerful and what is not?
>
> . . . .
>   the elephant is
>   that on which darts cannot strike decisively the first
>
> time, a substance
> needful as an instance
>   of the indestructibility of matter, it
>   has looked at electricity and at the earth-
>
> quake and is still
> here. . . .

In *Collected Poems* (1951) both "Black Earth" (now entitled "Melancthon") and "Elephants" rightfully were included; but the earlier piece was omitted from *Complete Poems* (1967). As a reader I can only say (to paraphrase Dryden) I admire "Elephants," but I love "Black Earth"[21]— among many other reasons for its quietly sophisticated rhythm. The omission of "Black Earth" is only one more example of the fact that intelligent readers of Marianne Moore's poetry will need all the editions until some day a truly complete one is prepared.

"Nevertheless," a poem that almost memorizes itself for you, moves from one startlingly natural visual image to another, the sequence proceeding along the line of a virtue all can comprehend. The poem does not take off from any uncommon knowledge of natural history first encountered in a museum, a zoo, or travel film. For everyone has seen a strawberry that's had a struggle, and a cherry tree could grow in your own back yard, or over a neighbor's fence you could see how the grapevine's tendril

ties a knot in knots till

knotted thirty times,—so
the bound twig that's under-
gone and over-gone, can't stir.

Because of these familiar things—all but the "kok-saghyz stalks"—the poem has an appealing homeliness, attired in its deft three-line stanzas, the second and third line of each openly rhymed. This piece, and "The Wood Weasel," which follows it, lead the reader persuasively into a book where profundities loom before him at the end, when he comes to "In Distrust of Merits" and "The Mind is an Enchanting Thing." Yet "Nevertheless" is an overture to these later poems, and in fact it is not easy to fathom the implications of "Victory won't come / to me unless I go / to it," or of "The weak overcomes its / menace, the strong over- / comes itself." The title poem of the volume *Nevertheless* is in fact a spirited prologue to the stalwart explorations of peace and war that follow, in "Elephants" and "In Distrust of Merits."

The remarkable variety of the six major poems contained in this small book manifests one aspect of Marianne Moore's unceasing inventiveness. "A Carriage From Sweden" exemplifies the ease of her new forms of composition. As a theme the treasured exhibit of handicraft is potentially inert; but here it was the source quickening glance of a vital portrait. "A Carriage From Sweden," like "Spenser's Ireland," takes the reader to a land the writer had never seen: both poems differ from the place known at first hand and sharply observed. To create an imagined place or people successfully in poetry requires different skills—as Shakespeare's Bohemia or Forest of Arden evoked poetry different from that of the English scenes in the Henry IV plays.

Although the carriage is described in the second stanza as "a put-away museum piece" the reader has been prepared for different sensations by the first stanza. "They say" is a storyteller's beginning, the fabled "sweeter air" of Sweden is offset by the seemingly irrelevant remark that "there is in Brooklyn / something that makes me feel at home." This mood, far from contradicting the possible artificiality of a "country cart," brings "inner happiness made art." The "freckled integrity" of the American city has made room for the resined straightness of its northern opposite and counterpart. But the surprising invocation, "Washington and Gustavus Adolphus, forgive us our decay," almost confirms a momentary feeling that this poem is a digression from the others in *Nevertheless*. When we have read the whole text, however, "A Carriage From Sweden" falls into its true place in this book. Its varying perspectives converge on the unavoidable wrong of war, yet acknowledge that in a time of contest with mindless power, all that is fair declares itself against what is destructive of humanity. And— as in the deeper reverberations of "In Distrust of Merits"— peace is seen through the maze of beauty, of freedom, of risk-taking generosity. The very structure of the carriage, even the "crustacean-tailed" ornaments on the axle-tree, connote an "unannoying romance," and suddenly there is the beauty that becomes the climax of "In Distrust of Merits":

> ... And how beautiful, she
> with the natural stoop of the
> snowy egret, gray-eyed and straight-haired,
> for whom it should come to the door,—
>
> of whom it reminds me. The split
> pine fair hair, steady gannet-clear
> eyes and the pine-needled-path deer-
> swift step; that is Sweden, land of the
> free and the soil for a spruce-tree—
>
> . . . .
>
> The deft white-stockinged dance in thick-soled
> shoes! Denmark's sanctuaried Jews!

The life, the beauty, the clarity of an individual person, of the land itself, justify as a climax Sweden's voluntary offer of asylum to the Jews threatened by Hitler's conquest of Denmark. The salient fact is that Marianne Moore revised the poem—which was the last to be composed of any in *Nevertheless*—when it had already been accepted by the *Nation* and she was reading the proof. She wrote to Warner on March 1st, 1944:

> I set to work this P.M. to mention Kg. Gustav V's "opening the doors of his country to the Jews of nearby Denmark" to get it introduced *though my poem is in proof*—Bless me, what a narrow shave. The poem is *greatly* improved & Margaret Marshall I *think* will help me. I signed the letter requesting the change "timorously yours. . . ."

Washington, who had attended the first Jewish synagogue in Newport, Rhode Island, and Gustavus Adolphus, who stood for religious toleration in the Thirty Years' War, no longer seem surprising personages in the poem. "A Carriage From Sweden," like the other pieces in *Nevertheless*, incorporated what the poet herself called "peremptoriness," a deep sense of conviction that the central issues of World War II held their place with eternal questions of peace and freedom, the willingness to take a stand on them affirming our knowledge of every other kind of value.

In arranging the poems in *Nevertheless* Marianne Moore did not follow the chronological order of their composition: she made "The Mind is an Enchanting Thing" and "In Distrust of Merits" the last pieces for the reader to meditate upon. Although this was, I believe, right for the book itself, I prefer to discuss "In Distrust of Merits" as one of her mightiest self-discoveries, and a discovery for others of what the war challenged and what it revealed. Discussion of "The Mind is an Enchanting Thing" will follow, as a forecast of surprising poems to come.

Like the poem "What Are Years?" the lines of "In Distrust of Merits" are a distillation of feeling, of questioning and search for understanding, that began long before the poem was written. The actual text, however, did not evolve from many drafts different from the final one. It could not have, for the actual events of the war dominate its structure. But the underlying soil was prepared by many exchanges of thought with her brother about the book of Job and dialogues with her mother about the human propensity for intolerance, or desire for personal power as a root cause of conflict and injustice to others.

The germ of the poem occurs in a letter to Warner written on November 19, 1939. Addressing him as "Dearest Mongolian Gazelle" (his ship was returning from the Pacific), she describes going with her mother to see the movie *Pygmalion* at the Pratt Institute in Brooklyn, and then offers (as she frequently did) suggestions for possible sermons. Then she adds,

While waiting for the movie last night I read Bear a piece from The Spectator by Reinhold Niebuhr on Germany's condition as a race—in persecuting & being subject to Hitler, & though Bear says we already know it, he reminds us that intolerance is at work in us all *in all* countries,—that we ourselves "persecute" Jews and Negroes & submit to wrongful tyranny. Or at least feel "superior" in sundry ways.

This theme—"the warfare within"—occurs most explicitly in the conversations with her mother that Marianne records in one of her conversation notebooks, kept from 1935 to 1941, although there are a few later entries.

When *Selected Poems* appeared in 1935, a paragraph called *A Postscript* preceded the notes at the end of the book, and here, without mentioning her mother specifically, she wrote:

> Dedications imply giving, and we do not care to make a gift of what is insufficient; but in my immediate family there is one "who thinks in a particular way;" and I should like to add that where there is an effect of thought or pith in these pages, the thinking and often the actual phrases are hers.[22]

Since the conversation notebook of 1921-1928 has been lost, we cannot observe at first hand the translation of Mrs. Moore's sayings into lines, or parts of lines, in her daughter's earlier poetry.[23] I use the word translation deliberately. For even when the words are Mary Warner Moore's, the effect in the poem, especially the tone of the observation *as a whole* in its complete context, strikes very differently upon the ear. At first one is astonished to find that some of the most unforgettable images and phrases of "In Distrust of Merits" are entered in this notebook of the sayings of her mother. But their distinction in the poem belongs wholly to Marianne Moore's skill in composition and increasing ability to simplify and to connect. One reason for the difference between the impact of the initial sayings and the lines in the poem arises from the overt piety characteristic of Mary Warner Moore's utterances. They are thoughtful, witty, decisive, occasionally sarcastic; yet the intention of the minister's daughter—who might herself have wished to be a minister—prevails. One cannot help wondering if Marianne may not sometimes have felt, as Wilfred Owen did, a dislike of being prayed over by a zealous parent.

If she did, her underlying love of "Bear" suffered no fundamental impairment, nor did the humour with which she invested their shared life and its fortification by Badger's loyalty, his own humour, his sharing of his adventures with them, his unremitting attention to their needs. On his account, as well as their own opposition to the rising power of Fascism and Nazism, both Marianne Moore and her mother felt a strong commitment to the cause of the Allies. That conviction had to be reconciled with devotion to peace as inherent in Christian belief. But the moral conflict could not be gainsaid. Against this background we can perceive the art by which Marianne Moore incorporated many of the sayings of Mary Warner Moore into "In Distrust of Merits."

In June 1938 Marianne noted her mother's expression, "The dust of the earth that walks so arrogantly," and another on the same page "War—there is one answer—*the warfare within.*" In August, there is an entry that anticipates one of the themes of the poem, "The seeing who have no sight." The thought recurred in April 1942, "None are so frightening as the blind who can see"—the *morally* blind whose possession of military power threatens all. As the fighting in Europe intensified, Mrs. Moore's effort to grasp its meaning in Christian terms continued. Earlier (April 29, 1941) Marianne had entered her mother's comment, "We are thankful to have these thoughts put in our minds . . . that God is greater than war. . . . How ineffectual we feel against the evil that makes people evil (who do what we call wrong)," and then wrote above the first line and in the margin "Psalm xxix and last ch. of Vera Brittain England's Hour."[24] Psalm xxix exalts the voice of the Lord which "divideth the flames of fire," and promises that he "will bless his people with peace."

As further evidence of their interest in Vera Brittain's book, there is a letter of May 3rd 1941 to Warner Moore recommending it to him:

> Dearest Webfoot,
>
> . . . . After prayers—no, before—Bear and me read the last chapters of Vera Brittain's *England's Hour* & in it she says, though St. Paul's has been bombed and other churches and countless homes, victory is to be in vain if we can't forgive. If we can't love, if we can't see our sins & pray for penitence.

Vera Brittain's is indeed an impassioned book, much concerned with "the warfare within," animated by the conviction that the energies summoned by war could have been, and in future must be, "dedicated to revitalizing the Church; rebuilding the slums; reinvigorating literature, music, and art; reorganizing from top to bottom the economic system based on power and privilege; tackling the vexed problem of distribution; making equal education and opportunities available for all."[25]

A few days after the entry about Vera Brittain's book we come with a start upon the title of the poem that was to be written two years later. This new entry reads simply "In distrust of merits. Psalm—" Now it is unquestionable that the majority of the material in the Mary Warner Moore notebooks consists of things she said that Marianne wished to preserve. I myself believe, however, that *sometimes* the entries represent the poet's recapitulation in her own terms, her own language, of questions they had discussed. This seems to be particularly true of "In Distrust of Merits," for this entry follows immediately a brief note on Elizabeth Bishop's having seen a certain kind of bouvardia for the first time in Key West. The phrase "In distrust of merits" occurs again, in parentheses, on the next page—seemingly as a general theme to which particular comments could be related.[26] Or on other occasions, an expression that carries extraordinary power in the poem is set down beside a reflection of vague moral import with which it has no necessary connection—for example "We are not competent to make our vows" or "We are fighting fighting fighting."[27] Two striking examples are set down side by side although separated by a period of six months:

October 1941 Faith is an affectionate thing—a patient thing.
April 26 [1942] The dust of the earth that walks so arrogantly. These bodies may do wrong or may resist it.

Again in April of that year Mary Warner Moore reverted to the idea of the blind man who can see and on May 20 made the statement "Dust of the earth has been our enemy. It is our enemy and we are dust." By this time, of course, the United States was engaged in the war. After notes for a letter to Warner, and thoughts on the blackout ("Trust in the blackout, trust in the light that searches through the waves") we notice that the last remark is *revised* with alternate phrases by Marianne. When therefore at the foot of the page we find

Trust begets power
Positioned victories

marked with a number in the margin, it would appear that she was already converting into material for her poem ideas that were differently expressed by and had different connotations for her mother. The poet's taking over from some prayers and general adjurations expressed on May 25, 1943, the triplet "patience patience patience" impresses me as another example.[28]

The poem itself, "In Distrust of Merits," is like a magnetic field that assembles particles emitted from many different sources of experience. Other poems assimilate sparks from the words of writers or of people she knew. But here, because so many phrases were set down in this Mary Warner Moore conversation notebook, we have an unusual chance to discover how unity was achieved in the poem, how it sustains the profound emotion, the character of thought, that impel it to its unforgettable conclusion.

The publication of *Nevertheless* brought Marianne Moore wider recognition than she had hitherto achieved, because "In Distrust of Merits" spoke to the condition of a great many people who knew that war is wrong and yet believed that World War II had to be fought. For them there was no other way for the worldwide threat of totalitarianism to be overcome. That is why readers, reviewers, other poets regarded "In Distrust of Merits" as the greatest poem of the war. For, unmarred by nationalism, it is a war and peace poem, a poem about the force of evil and the costly struggle against it, a poem about doubt, and about undying belief.

It was born by the shaping into original form the continuous dialogue and the years of meditation, and born equally of agonized response to immediate events. Marianne Moore said with utter conviction that a picture in a newspaper of a slain soldier (the "quiet form upon the dust, I cannot / look and yet I must") made her feel she must write the poem.[29] It outlasts, and reaches beyond, those tremendous events of the nineteen forties; but those events gave life and passion to it.

The title has an inscrutability like that of Milton's "two-handed engine at the door." In distrust of *whose* merits, we must ask? And reading the whole text as I have many times, I think that the title and the poem are like the two-edged sword of *Revelation*. The merits distrusted begin with those of the morally blind who can physically see, those whose gunsights aim violence against humanity—Mussolini's initial aggression against Ethiopia, Hitler's against the Jews, and against civilization itself. This is the utmost outward evil. Parallel to it, different from it, more insidious than a physical threat, the poem envisions the suffering caused Job by the false comforters, those self-righteous ones whose routine belief enshrines hypocrisy. The presence of Job in the poem links the merits to be distrusted with the truth that distrust of them confirms. In this respect "In Distrust of Merits" bears comparison with Donne's Third Satire.

The ultimate distrust to be learned is the one that unites the various parts of the poem with the final lines: we must dismiss any idea of our own merit, in the face of eternal value. If we can see how this dramatically presented self-questioning is linked also with the figure of Job, we will understand the meaning of "Iscariot-like crime." Then the organic structure of the poem should emerge, the whole being implicit in every part.

The opening question is an incomplete sentence ("Strengthened to live, strengthened to die for / medals and position victories?"). It needs no completion but the answer that immediately follows in the first statement of the theme.

> They're fighting, fighting, fighting the blind
>   man who thinks he sees,—
> who cannot see that the enslaver is
> enslaved; the hater, harmed. . . .

The pain of contemplating the danger, the losses of the fighting men immediately evokes the image of the star:

> O
>   star of David, star of Bethlehem,
> O black imperial lion
>   of the Lord—emblem
> of a risen world—be joined at last, be
> joined. There is hate's crown beneath which all is
>   death; there's love's without which none
>   is king; the blessed deeds bless
>   the halo.

The symbols here for the unity of man without which no love can be exalted (the Jewish star of David, the star leading to the discovery of Christ, the lion epitomizing Haile Selassie's fight for the freedom of black people)[30] strongly introduce the truth that surpasses any individual merit, and disallows the assumption of superiority by any race or nation.

The line "the blessed deeds bless the halo" has exceptional interest, and may remind us of the luminary qualities of the halo in some of Dürer's late work—no mere traditional symbol of holiness, but a visionary summation of goodness—as in Dürer's engraving of St. Jerome or of Christ in the Agony in the Garden or the Last Supper.[31]

For merit, if to be distrusted, is not to be denied when it leads to what defines it. As "What are Years?" united contrasting questions in a form resembling plainsong, so the polyphonic structure, the counterpoint of "In Distrust of Merits" achieves its victory by an extraordinary transition from distrust to trust. Here we may see, if not wholly comprehend, the indefinable genius that elicited new meaning from some of the phrases in the notebook containing her mother's sayings. The theme of trust (which ultimately prevails) spreads across several stanzas.

> As contagion
> of sickness makes sickness,
>
> contagion of trust can make trust. . . .
>
>
> . . . O alive who are dead, who are
> proud not to see, O small dust of the earth
> that walks so arrogantly,
> trust begets power and faith is
> an affectionate thing. We
> vow, we make this promise
>
> to the fighting—it's a promise—"We'll
> never hate black, white, red, yellow, Jew,

136

Gentile, Untouchable." We are
   not competent to
make our vows. With set jaw they are fighting,
fighting, fighting,—some we love whom we know,
   some we love but know not—that
     hearts may feel and not be numb.

The tragedy of love for the known and unknown soldiers fighting will be with us forever as long as it is a separate love for black, white, red, yellow, Jew, Gentile, or Untouchable. We are not able to trust until love itself, never singular or tribal, may be trusted. "In Distrust of Merits" denies no virtue, because merit is not a virtue. "In self-trust lie all the virtues," Emerson said; and I do not believe that the realities of Marianne Moore's Calvinism were meant to contradict this, because Emerson's self-trust was for every man. The expression "some we love but know not" corroborates a sentence in one of her letters to her brother when, after briefly stating that the son of one of her friends had been killed in the war, she added, "It shakes life into perspective."[32]

Some comments on the book of Job that she relayed to her brother enlarge our understanding of the central place of Job in the poem. The crucial passage is a brief one: "Job disheartened by false comfort knew / that nothing can be so defeating / as a blind man who / can see." Perhaps for those who know the book of Job well, any comment is unnecessary. But—though not wholly ignorant of it—I found that some of the passages she quoted or summarized from Genung's *Epic of the Inner Life* afford an insight to the connection between the Calvinist realism of some lines and the conclusion of the whole poem.

On May 3, 1940, having in mind a service her brother was to conduct, she wrote, "I enclose some of the statements made in Genung's Epic of the Inner Life (which the Bear and I are reading Sundays from time to time)." The ones that seem clearly relevant to "In Distrust of Merits" are these:

... the book of Job is too much like real life to be a didactic teaching with a single self-evident answer to its problem. . . . Why does suffering upon suffering befall the righteous—is unsatisfactorily answered in the apparent fluctuations of its reasoning, the unity of the book being centred in a person—Job.

Not why & how God deals with man, but what Job *is*, is the vital question . . . the book is an epic of the inner life—a drama within the individual soul.

And if Job has wrought out the answer, then the answer exists in humanity—: Answer: *There is a hunger for God and a loyalty to him, which survives loss and chastisement.*

But the answer is not put in words. It is *lived*

. . . .

Job sees as God sees, that the visitation was causeless— in so far as just punishment was concerned.

. . . .

chap. 42 The experience has brought Job nearer to God and there is all the difference between sight and hearsay. Job's repentance or contrition is not repentance for an error in which he was proved wrong but from the sense of earthly impurity, which rises when the heart is laid bare before infinite Holiness.[33]

Job is the fulcrum of the poem because he rightly distrusts the presumption of merit by the false comforters who attribute his misfortunes to sins he did not commit, wrongs he did not do. But the insight he ultimately affords the reader, because the poet directs that insight to a modern dilemma, is "the sense of earthly impurity, which rises when the heart is laid bare "before God. There are lines in the poem that to many readers may at first seem strangely self-accusatory and to attribute to the fighting men a purpose which few would have professed, or even been aware of:

> They're
> fighting in deserts and caves, one by
> one, in battalions and squadrons;

> they're fighting that I
> may yet recover from the disease, My
> Self. . . .[34]

But these lines make of the brave assembly a Job who "has wrought out the answer . . . that exists in humanity."

The final movement of the poem defies praise by its resolution of all the preceding themes, and its fitting climax. "Fighting fighting fighting" takes on an aspect not limited to this or any single struggle.

> "When a man is prey to anger,
> he is moved by outside things; when he holds
> his ground in patience patience
> patience, that is action or
> beauty," the soldier's defense
> and hardest armor for
>
> the fight. The world's an orphans' home. Shall
> we never have peace without sorrow?

And a few lines later the small dust that walks so arrogantly, the death-in-life of the enslaved hater, is overcome by the quiet form upon the dust, the life-in-death of the patient soldier who helps man to conquer the hatred and prejudice of the warfare within. The climax proves Thoreau's statement that a writer must learn to be extravagant, extra-vagant, enough. The poet-warrior in "In Distrust of Merits" is entitled to resolve

> I must
> fight till I have conquered in myself what
> causes war, but I would not believe it.
> I inwardly did nothing.
> O Iscariotlike crime!

—Iscariot's crime being to desert the teaching of love. In writing the two lines that follow Marianne Moore again evinces a modest audacity. She knew she might well have chosen another word than beauty. That dust is for a time—

139

the dust of the hate-hardened aggressor as well as of the patient soldiers of freedom, the dust of common mortality— the whole poem recalls. But beauty? Too many words have been written to say why Keats wrote that "Beauty is truth"; of course Marianne Moore was aware of his lines. Any poet ascending such difficult passes knows that he has footsteps ahead of him; but his footsteps, though guided by his predecessors, must take a slightly different route. In an early reading diary Marianne Moore had copied the lines from "Peter Quince" that she often liked to quote:

> The body dies; the body's beauty lives.
> So evenings die, in their green going,
> A wave, interminably flowing.

She knew that she too was writing something to be read in "patterned correspondences" and with a not wholly opposed, although necessarily different, tenor of meaning.[35] I think (because in her poem she attributes beauty to the soldiers' *action* as well as to their patience) that she was also aware of Hopkins' "Brute beauty and valour and act" from "The Windhover," and of the lines from "The Leaden Echo and the Golden Echo," "Give beauty back, beauty, beauty, back to God, beauty's self and beauty's giver."[36] And, admirer of Dürer as she was, she would not have objected to anyone's setting down a quotation from him: "But what absolute beauty is, I know not. Nobody knows it except God."[37] It may stand as a not unworthy accompaniment to the quiet crescendo that concludes "In Distrust of Merits."

Profound as it is, difficult in the best sense, as the music of Bach is difficult to understand in all its inner relationships, *In Distrust of Merits* enters a domain of feeling that arose from a new kind of experience of war. There lay an encounter like a battle between the mind of the civilian and the fighting men whose suffering he could only share by a rebirth of himself. Her poem does not convey the testimony of men on the firing line as Wilfred Owen's "Exposure" does, nor the experience of civilians warred upon in the bombing of London (or other cities), to which Edith Sitwell gave the signature of tragedy in "Still falls the rain."

Still falls the rain
Dark as the world of man, black as our loss. . . .
Still falls the rain
At the feet of the Starved Man hung upon the Cross. . . .
　　　　　　　Still falls the rain

. . . .

Then sounds the voice of One who like the heart of man
Was once a child who among beasts has lain
"Still do I love, still shed my innocent light, my Blood,
　　　　　　　for thee."[38]

In contrast, supporting the rare and universal insight of "In Distrust of Merits" is a tough underlying logic, controlling the movement of thought from one stanza to the next, so that the whole poem possesses what T. S. Eliot called the logic of emotion. The logic of emotion in her poem confronts the psychological conflicts from which wars stem.[39] Although different from any of the *Four Quartets* in tone, structure, and the quality of experience it objectifies, "In Distrust of Merits" has more in common with "Little Gidding" than with the fierce pity of Owen or of Edith Sitwell's great lament.

I have reserved for a final discussion of the work in *Nevertheless* a wholly different poem, "The Mind is an Enchanting Thing." For although "In Distrust of Merits" is a landmark in Marianne Moore's work it has no successor poems—in the nature of things it could not have. And like any poem that is at once the voice of great historic events and the response to them of a unique sensibility, it will as time goes on have to be read in a historical context. We can still recognize the power of Milton's sonnets to Sir Henry Vane or "On the Late Massacre in Piedmont" but we cannot plumb their meaning without some acquaintance with the circumstances of the time. But we need not enumerate the far greater number of poems that are self-dependent, self-sustaining.

To this group of poems "The Mind is an Enchanting Thing" belongs. And it possesses extraordinary interest because we may see here a development from "Spenser's Ireland" to the unanalyzable music of ones yet to be achieved, like "Propriety," "Armour's Undermining Modesty," and others still to be discussed.

"The Mind is an Enchanting Thing" brings evidence of a quality in Marianne Moore's poetry that has been noticed in other poems, and that Eliot referred to in his introduction to *Selected Poems* when he said that the range of association is very wide. One might wish to modify this statement, even though it makes good sense taken by itself. But something more elusive creates the wholeness, the inevitability of the sequence of images, and of statements that are essentially themselves images, in "The Mind is an Enchanting Thing." For we do not see here a range of association comparable to Virginia Woolf's in *Jacob's Room, Mrs. Dalloway*, and *To the Lighthouse*. Rather than circles moving out from the stone dropped in the water, we see a magnetic center defined by the centripetal movement of comparable although diverse phenomena—trued by the gyroscope of the governing insight. Coleridge's "unity in multeity" seems to describe such a power better than "range of association."

Sometimes, Marianne Moore chose a major image as shorthand for identifying a poem—writing to her brother for example of "my strawberry" ("Nevertheless") or "my kiwi." "The Mind is an Enchanting Thing" does not start from the kiwi, but that extraordinary creature leads to the most cryptic and enlightening part of the poem. Its field-marks (apteryx awl and rain-shawl) tell—without our ever being quite aware of how they do so—how to understand the concept of the mind that walks with its eyes on the ground.

In an early obviously incomplete draft (possibly the first draft) of this poem the kiwi has no place.[40] This time—in contrast to the early drafts of "What are Years?"—the first line of the poem and its central intent stand out clearly. What will fascinate any responsive reader is that two of the other images that carry the burden of the poem's meaning were there from the beginning, and to Gieseking's playing of Scarlatti is attributed a virtue, "conscientious inconsistency," that later characterizes the entire sequence. Then a potential conclusion, inherent in the finished poem, was eliminated because there was no need to state it. Even in this very tentative draft, the first five lines are essentially as they now stand. But instead of parallelling Gieseking's playing of Scarlatti with the apteryx awl of stanza two, initially the poet thought of the musical performance as one of "regnant certainty," as well as "unequivocal, conscientious inconsistency," and then felt around for something comparable, introducing "sun on the neck of the dove." As in the manuscripts of most good poets, the embryo of meaning was always there in some of the words and images, and the poet's delight is to find their true order while the indispensable missing elements come to take their place with the others. Thus, we find the statements (variously phrased) in this early draft:

How

Quickly beauty enters
it is an enchantment
of power like sun on the dove's neck

and

It is an enchantment of strong power
How quickly beauty enters it

These are superseded by the marginal correction "It has the power of strong enchantment," very close to the line as finally written. "How quickly beauty enters it" was deleted; it was unnecessary to declare since the whole poem creates that sensation.

The ability to perceive "unity in multeity" appears also

in the unexpected but perfect sequence of seemingly unlike images: the katydid's wing, Scarlatti's music played with masterly awareness of tempo, the kiwi with awl-shaped beak and feathered rain-shawl aiding its concentration on the ground, sun on the dove's neck. The final resolution of images is derived from the opening line (which, as in so many cases with Marianne Moore, begins with the title). The kiwi, by which she affectionately identifies the poem in her letters, accommodates itself surprisingly well with the katydid—yet from what distant sources in experience they are derived! Nearly everyone has *heard* katydids on a summer evening; how many have seen them? On a visit to Woodbury, Connecticut, her observant eye detected a katydid in the daytime "among the petunias," as she reported to her sister-in-law in a letter that also described seeing a tree toad and included a drawing of the jerboa and of a hawk's-head moth.[41]

This letter was written in September 1932. An earlier one to her brother has a drawing at the top of the first page of a kiwi staring at a solitary egg, and "Dear Pago-Pago" was asked "Know what this is?" She tells her brother she had gone to the Museum of Natural History to investigate the jerboa, the basilisk, and the fawn-breasted bower bird. Neglecting nothing, after her inspection of lizards and other reptiles she proceeded to the part of the museum where birds were displayed and found "the ostriches, cassowaries and kiwis" a fine exhibit.[42] But to an inveterate spectator of movies and illustrated lectures about the animal kingdom, the next best thing to a visit to New Zealand was to see the slides shown at the Pratt Institute by an "internationally awakened man" who showed a kiwi . . . and "kiwi feather capes." Summarizing the lecture for her brother, giving details about penguins, pilot fish and dolphins, she again singles out the kiwi. It "has the longest nose of any bird, with the nostrils at the end of the beak (under the beak) at the tip, for smelling worms. . . . The kiwi, I should add, weighs 2 pounds and lays an egg weighing about one pound, so it does not suit it to lay more than one at a time."[43]

Kiwi is the name given by the New Zealand natives to the flightless bird named apteryx. (The name imitates its cry.) It would not, of course, have escaped Marianne Moore's attention that T. S. Eliot signed a few of his shorter pieces written for the *Egoist* with the pseudonym Apteryx. Well-trained in biology, she knew what apteryx meant.

In short, this central image, metaphor, and symbol in "The Mind is an Enchanting Thing" had perhaps been stored in the poet's consciousness for thirty-five years before it found its true place in the poem written in 1943 and first published in the *Nation* in December of that year. It is a central symbol because it is *like* the kiwi that

> the mind
> feeling its way as though blind,
> walks along with its eyes on the ground.

We remember Shakespeare's differently used expression, "in the eye of my mind."[44] And the sequence of metaphors that follows in this poem resembles Shakespeare's power to bring universal but seemingly abstract qualities to life by some strange visual phenomenon. One cannot remotely hope to give even a faint equivalent in other words for "pity like a new born babe striding the blast" or "strong toil of grace." In her poem, "memory's ear / that can hear without having to hear" is a power of the enchanting and enchanted mind that

> tears off the veil; tears
> the temptation, the
> mist the heart wears,
> from its eyes,—if the heart
> has a face; it takes apart
> dejection.

Surely, when we read these lines, we know that the heart has a face, introducing the mind to imagination.

The mysterious phenomena summoned to bear witness to the mind's power of enchantment are united by the theme from which the first draft took off: the "conscientious inconsistency" heard in Gieseking's playing of Scarlatti, but now given to the mind itself. To maintain constant direction, the gyroscope must shift position; the fire in the dove's neck's iridescence is a play of changing colours; and the concluding lines have a profounder meaning because they are the outcome of these interrelated symbols. The mind, when true to "conscientious inconsistency," resembles "unconfusion that submits its confusion to proof." And because "it's not a Herod's oath that cannot change" it never intends, has nothing to do with, death as Herod did by refusing to change his oath. The mind sustains life itself by the power to change sensation into understanding, to abstract itself from the quotidien, the temporary, by walking with its eyes on the ground, and hearing like the Mother of the Muses without having to hear, listening to the inward, not only to the outward, summonings.

The musical pleasure of "The Mind is an Enchanting Thing" begins with the significant change down of pitch from "enchanting" to "enchanted." As in "Spenser's Ireland:" every word "is a tune." Her attention to musical form is evident. After describing a concert at the Pratt Institute in a letter to her brother, she added that she went to these concerts to get ideas for her writing.[45] She had attempted—in a necessarily different and briefer mode of expression—structural possibilities similar to a fugue in "The Jerboa." The song-like quality of "Spenser's Ireland" and "The Mind is an Enchanting Thing" brings something different into her poetry. If I. A. Richards did not err in attributing to "The Waste Land" a music of ideas, these poems and some later ones of hers present ideas in a natural music. Marianne Moore did sometimes have in her mind a tune or motif while writing a poem.[46] That this was the case with a later poem, "Propriety," a manuscript of it confirms.

146

The response of readers and critics to *Nevertheless* brought welcome encouragement. "The *Nation* had a most remarkable review of me by F. W. Dupee the week before Christmas," she wrote her brother, and told him also of "some awful nice letters from Alfred Barr, Wallace Stevens and others." In this letter, which had characteristically begun with the news that "Bear" had "ketched its first crab a great big thing with blue claws, at Charlie the fisherman's today," she was able to say of *Nevertheless*, "On the whole, I take more interest in it than in any of my other books."[47]

Having to be extremely economical, Marianne Moore and her mother felt some impatience at the demands for complimentary copies for which they had to pay (though they were always generous in giving them to close friends or relatives). Interviews and a broadcast for station WNYC brought further attention to the book.[48] Best of all, word from London: "T. S. Eliot says after the war (if a publisher may do what he wishes) he will have *Faber & Faber* publish a "Collected Poems" for me, of my *Selected Poems, What Are Years*, and *Nevertheless*."[49]

Her work was sought for the first time by the *New Yorker* and she felt this to be a challenge. "The New Yorker, Bible [her brother's wartime nickname], has ast me—nay urged me to contribute, and I must do so when I can write anything they'll take!"[50] And two days later, in a letter full of anxiety about dangers of the advance of American forces in the Pacific, and "the possibility of sudden death in those areas" from which her brother was now returning, she interpolates "I am much toaded up that Mrs. White and Louise Bogan of the *New Yorker* are so earnest about me writing for them and I must try."[51] The first of her poems accepted by the *New Yorker* was "Tom Fool at Jamaica," published in 1952.

For Marianne Moore the years between the triumphant success of *Nevertheless* and the edition of her *Collected Poems* in 1951 presented many difficulties, as well as challenges and opportunities that she welcomed. During this time she undertook the translation of the fables of La Fontaine—the arrangements for that book will be discussed in the chapter dealing with the fables. She postponed the effort to collect some of her prose—as no publisher at that time showed any enthusiasm for the plan. She accepted a Guggenheim Fellowship,[52] and used it for work (with a collaborator) on a translation of a tale by Adelbert Stifter, *Rock Crystal*. She endured the ordeal and sorrow of the final illness of her mother, who died in 1947. It was the end of an extraordinary relationship for which I can think of no comparison. Not only had Marianne Moore given unremitting attention, during the more than thirty years they lived together, to the needs of "the Bear": she had with patience and understanding accepted Mrs. Moore's efforts to revise poems and articles, as well as, it seems, her habit of reading the letters that she (Marianne) wrote to others in the family, and to editors and publishers.[53] In a brief letter expressing his sympathy, T. S. Eliot said that he recognized the help that Mrs. Moore had given by being "an acute and ruthless critic."[54] The equal of Mary Warner Moore, her integrity, her wit and tenacious accuracy, and a goodness of heart almost disguised by her fierce economy and disdain of pleasure, is not likely to be seen again. There can be no question that she imparted strength to her daughter, and the ability to survive many trials. If uncommonly demanding, and possessive, "the Bear" was also a shield, and an example of love.

The years from 1945 to 1951 were never easy ones. Yet during them Marianne Moore wrote twelve new poems, of which nine were included in the collective volume. Of these, several compete with the finest work in *What Are Years* and *Nevertheless* as evidence of the poet's advance. It seems appropriate to discuss them here, in order to observe the consanguinity of, for example, "Propriety" and "The Mind is an Enchanting Thing."

Two poems in particular pay tribute to her mother—but without naming her, and with the reticence and simplicity poets do not always find easy to achieve. "A Face" takes off from a realistic remark, probably close to something her mother said.

> 'I am not treacherous, callous, jealous, superstitious,
> supercilious, venomous, or absolutely hideous':
>> studying and studying its expression
>
> . . . .
>
>> though at no real impasse,
>> would gladly break the glass; . . .

The convincing ordinariness of this beginning adds to the pleasure of the ending:

> Certain faces, a few, one or two—or one
> face photographed by recollection—
>> to my mind, to my sight,
>> must remain a delight.

Characteristically, she selected "A Face" for inclusion in *The Poet's Choice*, a volume in which the contributors were requested to "select a favorite or crucial poem from their own work and comment on it."[55] Likewise, she included it in her Caedmon record.

The other poem I believe to give a sense of the meaning to her of both her mother's life and her brother's, is "By Disposition of Angels." It differs from her other work in its close approach to the mysteries of relationships between human faith and the indefinable subject of that faith. The uncommon form of the poem aids its purpose—if we can ever appropriately speak of the purpose of a poem. The questions by which it begins, and proceeds, have no resemblance to the ironic or disdainful ones from which "In Distrust of Merits" or "The Paper Nautilus" take off. Those questions require the reader to reject the possibilities they characterize in order to prepare to recognize something closer to reality. But the questions in "By Disposition of Angels" serve, better than declarative statements could, to express a feeling of wonder, a discovery in a different mode of faith that is "the evidence of things unseen."

149

To query whether intuitions of communication are possible gives greater impact to the careful understatements or guarded affirmations that conclude each stanza. The unusual pattern (a second stanza in which the first five lines end with the same rhymes as those of the first stanza, a change occurring only in the final couplet) suits the inquiry. The opening questions,

> Messengers much like ourselves? Explain it.
> Steadfastness the darkness makes explicit?
> Something heard most clearly when not near it?
>
> [Stanza I]

and

> Star that does not ask me if I see it?
> Fir that would not wish me to uproot it?
> Speech that does not ask me if I hear it?
>
> [Stanza II]

waken the reader's mind so that the following lines open the way to things beyond the ordinary range of feeling:

> Above particularities,
> These unparticularities praise cannot violate.
> One has seen, in such steadiness never deflected,
> How by darkness a star is perfected.
>
> [Stanza I]

> Mysteries expound mysteries.
> Steadier than steady, star dazzling me, live and elate,
> No need to say, how like some we have known;
> too like her
> Too like him, and a-quiver forever.
>
> [Stanza II]

The image in the first stanza of a star perfected by darkness gives climactic force to "star dazzling me, live and elate;" the formal understatement—"no need to say" lends unspoken beauty to the ending. The choice of the title "By

Disposition of Angels" discreetly allows mysteries to "expound mysteries" here. Perhaps one may think after reading this poem, of the "disposition" of other angels in modern poetry: in Rilke or in Lawrence. They are not survivals from a past tradition—any more than Marianne Moore's are—but symbols of a kind of experience requiring something beyond the mundane. The modern cliché, extra-sensory perception, is unhelpful only because extra-sensory perception is not really extra-sensory.

Two poems in the "Hitherto Uncollected" group that rounds out *Collected Poems* of 1951 possess such striking individuality as to merit being the keynote of a separate book—as "What Are Years?" had been, and "Nevertheless." "Armour's Undermining Modesty," the last of the poems included, bears the signature of Marianne Moore in every line. The informal, mild beginning ("At first I thought a pest / must have alighted on my wrist") takes the reader into a bravura of descriptive pleasure—the "backgammon-board wedges interlacing / on the wing— / like cloth of gold in a pattern / of scales. . . ." Once again, the intently noticed texture and pattern of a familiar creature like a moth finds a parallel in an artifice, cloth of gold. But the description is brief; and satire intervenes provocatively:

> . . . Once, self-determination
>   made an axe of a stone
> and hacked things out with hairy paws. The consequence
>   —our mis-set
> alphabet.
>   Arise, for it is day.
>   Even gifted scholars lose their way
> through faulty etymology.

A well-aimed dart. And after disowning stars and harps and the new moon (allowed to be at home in other poems such as "Spenser's Ireland" or "By Disposition of Angels") the writer chooses a homely armour, preferring, if tributes cannot be implicit, "diatribes and the fragrance of iodine."

151

One reason why "Armour's Undermining Modesty" represents something different—as well as a firm new version of qualities we have earlier recognized—is that it was written when Marianne Moore had already translated many of La Fontaine's fables. In these translations—to be discussed in the next chapter—she developed experiments in rhyme and patterns of language that one does not find in the earlier poetry. Some lines in "Armour's Undermining Modesty" pick up a wonderful accentuation from these devices: one that might be termed alliteration of syllables rather than merely of letters, another a combination of internal rhyme and partial rhyme in a sequence resembling the Welsh *cynghanedd*.

> the cork oak acorn grown in Spain;
> the pale-ale-eyed impersonal look
> which the sales-placard gives the bock beer buck.

And just as the reader is looking at the poster promising a supply of bock beer in the corner store, he is spirited away by the concluding line of this stanza, "What is more precise than precision? Illusion." In this line and the later stanzas, "conscientious inconsistency" expands the theme announced by the title. The uncanny examples of the opposition between insistent display and "unhackneyed solitude" almost outpace the reader before he is rescued by the final line, "There is the tarnish; and there, the imperishable wish." The implications of this line require one to recall that the armour in the poem is the spiritual armour described by St. Paul (Rom. 13:12 and Eph. 4:13-17); its undermining modesty is humility. The tarnish on the armour is man's imperfection; the imperishable wish, his resolve.

As early as November 1944, only a month after *Nevertheless* came out, "Propriety" was published in the *Nation*, a poem that belongs in the company of "The Mind is an Enchanting Thing," "Style," and "Logic and the Magic Flute."

The form and theme of "Propriety" correspond. The opening sentence, "Propriety / Is some such word / as the chord / Brahms had heard / from a bird, / sung down near the root of the throat," is a musical definition. The composition remembered here is, probably, one of Brahms' *Liebeslieder Waltzes*, called "Ein Vögelein." The other piece that is referred to in the first part of the poem, C.P.E. Bach's *Solfegietto*, was an invention for teaching, and Marianne Moore must have learned it when she played the piano in Carlisle. For some reason it had a special meaning for her —the opening passage is entered in two of her notebooks. The typescript of an early draft of "Propriety" has musical notes for the opening stanzas, beginning with this score (Fig. 3). These notes do not seem to me to be a suggested setting for the poem, but rather the way that the writer heard it in her mind.

We owe some of the pleasure given by "Propriety" to the curious way that colour and motion—the downy woodpecker "spiraling a tree— / up up up like mercury," or "resistance with bent head, like foxtail / millet's"—match the musical proportions. Trusting itself and the reader from the start, "Propriety" has a kind of winsomeness; everything chosen to convey this virtue is attractively scaled. The rhythm becomes a master metaphor, from the lightness of the "not long / sparrow-song / of hayseed / magnitude" to the "fish-spine / on firs, / on / sombre trees / by the sea's / walls of wave-worn rock. . . ." These unexpected congruities are temporal progressions to the final part, reintroducing Bach and Brahms. To thank Bach

> for his song
> first, is wrong.
> Pardon me;
> both are the
> unintentional pansy-face
> uncursed by self-inspection; blackened
> because born that way.

In Marianne Moore's reading aloud of the poem certain lines ("Pardon me," for instance) had a deliberate throw-

Marianne Moore
260 Cumberland Street
Brooklyn, New York

Propriety

It's a chord
like one word
Brahms had heard
from a bird
warbling at the root of its throat.
It's the little downy woodpecker
spiralling a tree
up up up like mercury.

A bird song
is not long,
a wayside
of hayseed
tune; a reticence with rigor
from strength at the source. Propriety's
Bach's Solfegietto,
harmonica, and basso.

The fish-spines
of fir pines --
sombre trees
by the sea's
walls of waveworn rock -- have it; and
a moonbow and Bach's cheerful firmness
in a minor key.
It's an owl-and-a-pussy

both-content
agreement.
Come, come. It's
mixed with wits;
it's not a graceful sadness. It's
resistance with bent head, like foxtail-
millet's. Brahms and Bach,
no; Bach and Brahms. To thank Bach

for his song
first, is wrong.
Pardon me;
both are the
unintentional pansy-face
uncursed by self-inspection; blackened
because born that way;
blackened because born that way.

Figure 3: Draft of "Propriety" with Musical Notation

away effect, protecting the implications of "a tuned reticence with rigour" and of the final lines, where I believe she may have had an individual in mind, as well as both J. S. and C.P.E. Bach, and Brahms.

The twenty-six poems included in *What Are Years, Nevertheless*, and the "Hitherto Uncollected" group, added to the *Selected Poems* of 1935, made the new volume that T. S. Eliot had promised to issue after the war; he also arranged for its publication in America by Macmillan.[56] The appearance of *Collected Poems* in 1951 was a landmark in Marianne Moore's achievement. But this does not imply that the earlier work is less good. Poems like "The Fish," "A Grave," "Part of a Novel," "The Jerboa," to single out a few, are not surpassed. But the work published between 1935 and 1950 could not have been written earlier, and differs in discernible, if varying, ways from even the best pieces in *Observations* or *Selected Poems*. Some of the differences are technical, having to do with the sequence of images, with new metrical patterns, and ways in which the nature or placing of rhyme affects the rhythm. Let us say that the weave of meaning may be closer and the spoken texture more open, if that is possible; the rhythm is firmly controlled, yet now more fluent.

None of the longer poems now has the same kind of complexity as "An Octopus" or "Marriage," but from writing these poems there came a mastery of development noticeable in "Virginia Britannia," for example, where the horizontal lines of things in the living present intersect the vertical ones of the perceived past. If in the "serial poems" and ones like "The Plumet Basilisk" images and forms are stacked up to build a tower of inspection, in "The Paper Nautilus" or "A Carriage From Sweden" lines of vision run freely, have more open space to move in. In "The Pangolin" or "Elephants" the habits of animals resembling human traits (or the converse) are more simply related to each other, as is the dark to the light in their consciousness.

The poems "What Are Years?" and "In Distrust of Merits" have access to a widened range of human action. Eliot had said of her writing down to the time of *Selected Poems*, that "for a sensibility so reticent, the minor subject, such as a pleasant little sand-coloured skipping animal, may be the best release for the major emotions." The reticence was never lost; yet *What Are Years* and *Nevertheless* recreate themes that from Biblical times on have held meaning for all men. The contrast in form of the earlier and later poems shows an increasing ability to liberate feeling by the searching discipline of language and rhythm. She could always suggest the prehensile reaches of meaning in the fragments of time that are humanly encountered; but she now commands a hard-won simplicity of utterance.

"Spenser's Ireland," "The Mind is an Enchanting Thing," and "Propriety," mark the poet's advance, and chart another course for poems still to be written. They mark another change: a willingness to let the poet's own mood and individual humour appear more informally in what she is writing. This is done with a mimetic skill; the performer has a place in the poem, though speaking only occasionally, and from the wings, not the center of the stage. The readings she now more frequently gave certainly contributed to this. Thinking back to the days when Harriet Monroe and others found Marianne Moore's poetry "too abstract," too intellectual, one is ready to laugh them out of court. Writing of Sir Isaac Newton, J. M. Keynes presents him as not primarily a pioneer of rationalism in modern science, but rather "the last of the magicians." When one considers Marianne Moore's way of composing a poem that she had long lived with in her meditations before writing it down, Keynes on Newton is enlightening:

> I believe that Newton could hold a problem in his mind for hours and days and weeks until it surrendered to him its secret . . . it was his intuition which was pre-eminently extraordinary. There is the story of how he informed Halley of one of his most fundamental dis-

coveries. . . . "Yes," replied Halley, "but how do you know that? Have you proved it?" . . . "Why, I've known it for years," [Newton] replied. "If you'll give me a few days I'll certainly find you a proof of it"—as in due course he did.[57]

The poems—their composition—were the "proofs" Marianne Moore had to find for things she had known for years. As time went on, the proofs became more comprehensible to the reader, as the poet's increased ability to communicate her moral insight accompanied her inventiveness in musical and metrical form. Her magician's skill controls language by attention to both its changing values and inherent constancies. If we compare the company of words that Marianne Moore chose for the route of her observation in a poem like "Those Various Scalpels" or "Snakes, Mongooses" with the different air of "A Carriage From Sweden" or "The Mind is an Enchanting Thing," we will see at once that responsiveness to these changing values kept her work alive. As Virginia Woolf described them, words

> hate being useful, they hate making money, they hate being lectured about in public: in short, they hate anything that stamps them with one meaning or confines them to one attitude, for it is their nature to change. Perhaps that is their most sriking peculiarity, their need to change. It is because the truth they try to catch is many-sided, and they convey it by being many-sided. . . . And it is because of this complexity, this power to mean different things to different people, that they survive.[58]

The power that Virginia Woolf here attributes to words is a criterion set by Wallace Stevens for poetry, that "It Must Change." The translation of La Fontaine that Marianne Moore had now begun was a passport to further diversity in the poems of her later years, accomplished by a writer willing to be surprised "each day, each day," as new experience renews the self, and unexpected harmonies improve the ear.

6

"My Fables"

FOR Marianne Moore the decision to translate the fables of La Fontaine meant an unpredictable experience, a willingness to subordinate her imagination to that of another writer, and to place all her skill at his command. Yet she committed herself to this task with no hesitation, almost casually. W. H. Auden, who was then teaching at Swarthmore, was preparing an anthology of verse translations, and sent a mimeographed letter to a number of writers, asking for suggestions. On the copy mailed to her he added in his own hand, "Have you done any translations. What translations appeared in The Dial?"[1]

"I have done no translating," she replied, "except as I interfered with translations published by The Dial . . . prose translations for the most part."[2] A month later she sent him a list of English verse translations that she admired. It included, as we might expect, Pound's "Donna mi Pregha." She had published this revision of his earlier translation from Cavalcanti when she was editor of the *Dial*. She also listed examples from Rossetti's *Italian Poets Chiefly before Dante*; Roger Fry's Mallarmé; some Nabokov versions of Pushkin and other Russian poets. But far beyond the significance of the examples given are indications of the principles she felt essential. From Pound's book *Instigations*, she cited his praise of Gavin Douglas's *Aeneids* and Golding's *Metamorphoses*, "a new beauty having been in each case created." And in listing as worthy of attention F. S. Flint's translation of the *Mosella* of Ausonius, her comment was that it "had attractions" for her, "but it shows that it is translated."[3] One must reckon from the start with the concept of translation implied here: a good translation must create a new poem in English, rather than a competent but more literal conversion from one language to another. This is a point that deserves full consideration in any reading of the Moore-La Fontaine fables.

Soon after his initial inquiry, Auden had suggested to one of the editors at Reynal and Hitchcock that she be asked to translate La Fontaine. She entered upon this project with enthusiasm and only a minimal awareness of the difficulties that would attend it. The first one, arranging for its publication, seemed deceptively easy. She wrote to her brother:

> Bible, we are kind of excited over a job I seem to have give' me. Walter Pistole of Reynal & Hitchcock has wrote me that Mr. Auden recommended me for translation of La Fontaine! I love them fables and no one has translated them into English verse! So I set about a sample of the book they have sent me,—did this tonight [and] think it looks possible.[4]

But her editor at Macmillan's did not like her undertaking a translation for another publisher. Her book *Nevertheless* was already being reprinted; she had acquired many new readers. A subsequent letter to her brother described how Mr. Putnam had "carried on yesterday" when she telephoned him to report Reynal and Hitchcock's offer of a contract for the fables. "He said . . . 'I'm swept off my feet by this. A publisher's wealth, you know, is his authors' *creativeness*. I think it's a little selfish of Reynal and H. to . . . ask you to put your *time* on translation when you should be doing creative work'!!!"[5] Later, Mr. Putnam called back to say that Macmillan's option on her next book of poetry did include the La Fontaine; and she countered by replying that a translation was not her own poetry. He astutely rejected this argument. " 'Oh yes it is,' " he said. " 'It's yours and it's poetry, but I can get a release for you to do this special piece of work.' "[6] But for a while he held up the re-

lease, although advising her to go ahead with the transla-
tion.

As with speculations on the kind of poems Keats might
have written, had he lived longer, her publisher was raising
a merely hypothetical question. Would she not be wiser to
proceed with poems of her own? But Macmillan's lack of
interest in publishing the translation made her indignant,
as many of her friends can testify. When Reynal and Hitch-
cock relinquished its contract with her, and Viking made
her an offer,[7] she stayed with her new publisher for all the
work she did after 1950. Mr. Putnam's statement that "it's
yours and it's poetry" was intended merely as an affirmation
that Macmillan could legally take up the option it held on
her next book of poems. Had he believed that her La Fon-
taine would in all truth contain remarkable new poems of
hers, he would never have let it go.

If Marianne Moore, on the other hand, had realized that
her translation would occupy her for eight years, might she
have chosen otherwise? This, again, is unanswerable. My
own conviction is that some of her finest work is in that
book, and that the nature of the task invested her with
skills different from those of her earlier poetry. She was
fifty-eight years old when she began her translation, and
sixty-four when she reaffirmed her decision to complete the
work.[8] Had she not felt an incentive, and the power to sus-
tain it, she might not otherwise have had the creative im-
petus to write "Tom Fool at Jamaica" or "Logic and the
Magic Flute." In these poems we can see that she could
translate new experience of her own into figures of sound
perfected by her encounter with La Fontaine.

Translations and adaptations of poetry written in an-
other language have been a stimulating enterprise for many
English poets, and have often produced poetry worth read-
ing for its own sake. At times, as W. H. Auden pointed out,
some translations have affected the development of English
poetry itself.[9] But to understand their value the reader must
keep in mind that a real translation of poetry is virtually

impossible. One language differs from another in ways that make similar effects of rhythm and diction attainable only by some improvisation in the treatment of meaning. Literal translations, attempting to give as exactly as possible the purport of the words, the grammatical and syntactical structure of the original, cannot hope to convey a vivid impression of the sound of the other language in the tone of the original writer. Without that, an essential part of the meaning is sacrificed.

The utilitarian translation allows the reader lacking knowledge of Russian, or Portuguese, to understand the characters, the action, the themes of *Eugene Onegin* or the *Lusiads*. But when Wyatt translated Petrarch, for example, he not only brought the form of the sonnet into English verse, he made some poems of great beauty:

> My galley chargéd with forgetfulness
> Thorow sharp seas in winter nights does pass
> Twixt rock and rock.

These lines have the intonation, the feeling present in Petrarch, but to achieve this naturally Wyatt had to rely on his own poetic energy, forgoing Petrarch's "Scylla and Charybdis."

As a translator, Pound availed himself of a similar freedom. He sometimes had to expand or contract a phrase; he was often hard pressed to find an English equivalent for an Italian word. He resorted to archaic forms and to an inversion of noun and verb in order to get something closer to the alliterative pattern of "The Seafarer" ("Bitter breast cares have I abided") or to the sequences of rhyme and rhythm in the troubadours ("sith no thing is but turneth into anguish / And each today 'vails less than yestere'en"). For Marianne Moore, Pound was a model translator; she was aware, of course, that his knowledge of Italian and of Provençal surpassed her knowledge of French. The succinct preface to her *Fables* records her loyalty. For rhythm and syntax, she said, "the practice of Ezra Pound has been for me a governing principle—as deduced from his 'Guido Cavalcanti,' his 'Seafarer,' and certain French songs: the natural order of words, subject, predicate, object; the active voice where possible; a ban on dead words, rhymes synonymous with gusto."[10] In fact, these principles govern her own earlier poetry as well as her La Fontaine more surely than they do Pound's early poetry or his translations. The principle that she did accept is the one quoted in her letter to Auden, that in a good translation a new beauty can be created. Without this stimulus, translation could only be an onerous task.

But she felt equally convinced that she must express La Fontaine's meaning as accurately as possible. For that reason she asked Reynal and Hitchcock to enlist the aid of Harry Levin, Professor of Comparative Literature at Harvard.

Aware of the need for closer study of the French language and of La Fontaine's prosody, was she aware of any questions about the genre, *fables*?

Had Auden suggested the right poet for the wrong reason? Did he think, and others agree, that because Marianne Moore had written extraordinary poems about animals, in which observations on human qualities appear, she therefore was a fabulist? The parallel is sufficiently real to be relevant; but the geometry of poetry is Euclidean, where parallels do not meet.

The animals of the fabulist, whether Aesop, Phaedrus, or La Fontaine, behave like human beings. The animals in Marianne Moore's poems behave like animals. They do not compete for the rôle of monarch; the jerboa does not make trouble for himself by playing tricks on the monkey or the mongoose. We are explicitly told that the ostrich does *not* hide its head in the sand.

None of her animals is invented to satirize man's behavior, although man may observe in animals ways of behaving that he can admire or emulate. To notice an animal "too intent to cower" differs from describing a crow who opens his beak to respond to a fox's flattery, thus dropping his piece of cheese for the fox to eat. We all know that crows don't eat cheese; and foxes don't eat grapes; and goats do not jump to bottoms of wells when they are thirsty. These little stories were popular, and lent themselves to the transmission of a somewhat prudential morality.[11]

An additional challenge lay in the fact that the fable as a kind of writing was popular in the age of La Fontaine, but for adult readers is not so in modern times. French readers in the seventeenth century, on the contrary, had developed a taste for writing of this kind. As Pierre Clarac pointed out in his study of La Fontaine, "Vers 1660 Esope est à la mode."[12] This popularity led to the reprinting in 1660 of the major collection of Aesopian and later fables that had earlier been published by Névelet in 1610. Aptly given the title *Mythologia Aesopica*, it contained the fables attributed to Aesop, the fables in Latin verse by Phaedrus, as well as prose fables in Latin and others grouped with them.

La Fontaine, therefore, was writing for people able to recognize at once a fresh treatment of familiar themes, and the way that his subtle ironies overcame the prudent moralizing of the Aesopian tradition. Readers of his age likewise could see with what mastery La Fontaine drew upon Rabelais, upon Montaigne and Regnier to achieve a more lively and natural tone and diction. Some at least would have been aware of the way that his lion, his fox and his wolf, stemming from the medieval *Roman de Renart*, were transformed into characters enacting a satiric comedy with a direct bearing upon the manifestations of absolutism in the régime of Louis XIV.

In short, La Fontaine's fables are a highly original development of an already popular genre. Then, too, his readers could immediately respond to the virtuosity of his rhyming and to the successful experiments that changed the traditional rhythmic patterns of French poetry. American and English readers of Marianne Moore's translation grew up in a different world, where a few of Aesop's fables were proverbial, and some of La Fontaine's might have been read or memorized in school. Most would not have known *all* of La Fontaine's fables. And how many of those who are well-acquainted with her poems have read her translation in its entirety?

If they have not, the reason is their failure to recognize why she was an ideal translator of La Fontaine: not because she liked animals and had written about them herself, but because, like La Fontaine, she could produce consonances, melodies, syncopations varying the patterns she had already mastered. And if there were great differences between her social milieu and La Fontaine's, she shared with him a love of simplicity and an aversion to the exploitation of human beings, to vainglory and hypocrisy. Like him, she enjoyed the comedy of errors in which we all play a part.

When she asked her publisher to enlist Harry Levin as consultant, she was anxious primarily to insure accuracy. But more was involved than she realized; and she could not have chosen more wisely. Mr. Levin instantly perceived the inherent value of such a translation, and offered encouragement without minimizing the difficulties to be overcome. Returning the samples that Reynal and Hitchcock had sent him, he commented that "if anyone in English can manage La Fontaine's intermixture of the casual and the artful, innocence and urbanity, it must be Miss Moore, and she has demonstrated it here." After praising certain versions, he quickly indicated some errors in a tactful way: "*Parents*, if you'll forgive my pedantry, would be 'family' rather than 'parents.' And the *chanteur* would not be chanticleer but the mythological figure of Arion, less *renommé* in English than in French." Helpfully suggesting ways to cope with some of the inevitable problems, his conclusion must have encouraged her, as well as her publisher. "I am now sure," he wrote, "[that] Miss Moore can give us a translation worthy of La Fontaine."[13]

Refusing her offer of a fee for his assistance, Mr. Levin

generously gave time to the scrutiny of versions sent to him by Marianne Moore at intervals until the work was completed. He brought to this enterprise not only a greater knowledge of the French language and of seventeenth-century France, but the insight of a critic whose reading of poetry has always been imaginative. In addition to his own careful reading of her drafts, Mr. Levin arranged a meeting of Marianne Moore and the French essayist Pierre Schneider, who was then a graduate student at Harvard. For, as the scholar pointed out, only some person born to the language could "quite hear all the relevant nuances."[14] The meeting with Schneider took place in 1949, when she was halfway through her task. Levin also urged her to test the effect of her lines upon another poet whose native tongue was English. Ezra Pound had read some samples of her early translations, and made suggestions for improving them; but as she continued with the work he sent word that he felt "unable to concentrate."[15] The Viking Press, however, provided Malcolm Cowley as one more adviser. And there were others who were called upon, whose help she acknowledged in her preface.

One wonders how the animation and grace of the best versions she produced could survive the demands of so many, but as she wrote to the ever-faithful and encouraging Mr. Levin, "If what you call harshness, is not my salvation, I don't know what is." She praised him with justice for his "collaborative valor," and "unestranged magnanimity."[16] There can be little doubt that of her various advisers she owed most to her "years as a Harvard student" with Harry Levin.[17]

Before considering the result of her translation, one needs to recognize specifically the technical demands she made upon herself. She had decided not only to follow the metrical pattern of the original, but to offer an equivalent of the rhymes as well. On the whole, she obeyed these self-imposed imperatives.

A curious paradox challenges the reader willing to study

the symbiotic relationship of Moore and La Fontaine. (By the term symbiotic, I mean that studying her translation in comparison with the original adds to the enjoyment of reading La Fontaine, and that the pursuit of this difficult task gave birth to different energies in her own poems.) The paradox that must be explained is this. La Fontaine in his early poetry, especially *Adonis*, conformed to and had mastered the "rules" of French prosody, rules governing the writing of Alexandrines with careful placing of the caesura and observing consistent patterns of rhyme. Paul Valéry has shown that in the language of *Adonis*, La Fontaine controlled tones that could treat subjects ranging from the simplest to the most lofty, in this respect anticipating Racine himself.[18]

But when he was ready to write the *Fables* and the *Contes*, he brought an ease, a grace, into French prosody that remains unrivaled. In the "Avertissement" at the beginning of the *Contes*, he explained his choice. He had asked himself what might be the most appropriate kind of rhyme for these tales, and had come to believe that "les vers irréguliers ayant un air qui tient beaucoup de la prose, cette manière pourrait semble la plus naturelle, et par conséquent la meilleure."[19] Valéry, in his discussion of La Fontaine's meter, uses the term *vers varié* instead of La Fontaine's *vers irrégulier*; for the English or American reader this is preferable.

There is nothing "irregular" in the meter of either the *Contes* or the *Fables*; what La Fontaine accomplished was a sophisticated variation of the line length and the sequence of rhymes, appropriate for the dramatic scenes he presents, and, as Valéry pointed out, reflecting the inner changes in his own sensibility.[20] Therefore, although in the *Fables* he emancipated himself from the "rules" governing French prosody at that time, he maintained consistent patterns of rhyme and demonstrated the utmost skill in the placing of the caesura.

One can see now why Marianne Moore was uniquely

qualified to be a translator of La Fontaine. She had invented her own kind of *vers varié*, and had no doubt a sense of inward amusement when some reviewers complained of the qualities of prose writing evident in her poems. She had another resource that would aid her La Fontaine translations: a skill in the acceleration of rhythm. You can hear this in the last four words of a line in an early poem, "To a Chameleon,"

> An emerald as long as
> The Dark King's massy
One,
Could not snap the spectrum up for food as you
> have done.

Many examples from later poems could be cited. The power to control, and to change tempo, was quite as important as her long-practiced skill in syllabic patterns.

She had at her command another necessary power, that of making conversation into poetry. She had often introduced words spoken by another person into the texture of her own compositions. But she had not written narrative poems including dialogue. Here, it would take practice to reproduce the movement in La Fontaine's verse, and even practice could not always catch the effect of colloquial French, or of expressions taken from dialect, or of the occasional archaic word. And she now would have to employ all her skill in the service of meters, patterns, themes not chosen by herself. In effect, she had to submit to the kind of discipline La Fontaine himself had adhered to in his early work, to create English poems suggesting the innovations of his fables.

The small group of fables included in her *Complete Poems* gives the reader only a slender chance to sample either the best La Fontaine or the best Moore fables. It comes as no surprise that each of these poets could produce a witty version of a typical Aesopian piece like "The Ant and the Grasshopper." Two of the sample translations that she submitted to publishers before undertaking the whole

167

venture, "The Lion in Love" and "Bitch and Friend," present an instructive contrast.[21] La Fontaine's "La Lice et sa Compagne" begins more economically, stating simply that a female hound, having reached the time to deliver her litter and not knowing where, persuaded a companion to lend her its hut. There the bitch shut herself in. The terse beginning of this little narrative contains a subtle interlacing of rhyme and assonance. The Moore translation begins with a flourish:

> A bitch who approached each hutch with a
> frown,
> Since a-shiver to shelter an imminent litter,
> Crouched perplexed till she'd coaxed from a vexed
> benefactor
> A lean-to as a loan, and in it lay down.

(II, 7)

Here we have an almost pyrotechnical display of skill, reminiscent of the "cork-oak acorn grown in Spain" or the "pale-ale eye'd impersonal look / that the sales placard gives the bock beer buck," in the poem "Armour's Undermining Modesty."

La Fontaine's essential meaning has been conveyed, with some expansions; the French animal does not approach a hutch with a frown nor does she crouch perplexed. But who would forgo this variation, in which the event is not generalized as in La Fontaine, and the sound of the lines dynamically intimates the humour to come? For when the "friend" finally tries to reclaim her hut, after having once extended the loan, she is reminded all too forcefully of her dilemma. The bitch and family will leave if she can put them out; but "the puppies were by then tall curs." One notices how the English version comes as close as possible to the French rhyme, La Fontaine's "hors . . . forts" becoming "doors . . . curs." Earlier, the play of internal and end rhyme in La Fontaine (Fait si *bien* qu'à la *fin* . . . / sa compagne re*vient* . . . *quinz*aine, and many other examples) afforded ample precedent for parallel entertainments in English.

In this fable there is a minimum of dialogue; the moral, hardly needed, is somewhat lengthy, even discursive. "The Lion in Love" (IV, 1), one of the prefatory fables that La Fontaine placed at the beginning of each book, has a quite different tone. The courtly compliment to Mademoiselle de Sévigné offered in the opening lines seems a little stilted in the English rendering. "Mademoiselle—goddess instead— / In whom the graces find a school / Although you are more beautiful" hardly captures the sophisticated ease of "Sévigné de qui les attraits / Servent aux Grâces de modèle, / Et qui naquîtes toute belle." But it would have been almost impossible to achieve a similar finish in our language, or to give a twentieth-century realization of the underlying resonances of meaning. Like her more famous mother, who had known La Fontaine since his youth, Mademoiselle de Sévigné was an admiring reader of his fables. She had at one time acted in a royal ballet whose theme was the birth of Venus. Some of the resulting ironies of La Fontaine are not transportable. But Marianne Moore's own wit held sway when the meaning was human rather than topical. How better translate the line "A votre indifférence près" than "Even if with averted head"? A precise image of the vanished beauty comes swiftly into the reader's mind.

The body of the fable (as La Fontaine called the narrative part) is firmly established in the translation, although in some lines the effort to maintain a similar sound in the rhymes detracts from simplicity in the rhythm. Nevertheless, the conversion of the lion's "belle lure" into "manes like haloes" creates a more vivid image; the translator's eye is on a real lion, not La Fontaine's allegorical one, who suggests the lion-king, Louis XIV. Her own eye also sees the "shaggy shoulder fur," much more concrete than "a longue crinière." And in "The Lion in Love," the moral (defined by La Fontaine as the "soul" of the fable) finds such a genuine equivalent in Marianne Moore's lines that the difference between the two languages reaches the vanishing point:

> Amour! Amour! quand tu nous tiens,
> On peut bien dire: Adieu prudence!

> Love, ah love, when your slipknot's drawn,
> We can but say, "Farewell, good sense."

(IV, 1)

The translation of these two fables, "Bitch and Friend" and "The Lion in Love," required quite different kinds of skill. The intricacy and variety of La Fontaine's compositions would continue to demand the utmost inventiveness on the part of the translator.

In a study of her poetry, comparisons of her translations with the La Fontaine text must yield to examination, for their own sake, of the resulting English poems. Readers will find many of them wholly successful. Some of the early ones that might be tested in this way are "The Fox and the Stork," "The Miller, His Son, and the Ass," "The Cock and the Fox," "The Dove and the Ant," "The Eagle and the Beetle."[22] All these fables contain a theme congenial to the translator, and in each of them the language is natural, the rhymes ingenious.

In others the exigencies of adhering to La Fontaine's meter and of finding rhymes similar to his sometimes caused awkwardness or even artificiality of expression. "The Peacock's Complaint to Juno" exhibits some unevenness for these reasons. In French, the peacock speaks to the Goddess with royal ease: "Déesse, . . . ce n'est pas sans raison / Que je me plains, que je murmure," whereas in English she "experience[s] pain . . . and exhibits righteous ire." One would never expect to find the last expression in one of Marianne Moore's own poems. The peacock's further complaint, that to the nightingale "Est . . . seul l'honneur du printemps," is expressed in English as "Announcing to all that fair spring has begun," losing the telescoped beauty of

170

the idiom. But in our language the nightingale's privilege could not have been so concisely described. Elsewhere in the translation of this fable, we find lines notable for imagery, control of rhythm, and lucidity of sound:

> You have dared to envy the song of the nightingale?
> Though your sapphire necklace grows dark by turns
>   and pale—
> With a thousand rainbow tints that nearly fade, then
>   stay;
>   You flaunt or fold your fan away. . . .
>
>   (II, 17)

And many of the Moore fables, even those that give evidence of being translated rather than recreated, contain lines of distinction comparable to La Fontaine's.

All of them deserve attention from the student of poetry—or for that matter of prose. When "Le corbeau sert pour le présage" becomes "The crow warns from the wood" (II, 15), imagination has been at work—the echo of *Macbeth* lending something to it. In the same fable, the translation of "Sur la branche d'un arbre était en sentinel / Un vieux coq" as "An old cock perched on a branch which made all visible" has a logical aptitude approaching the effect of metaphor. What one misses at times in the Moore translations from the first six books, is a certain sophisticated simplicity that generates the humour, as in "La Chatte Metamorphosée en Femme":

> Un homme chérissait éperdument sa chatte
> Il la trouvait mignonne, et belle, et délicate
>   Qui miaulait d'un ton fort doux.
>   Il était plus fou que les fous.
> Cet homme donc, par prières, par larmes,
>   Par sortilèges et par charmes,
>   Fait tant qu'il obtient du destin
>   Que sa chatte en un beau matin
>   Devient femme, . . .
>
>   (II, 18)

The English version, attempting to establish a similar series of rhymes and to carry the sense of this expert ridiculousness, seems heavy in comparison:

A man one time became dementedly fond of his cat—
The silkiest, daintiest, most exquisite, he thought.
   Indeed the mere sound of her miaow
   Thrilled him until he had somehow
   By tears and prayers of a touched brain
   Forged potent forces of a chain. . . .

Already, the added words have cast the opening lines into an explanatory vein; the swift little narrative has lost much of its charm. But among these early fables one can find many where La Fontaine's verve is caught by his deft translator. One of the best of these exemplifies the rhythmic acceleration and the exhilaration of spirit Marianne Moore could transmit:

   A devoted gardener—
   A not quite rustic, not quite citified one—
   Possessed in a village somewhere
A trim well-cared-for garden, by tillage he'd sown.
A snug hedge framed what he was growing with green.
Sorrel and lettuce grew at will within,
Flowers enough to make Betsey a bouquet should she
                                        wed.

The devoted gardener unwisely sought his squire's aid to rid him of a hare that devoured his plants. The scene need not be described, but left the kitchen garden past repair. "Farewell, chicory and leeks; farewell, all / That lends soup savour." The whole poem is a triumph in English as well as in French. Again, one senses that the ingredients of the fable[23] as well as its purport were as appealing to Marianne Moore as to La Fontaine—in this respect anticipating some of the opportunities of the later books.

The writing of his fables occupied La Fontaine over a period of more than twenty years—although during this time he had also published works of a different nature. The first six books of fables came out in 1668; the second collection (Books v-xi) was complete by 1679; Book xii was not published until 1694.[24] French scholars generally have agreed that the last six books differ considerably from the first six, and represent a major development in his art.

In his preface to the first group he had praised the virtues of his predecessors, while avowing his right to improve upon them. Modestly averring that he could not match the elegance and concision of Phaedrus, he felt he must "even things by imparting an added liveliness," and to these familiar stories he would lend "a certain piquancy—the desideratum nowadays—originality, humor."[25] And whereas in Aesop's day the fable was told simply, with the moral separate and always at the end, he would place it where most appropriate, or omit it at times. He stressed also his belief in the value of fables for teaching the young. In these aims he had succeeded. But no good writer wants to repeat himself. Fortunately, an infusion of new ideas and new experience refreshed his poetic energies and gave a different air to the second collection.

The men who frequented the salon of his patroness Mme. de la Sablière included not only his friends Molière and Racine, but the great voyager Bernier who had traveled in Syria and in Egypt, then lived in India for some years as physician to the emperor Aureng Zebe. From Bernier, La Fontaine heard of episodes he could convert into fables, and must have owed to him his newly acquired knowledge of the Indian fabulist Pilpay. But whether in treating material found in Pilpay or drawing upon older sources, La Fontaine now more often changes details in the narrative to suit himself.[26] And he brings into his poetic world themes and expressions of classical writers as diverse as Horace and Pliny, Virgil and Lucretius. In effect, he widens the limited genre of fable to encompass poems of a fundamentally different nature, whether elegiac in tone ("Les Deux Pigeons") or meditative ("Le Songe d'un Habitant du Mogol") or mordantly satiric ("Le Lion, le Singe, et les deux Ânes"). Marianne Moore as translator was sensitive to these new possibilities, no doubt finding most welcome of all La Fontaine's increased reliance upon his own stored impressions of the streams, the woods, the wild creatures and domestic animals of his native region.

The challenge of translating these last six books required an ability to grasp their underlying philosophy, based in part upon Gassendi and in part upon Lucretius. As Margaret Guiton presents it, La Fontaine's "disruption of our normal human sense of scale . . . expresses the underlying unity of all animate human existence—the plants, the insects, the animals—all dignified, and in a sense equalized, by their common participation in the workings of the natural universe."[27] This aspect of the later fables, and the element of self-portraiture in them, called for a deeper response from the translator. She was in fact better prepared to meet these challenges than she had been to match the sophisticated style of the earlier books. The greater realism in portraying animals and human beings, the closer attention to their physical surroundings, and the departures from traditional fable symbolism allowed her to rely more upon her own intuitions about human behavior. Whether she gave any thought to the influence of Gassendi or Lucretius or Virgil is immaterial. Her lifelong interest in unifying relationships in the natural world was at least equal to La Fontaine's, although derived from different sources in her training and experience.

The result is that many of the translations of these later fables come closer to La Fontaine's tone and diction. In "Le Héron" the French poet writes from observation, not tradition:

Un jour sur ses long pieds allait je ne sais où
Le héron au long bec emmanché d'un long cou.
   Il côtoyoit une rivière.

174

L'onde était transparente ainsi qu'aux plus beaux jours;
Ma commère la carpe y faisait mille tours
    Avec le brochet son compère.

(VII, 4)

Such a congenial subject induced the translator to write with comparable ease, and to convey the sense of a quiet hour along some stream.

A heron on wary stilts, though where I've not found
                       out—
Long beak thrust out on longer neck—stalked all about
    Where a river cooled the air.
The water was as clear as the fair morning hour;
With Dame Carp circling near as under magic power
    And a crony accompanying her.

The mood, the rhythm, the particulars of the scene come alive in English. The rhymes come close to the sonorities of the French words, but to obtain this the translator availed herself of some license—adding "under magic power" in the fourth line, and aptly using the term "crony" for "compère," but losing the exactness of "brochet" (pike). Still, we have as close an equivalent to La Fontaine's lines as could be expected in a different language, and this success is maintained throughout the double fable of the over-fastidious heron and the demanding demoiselle, each of whom rejects good chances, only to settle for lesser opportunities in the end.

When La Fontaine widens the scope of his fables to include meditative or elegiac poems, Marianne Moore again must have found this a stimulating change. For some of her best translations are to be found in this later group. A striking example may be found in *Les Deux Pigeons*, a fable dear to all French admirers of La Fontaine. Wisely choosing as the English title "The Two Doves," she successfully follows the path of the haunting narrative where, in spite of

175

mutual devotion, one of the pair wilfully set out to travel alone while the other stayed at home. After the sightseer had nearly been destroyed by unexpected dangers (storms, bird traps, predators), "She flew to the cote from whence she'd come," and was reunited with her mate. Instead of the ironic comment or query which often serves as the "moral," La Fontaine wrote a deeply felt individual conclusion. Who can say that the translator has failed to give it life?

> Fond lovers, since love is all in all, if you go away,
>   Come hastening home again:
> Each a beautiful world to the other of the two,
>   Forever strange, forever new.
> Love the world in each of you, unaware of all the rest.
> I who loved long ago, desiring nothing more,
>   Would not exchange the Louvre's vast store
> Of all that's rare—or heaven—for love confessed. . . .
>
> Are lost delights that made life sweet forever gone,
> Forsaking my soul in its dejected state?
> Ah! might my heart take fire once more in the old way,
> Alert even now to love's spark and, elate,
>   Beat fast as in a former day.
>
>   (IX, 2)

The translation is in places very free; some of the implications of the French lines are lost. "Fond lovers" does not capture the intimate tone of "Amants, heureux amants," or La Fontaine's nostalgic mood. But there is more than nostalgia in his introspective questioning—can he ever again experience transcendence of himself in love? The form of the question implies that he has not lost that power. (Something in the ending of this poem resembles Donne's "Study me then, you who shall lovers be / At the next spring.") The Moore translation loses the impact of some lines; but her transformation of the literal sense in the final part attains a simplicity uncommon in her own work.

176

The more often one reads the French text and the Moore fables side by side, the more evident it becomes how much was demanded of her; and one understands better why she so often succeeds in making a good poem in her own language and why from time to time she fails. The requirement of keeping close to the meaning of poems written in a different age, and the technical demands already discussed, placed the first hurdle. Then, the amazing diversity of La Fontaine's genius would for this true poet-translator inevitably mean a fresh testing of her own convictions, and pose the question whether or not she could share the direction of his irony, his pleasure, his pity, his intellectual range.

Probably even a partial answer to such a question would have to allow for the mood the writer-translator happened to be in. "The Heron" and "The Two Doves" translations show that Marianne Moore could reckon with marked contrasts in La Fontaine's sense of life. Her translation of the ambitious philosophical fable, "To Iris: Madame de la Sablière" is firm and readable; it maintains the skilful maneuvers of La Fontaine's answer to Descartes. The implicit rebuke to people who exploit or extinguish the lives of animals possessing talents equal or superior to ours would ring true to the author of "Elephants" and "The Pangolin." These are poems of Marianne Moore's that do not suffer in comparison with any of the fables of La Fontaine.

Others, that one might think congenial to her, do not possess, in her version, a comparable finish. I have in mind, for example, "The Shepherd and his Flock," or "The Monkey and the Leopard." Each of these contains unforgettable lines:

Now they've got Robin, the dear, the pretty one—
  Following me so dutiful
  Down thoroughfares for bits of bun;
He'd be hard at my heels till stars and pasture blend.

(IX, 19)

Or

177

". . . The king who has been here,
Were I no more, would wish to wear
A muff of leopard fur, cream, yellow, black or gray,
With chained rosettes that interplay
On fairy-footmarked fur moirée.

(IX, 3)

Yet the ending of each of these two translations has an awkwardness wholly uncharacteristic of her own writing. Constraint was imposed partly by the effort to express something she would not ordinarily say, and partly by her self-imposed requirement to use rhymes as similar as possible to the vowels and consonants in French. So we have the crowded final line in "The Monkey and the Leopard," "Flaunt garb for gifts but worth a glance!" No doubt, the more explanatory or unnecessary "morals" were irksome to translate.

This explanation is borne out by the perfect ending of one of the most enjoyable early fables, "The Lark's Brood and the Farmer." Here the moral begins the poem ("Make the task your own is a maxim that is sound"), a moral in accord with Marianne Moore's own convictions. The charming story that follows need not be strained to illustrate the principle. A lark, nesting in grain soon to be harvested, instructs her young to be on guard and listen to every word the farmer says. When the farmer tells his son that they must call on friends to bring their sickles the next day, the mother lark is not alarmed, nor is she the second time, when the farmer summons relatives to help. But when he decides that on the following morning he and his son must do the reaping themselves, she gives the alarm:

And the nestlings as quickly as if full grown
Fluttered and flapped and then had flown.
Not a larklet lurked in the wheat.

(IV, 22)

The English poem speeds through the story and ends with lines both musical and witty. The lark needed no moral to instruct her.

178

Both in the first six books and in the second group (VI through XI), we find Moore translations worth putting up as rivals or running-mates of the originals. Some of these are "The Miller, His Son, and the Ass" (III, 1), "The Dog who Dropped Substance for Shadow" (VI, 17), "The Fish and the Shepherd who Played the Lute," (X, 10), "The Mousie, the Cat, and the Cockerel" (VI, 5), "The Acorn and the Pumpkin" (IX, 4), "The Mogul's Dream" (XI, 4), and many others that delight without halting to instruct explicitly.

But in Book XII, published near the end of La Fontaine's long career, he gave the world several new poems of commanding interest. The dedicatory one with which the book begins (written for the son of the Dauphin, a boy of twelve), has the narrative form and the dialogue generic to the fable, and a "moral" that would seem appropriate for the instruction of the young prince. Nevertheless, although seeming to present a contrast between reason and brutishness, based on the myth of Circe, the poem in fact questions the supremacy of reason in man. Ulysses obtains from Circe permission to restore human form to the Greeks who had been transformed into beasts by her potion, but on condition that each one make the choice for himself. Speeding to his companions, Ulysses first asks the lion if he would not prefer to be a man again. But "with a kind of intimidating purr," the lion refuses.

Why renounce gifts to which all whom I know must defer?

. . . .

I am king; why submit to Ithaca's shrivelled laws
And a soldier's tedious round of indignities?
   I shall stay as I am and be at ease.

(XII, 1)

The bear also rebuffs Ulysses sternly; and his rebuttal gives this fable a skeptical irony comparable to Montaigne's in his essay "Des Cannibales." The bear asks, "Who shall say that one beast excels all the rest?" La Fontaine intensi-

179

fies this theme in the conversation between Ulysses and the wolf. When told to leave the woods, to "change, since you can / And instead of a wolf be an upright man," the retort of the wolf is decisive.

—"Is there such?" asked the wolf; "I see none for my part;
You have just now pronounced me a beast with no heart.
But who are you? Except for me would not you too
Have eaten those sheep whose loss grieves the neighbor-
hood?"

La Fontaine *appears* to reflect that the companions of Ulysses, who had been metamorphosed into animals and now preferred to range the woods and live as they pleased, had enslaved themselves. But his questioning of man's own claim to superiority is paramount. The Moore translation of this fable, like that of the "Discourse to Madame de la Sablière," faithfully and energetically delivers La Fontaine's meaning. In fact the turns of rhythm, the inflections of the dialogue, come closer to the original than in many other examples.

La Fontaine had offered a gentler version of the same theme in tribute to the great moralist, de la Rochefoucauld, in "The Rabbits" (xi, 14). Of all the Moore translations, this is the one I could least well dispense with. Like "The Companions of Ulysses," the poem bears little resemblance to the traditional fable. A theme is announced, "that man's counterpart / . . . Is almost always some animal he knows," because, the writer says, animals "have at least a semblance of mentality / In the mere corporal self, energized by something there." Instead of a little story about animals from which a moral can be drawn, the poem gives a first-hand account of the writer's own experience. Without doubt this approach and the episode itself evoked Marianne Moore's full imaginative power. "At an hour when stalkers stir, before the loiterer / Day has lighted their path upon the moor," the hunter has climbed some tall tree:

> . . . and from an eminence
> I am thundering with my gun
> At the rabbits crouching unaware.
> All disappear. I have startled them every one—
> On the green, in heather-sweet air—
> Bright-eyed, sharp-eared shadows that waited,
> Then sported; nibbling thyme-perfumed fare, enchanted.
>
> (x,14)

The expert placing of internal and end-rhymes, and other figures of sound, lend the whole passage an élan that would be impossible except as a work of love. One sees this best in fables that draw upon awareness and emotion natural to the translator as well as to La Fontaine.

"Crayfish and Daughter" in Book xii, a briefer composition, again suggests Marianne Moore as a collaborator rather than a translator, likewise "The Woods and the Woodsman" (xii, 16). Another, "The Gazelle, the Tortoise, the Crow, and the Rat" (xii, 15), a fantasy rather than a poem based on observation, breathes the generous spirit that Madame de la Sablière always evoked from her protegé La Fontaine; and the translation captures this radiance. Each of the creatures is threatened by some danger; by their disparate skills each in turn has a chance to rescue its fellow creature. When the gazelle has been caught in a snare, the crow and rat

> set off to try to rescue her—
> The lovable and faithful hind
> Their nimble little mountain friend.
> Obsessed with haste but at the rear,
> The poor tortoise dotted the scene behind. . . .

This "poor tortoise" is a cousin to the armadillo in "The Plumet Basilisk." The variety, the fresh departures of La Fontaine in his second collection of fables, and in Book xii, stimulated and emancipated the translator as well.

The translator needed that scope. When accepting with fervor Auden's suggestion that she begin the task, how could she have foreseen the many years it would take to finish it? The number of fables to be translated exceeded the number of poems she herself had written. And never before had she been required to satisfy the standards of several advisors. Yet as far as one can judge she never repented of this decision.

It was not without cost—literary as well as human. Her translation has been out of print for many years; and that means that modern readers do not know most of these poems. There has been little discussion of their place in her work as a whole. The principal reason for this neglect is the obsolescence of the fable genre and our failure to comprehend either the nature of La Fontaine's greatness or the real value of the Moore translation.

Taking myself as a sample, I confess that at first I had little relish for the lions, wolves, foxes and goats, cats, rats, and mice of the fable troupe. There are so many stories about each of them, and no fable of fables emerges to weave the whole into one fabric. Although La Fontaine is more subtle than Aesop, there remains a partial separation between the narrative and its moral intent. Only in the greatest fables of the second collection does he solve this problem.

Marianne Moore had not foregone the pungent aphorism, but allowed it to escape for itself. In her mature work, in "The Jerboa," or "The Pangolin," or "Elephants," the phenomena observed occupy the center of the composition. No moral is stated; different kinds of existence confront the world and question rather than instruct the reader. Moral perception "emerges daintily," like the wood weasel, and becomes a motif in a harmony of other events. As she advanced beyond her first book, *Observations*, the co-presence of animals and plants and of human beings is seen from a point of view that would be indefinable in terms of any single value. That is why her poems evade allegory, and terms like bestiary are irrelevant.[28]

To read her translation of the fables, we must re-encounter La Fontaine. The result will be to discover how the tone and movement, the syntax, the *vers varié*, the sonorities, the end rhymes and internal rhymes carry more of the intrinsic meaning than any moral can. In doing so, we share Valéry's belief that a modern poet can discover a source of improvement "pour son art," by a study of La Fontaine.[29] Then, and only then, will the reader be prepared to recognize how in the best Moore fables the sound liberates the sense, and why they also promise a benefit for poets of the future.

In many ways Marianne Moore resembles La Fontaine in sensibility, although her irony is less somber. The poetic field that he shared with his friend Molière is her habitat also—she had long admired Molière.[30] Her awareness of people perhaps comes closer to Molière's than to La Fontaine's. But these three as writers in different countries, in different centuries, belong to a commonalty that Valéry described (in a statement that she liked to quote): "It never was a lazy man's game to extract a little grace, a little clarity, something that will last, from the fleeting impressions of the mind, and to change that which vanishes into that which goes on."[31] So it is that the tempo, the phrasing, the rhymes, and the resources of language make the Moore variations upon La Fontaine a book for poets that the common reader may sometimes share with them.

Beyond that, should it be denied that the Herculean labor of eight years marked a detour from her own best work? If not, anyone will admit that although a detour delays a journey, it sometimes brings the traveler to good country bypassed by the throughway. Even while engaged in the voluntary servitude of her fables, Marianne Moore had written several major poems of her own, and one in particular that is unlike any other ("Tom Fool"). She came back from the detour to her own road forward.

7

The Poet's Pleasure

WE cannot make a sharp distinction between the poems written before the La Fontaine translation and the ones subsequently published; Marianne Moore always was creating something entirely her own. A remark in a letter to Margaret Marshall, then poetry editor of the *Nation*, expresses the need for independence: "Mr. Engel of the Viking Press is humane and reassuring but I cannot walk a tightrope my whole life. It is time I alighted."[1] The letter answers a question about "Armor's Undermining Modesty," and its date, March 23, 1950, indicates that this and other pieces in the "Hitherto Uncollected" section of *Collected Poems* (1951) overlap not only the *Fables* (1954) but poems in the books to follow: *Like a Bulwark* (1956), *O to be a Dragon* (1959) and *Tell Me, Tell Me, Granite, Steel, and Other Topics* (1966). Each of these books contains major poems and each resurrects some very early ones.[2] To observe the path of the poet's advance it is best to think of the new pieces as if all belonged to one rather sizable collection.

Readers will probably differ in their way of sorting them out, distinguishing the ones that belong with her most deeply conceived compositions from those written for the poet's pleasure in celebrating minor events. No matter what difference of opinion there might be in identifying the two kinds, one quality permeates all her later work: the place made in it for the emerging concerns of Americans in the latter part of this century. The diffusion of belief in the significance of the arts, loyalty to New York as a dynamic force for their continuity, absorption with sport (baseball, especially), a will to preserve the dignity of life symbolized by historic buildings, a recognition that the physical environment is part of the moral environment—all these find embodiment in poems like "Carnegie Hall: Rescued," "Hometown Piece for Messrs. Alston and Reese," "Old Amusement Park," "The Camperdown Elm," and in various lines of the fantasies and rhapsodies in her last three books of poetry, as well as in some of the prose in *Predilections* (1955) and *The Marianne Moore Reader* (1961).

One of the pleasures the later poems give to the reader is their novelty. Of course, in a general sense they resemble things in the work of her early and middle years; with few exceptions they would be recognizable as hers even if published anonymously. But the subjects vary from ones earlier chosen. Few of them are about animals; in fact none is comparable to "The Jerboa," "The Plumet Basilisk," or "The Pangolin." The porcupine in "Apparition of Splendor" gives the occasion for a complex visual design woven out of both memory and observation:

> Was it
> some joyous fantasy,
>
> . . . .
> of spines rooted in the sooty moss,
>
> or "train supported by porcupines—
> a fairy's eleven yards long"? . . .
> as when the lightning shines
> on thistlefine spears, among
> prongs in lanes above lanes of a shorter prong,
>
> . . . .
> —where needle-debris
> springs and shows no footmark;
> the setting for a symmetry
> you must not touch unless you are a fairy.

The last stanza of this poem reminds us that the porcupine is Maine's animal, and rather than fight an intruder "lets the primed quill fall." A mood that appears frequently in the notebook kept at this time also enters into the concluding lines ("Shallow . . . intruder / insister, you have found a resister"). But the poet's eye and the reader's do not see the animal in the center of things; they watch the thistlefine pattern of light and dark. The harmonies of rhyme conform to this, and justify the title "Apparition of Splendor."

It should not escape our notice that the word "fantasy" is present in "Apparition of Splendor." Although little explored as a critical term, fantasy has had attractions for a number of modern writers, and is often an important element in poetry—in Shakespeare of course, and in Blake. But it seems to be the governing form in "Then the Ermine." The notebook entries of the period when these later poems were written record (more than any others to which I have had access) the intermingling of the writer's moods with special moments in her life; they show that she then was thinking almost habitually in rhyme and that she was simultaneously pursuing related themes that emerged in a number of different poems.

The entries that by very skilful selection and ordering became the ingredients of "Then the Ermine" illuminate the nature of fantasy in this poem. In June 1951, she recorded "I saw a bat by daylight"[3] and subsequent entries in August show an effort to clarify or resolve conflicts such as those between timidity and bravery, or between the charm of discretion and "hammer-handed bravado."[4] Some of the most significant entries do not appear in any of the poems, yet are a part of the feeling that animates them. "Lapses fr[om] logical thinking. . . . What would we do without them" is attributed to John Edmunds;[5] a marginal entry on the same page, "Sensibility is sometimes at swords points w[ith] poetry"[6] finds an echo later in "Vis poetica: Yes[.] We are sentimental when unwary about that which we like because it is unsentimental."[7] Then, at the end of this page, "Charm like a garland / or jack of the green / circulating out and in," introduces central images of "Then the Ermine." Before long she copied the motto that carries the burden of the theme, *mutare vel timere sperno.*[8] But not until the following spring do the trial lines include the dynamic concept of *implosion*, and Dürer's violets.[9]

Take "Then the Ermine" as a whole: once more, not about an animal, not about a weasel. We cannot say what a good poem is "about," but we can indicate what kinds of experience were brought into relationship within it. The wavering jack-of-the-green motion of the bat charms the mind, as the modesty of *"Mutare sperno vel timere"* counteracts bravado. The "ebony violet" of the crow and the dignity of the shepherdess (a figure in La Fontaine) reassure the speaker, who is wary of intrusive praise or undesired attention. The "range of association" that Eliot remarked upon connects a new word from the vocabulary of nuclear energy with a remembered painting:

> Foiled explosiveness is yet
> a kind of prophet,
>
> a perfecter, and so a concealer—
>   with the power of implosion;
> like violets by Dürer;
> even darker.

In these two poems, "Apparition of Splendor" and "Then the Ermine," we enter the realm of fantasy in poetry. A novelist, Bettina Linn, said of fantasy in the novel that it can cross "the usual frontier of reality and bring back the meaning found beyond."

It can employ personification and symbols—a prophetic voice, a vision or a dream; and it can suggest a new perspective by setting the scale of measurement of a supernatural world against the ordinary scale of our perceptions. Some writers of fiction will need all these devices to handle the rich and intricate material about them. . . . These few writers . . . will find in the special form, fantasy, a way to suggest what they cannot define, to represent what they cannot identify, to . . . express [indirectly] the wonder and horror, the variety and mystery of what they know.[10]

Fantasy in the novel as Bettina Linn describes it here implies a story of some length; in poetry the few parallels would include the dream visions of Chaucer and the Pearl Poet, perhaps Donne's "Anatomy of the World," some of Blake's prophetic books, McDiarmid's *A Drunk Man Looks at the Thistle.* In the lyric fewer examples come to mind; we should have to think carefully about Christopher Smart, Emily Dickinson, Poe, de la Mare. But in a poem like "Then the Ermine" the combined symbol of jack-of-the-green and wavering daylight bat,[11] and the uncommon imagery, do suggest what could not otherwise be identified. Perhaps they also suggest "the horror, the variety and mystery" of what the writer sensed. I do not think there is anything quite like it in Marianne Moore's poetry before this.

In the same notebook where lines and images were being tested or involuntarily recorded for these two poems of fantasy, a theme returns that had been entered in a different notebook years before: "Letter perfect is not perfect." As far as I can judge, this proverbial saying was often repeated by Mary Warner Moore in her last years.[12] As an expression that might be relevant in a poem, it first appears in a rough draft of a few lines for "Efforts of Affection."[13] But these lines were discarded. And when the expression "Letter perfect is not perfect" recurs, it marks a time of struggle, of disenchantment with the labor of the La Fontaine translation, and of restlessness caused by unwanted attention from insensitive admirers. Below the entry "Letter Perfect is not perfect" the diarist set down "Elderly adolescents, hideous beauties, ordinary egotists and factualists with no more compassion than a crocodile."[14] And at the end of this page she wrote, "The thing must be admitted, I don't care for the books that were not worked on by her," unquestionably a reference to her mother and to the La Fontaine translation.[15] Sometime later, under the heading "The Poem," the note continues "Letter perfect is not perfect" and "Sensibility . . . is responsible for suffering."[16]

These reflections alternate with moments of reassurance, of renewed hope. "Letter Perfect is not Perfect" now appears as a title, with the provisional lines "We fail and fail and fail (there is a touch of portraiture in this) and after all, prevail."[17] Interspersed with these meditations on her own state of mind are phrases that became a part of "Armour's Undermining Modesty"—especially the motif that "the fragrance of iodine" is more pleasing than unwelcome tributes in this time of grief and inward struggle. The élan of the poem overcame its antagonists in her experience; and her natural relish for work was fortified by friends, by enjoyment of La Fontaine's "exquisitely careless accuracy,"[18] and by her religious belief, attested here by frequent quotations from her minister's sermons and from the Biblical texts he was interpreting.[19]

The notebook kept during these years gives evidence, then, that the theme "Letter perfect is not perfect" stood for a victory of sensibility over everything in one's self or in others that defeats life. Neither "Propriety" nor "Armour's Undermining Modesty" had exhausted this theme. At least two years before she wrote "Tom Fool at Jamaica," Marianne Moore's resolve not to spend her talent for irrelevant ends became associated with Jonah's unwillingness to prophesy at Joppa.[20]

"Letter Perfect is not Perfect" became a poem at last, published by the *New Yorker* with the title "Tom Fool at Jamaica." It is powerfully conceived, with a genesis as special as that of a champion race-horse. An unexpected request gave Marianne Moore the "objective correlative" to precipitate a concrete form for her inward musings. A now defunct magazine owned by Cowle Publications wanted a poem from her; it was suggested that she write one in the shape of an airplane. She replied that she could not do that, but might be able to produce one in the shape of a rivet![21]

After this exchange, she agreed to write one about a horse, and, accompanied by her faithful helper Gladys and Gladys' husband, she went to the race track at Jamaica. The resulting poem was eventually published not in *Flair* but in the *New Yorker*. Howard Moss suggested changing the title to "Tom Fool at Jamaica."

Celebrating victory in a race by investing it with myths chosen by the writer to offset pride and temporality resembles the challenge of a Pindaric ode. The long-meditated theme "Letter perfect is not perfect" summons the unwilling prophet for the opening lines:

> Look at Jonah embarking from Joppa, deterred by
> the whale; hard going for a statesman whom nothing
> could detain,
>
> although one who would not rather die than repent.
> Be infallible at your peril, for your system will fail,
> and select as a model the schoolboy in Spain
> who at the age of six, portrayed a mule and jockey
> who had pulled up for a snail.

Much of the Old Testament book of Jonah, itself an essentially humorous short story, is telescoped in this ironic warning, and the schoolboy's drawing is a comic reversal of the aim of horse-racing.

Then Victor Hugo's statement and the melody of an eighteenth-century French air, "Sentir avec ardeur" sound the note of victory in the only sense that the poem allows: the champion is one " 'who makes an effort and makes it oftener than the rest' "—his jockey's description of Tom Fool. But the "effort" is not like the Puritan work ethic; for the phenomenon of controlled speed has beauty:

> You've the beat
> of a dancer to a measure or harmonious rush
> of a porpoise at the prow where the racers all win
> easily—
> like centaurs' legs in tune, as when kettledrums compete;

nose rigid and suede nostrils spread, a light left hand on
the rein, till

well—this is a rhapsody.

In the musical sense, it is. In the last stanza the great pianist
Fats Waller with his "feather touch, giraffe eyes and that
hand alighting in / Ain't Misbehaving,"[22] and Eubie Blake,
whose musical comedy *Shuffle Along* Marianne Moore had
seen in 1921, are enrolled among the champions in this ex-
pertly complex poem, which ends, as it began, at some dis-
tance from the race track.

The *New Yorker* editors had queried the date in the lines
"out on April first, a day of some significance / in the am-
biguous sense," "We are not sure," Howard Moss wrote,
"whether you mean 'out on' to refer to Tom Fool, specifi-
cally. According to our checkers, Tom Fool didn't run until
April 25th, though racing began on the first."[23] She ex-
plained in her reply that Tom Fool appeared for practice
on April first when the training season began. The legend
of April first and the name of the horse combined to give
her the metaphor she needed to touch into the poem her
horror of gambling, without impairing the comedy of the
whole. The poem "does" the race-track in several voices,
that of the poet herself, Victor Hugo (as quoted by the min-
ister of the Lafayette Street Presbyterian Church),[24] the
French poet Madame de Boufflers, the track announcer
Signor Caposella ("It's tough . . . but I get 'em; and why
shouldn't I? / I'm relaxed, I'm confident, and I don't bet"),
and that of Ted Atkinson, the jockey.[25] The writer's com-
ment follows Caposella's statement: "Sensational. He does
not / bet on his animated / valentines—his pink and black-
striped, sashed or dotted silks" and introduces a vibrant
tone in the very center of this composition, which appeals
to all the senses, the love of colour, of sound, of touch, and
of motion.

In a review of Eliot's *Murder in the Cathedral*, Marianne
Moore had said that "originality is not a thing sealed and

191

incapable of enlargement . . . an author may write newly
while continuing the decorums and abilities of the past."[26]
Her later poems give evidence of that possibility. If, as I
have tried to show, the poems of fantasy are a different
kind of poem from her earlier ones, and "Tom Fool" an-
other new development, we may look at "The Sycamore"
to see how she now deals with the pattern of subject, coun-
ter-subject, and resolution that she had mastered long ago.
I think that the nonchalance, the "careless accuracy" she
admired in La Fontaine, characterize her writing in this
poem. Reading "The Sycamore" with "Camellia Sabina" in
mind will clarify this. The structure of "The Sycamore" de-
pends upon two contrasting images. The startling first one
is quickly developed: "Against a gun-metal sky / I saw an
albino giraffe. Without / leaves to modify, . . . it towered
where a chain of / stepping-stones lay in a stream nearby."

The transition from the "glamour" of the sycamore to the
second half of the poem changes its key and tempo: "A
commonplace: / There's more than just one kind of grace."
The counter-subject, a contrasting visual figure said to be
worthy of the simplicity of a miniaturist, is simply stated:

> clinging to a stiffer stalk
>   was a little dry
>   thing from the grass,
>   in the shape of a Maltese cross,
>   retiringly formal
>   as if to say: "And there was I
>   like a field-mouse at Versailles."

One remembers the wild mouse in "Camellia Sabina" with
a grape in its paw and its child in its mouth—a grape quite
different from the cherished ones of the wine-merchants of
Bordeaux. In both poems a statement after the counter-sub-
ject ends the poem. "And there was I / like a field-mouse at
Versailles" lingers in the mind as a humorous and dramatic
close.[27] The ironic dismissal of luxury in "Camellia Sabina"
(" 'Close the window' says the Abbé Berlèse") does not

speak so directly and lightly for the writer herself. "Camel-
lia Sabina" has a more elaborate structure; "The Sycamore"
a fluency and seeming rapidity of execution won by years
of discipline.

"Style," and "Logic and 'The Magic Flute' " present
new figures of sound confirming Marianne Moore's belief
that originality is "capable of enlargement." Most of her
poems, even when the dominating rhythm has overtones of
prose, obtain unusual musical intervals by the spacing and
variation of rhyming words. Although she had declared her
preference for rhyme to be "nested," she had also allowed
herself major open rhymes (in "The Fish," for example).
Acceleration and changes in tempo were discussed in the last
chapter. One of her La Fontaine fables had given her the
chance to experiment with a refrain achieved by repetition
of key words in a different order ("The Cat and the Mouse,"
Book XII). "Style" does not owe anything directly to that
fable. But the iteration of names of dancers, of instrumen-
talists, and of the court-tennis champion Etchebaster whose
own rhythmic placements and strategies were inimitable,
produce the sound that matches the subject, with special
modulations.

> . . . Entranced, were you not, by Solidad?
> black-clad solitude that is not sad;
>   like a letter from
>   Casals; or perhaps say literal alphabet-
>   S soundholes in a 'cello.

The poem speeds to its refrain-like effect from Rosario's
"guitar, wrist-rest for a dangling hand / that's suddenly set
humming fast fast fast and faster," to the metrical chant at
the end of the last stanza. For style,

> There is no suitable simile. It is as though
> the equidistant three tiny arcs of seeds in a banana
> had been conjoined by Palestrina;
>   it is like the eyes, ·

193

or say the face, of Palestrina by El Greco
O Escudero, Solidad,
Rosario Escudero, Etchebaster!

The meaning of "Style" is relatively transparent. The subject could have posed difficulties; but they melt away under the confluence of names and simile. "Logic and 'The Magic Flute'" may be read with equal ease; the development of the poem, however, is far more complex. The title begins to place the elusive illusion before the mind; the two terms "logic" and "magic" enter simultaneously. A performance is at the heart of this poem ("an intrusive hum / pervaded the mammoth cast's / small audience room"). But whose performance? Even without reading the appended note referring to a "colorcast" of "The Magic Flute" by the NBC Opera Theatre, we recognize characters and see them through a spectator's eyes.

Only Mozart's genius could have redeemed the confusing libretto of *Die Zauberflöte*; Auden and Kallman's English translation brings the principal themes into a truer relationship.[28] Marianne Moore's poem deftly abstracts the opposing forces of light and darkness in the opera. The scene of her lyric is not only the television screen but New York City; the action bridges the past and present in the viewer's life. The query "Up winding stair, / here, where, in what theatre lost / was I seeing a ghost" leads to a remembered image; "the magic flute and harp / somehow confused themselves / with China's precious wentletrap." The name of the mollusc *wentletrap* derives from a Dutch word meaning winding staircase; on a visit to the Marine Museum in Mystic, Connecticut, about six months before the telecast, she had drawn the spiral pattern of the shell in her notebook.[29]

The slender but strong narrative of "Logic and 'The Magic Flute'" takes the reader to the "abalonean gloom" of the Time-Life Building near the skating rink at Rockefeller Center, where "a demon roared," " 'What is love and / shall I ever have it?' " This line does not occur in the libretto, from which the poem has now escaped to make its own plot. There is a demon demanding love for himself opposing the pastoral role of Papageno. He becomes the "Trapper love with noble / noise, the magic sleuth," who "illogically wove / what logic can't unweave: / You need not shoulder, need not shove." The last line exemplifies "the art of defeating climax." Auden's reinterpretation of the role of Papageno and Mozart's music are the elected affinities of "Logic and 'The Magic Flute.' "

Underscoring its meaning are two earlier poems, "Marriage" and "The Paper Nautilus." The irony of "Marriage," like the shell of the crustacean, protects the trust that needs no statement. A conversation at a party for T. S. Eliot in 1950 also belongs to the background of "Logic and 'The Magic Flute.' " This little celebration of the success of *The Cocktail Party* was one of several where both Eliot and Marianne Moore were present, with friends, publishers, and others. As recorded in one of the conversation notebooks it runs as follows:

> Mrs. Reynal: "I bought a bird to match a lamp I had; Then I had 2 zebra finches—the female died; so I thought I should get the other a little wife to console him; but he would have nothing to do with her . . . and one day when the door of the cage had been left partly open, he flew away and never came back.
>
> T. S. A credit to his sex.
>
> Mrs. Reynal [continues about male birds taking advantage of "their innocent wives"].
>
> T. S. Are there no bird psychiatrists?[30]

Later, one of the guests spoke of a friend who had for twenty years lived with a woman to whom he was not married, and asked Marianne Moore if she thought the less of him for that. "Each's devotion to the other is all that matters—conventions are incidental," was her reply. This, the more generous view of the "institution," marriage, is reflected in "Logic and 'The Magic Flute.' "[31]

A particular event "afforded the occasion" necessary for

the writing of both "Tom Fool at Jamaica" and "Logic and 'The Magic Flute,'" although they are not "occasional poems" in the usual sense. But the category of occasional poems is a deceptive one. It can include labored salutes by laureates to a royal wedding or the birth of an heir apparent or the death of a national hero or a centennial. When such poems verge upon the official they are hollow—Dryden's "Threnodia Augustalis," Sir John Betjeman's poem for the silver jubilee of Queen Elizabeth II, some of Ben Jonson's tributes to the Stuarts. But what about Yeats's "In Memory of Major Robert Gregory?" Auden's "September 1939" or Hopkins' "Wreck of the Deutschland?" In such poems an event external to the writer's life, one that is either public or at least known to many others, may unexpectedly command a form for thoughts and feelings that a writer has long harboured, consciously or unconsciously. Whether such poems are relatively slight or of more far-reaching significance depends partly upon the nature of the occasion, but more upon whether the writer's response to it is compelling enough to command an appropriate form.

These later books of Marianne Moore contain a good many occasional poems. She had now become a public figure, "New York's laureate" as August Heckscher called her, and received more requests to read her poems than she allowed herself to accept. Perhaps "In the Public Garden" best illustrates the range of experience summoned by a demand of this kind. Having accepted an invitation to read at the Boston Arts Festival in 1958, she characteristically came with a new piece of work. As a spectator described the scene, "a crowd of something like five thousand persons . . . in the semi-darkness under the elms" waited for the poet to appear. When she arrived and began to speak "it was in the unhurried voice of the continuing and uninterrupted conversation with a next door neighbour. Nor did the fire engines that began to race around the outside of the Public Gardens, or the jet planes roaring overhead disturb her or

196

the audience whom she held insulated from all extraneous sensation."[32]

> Boston has a festival—
> compositely for all—
> and nearby, cupolas of learning
> (crimson, blue, and gold) that
> have made education individual.

Boston's festival (the word giving the key for the rhyme that continues throughout) is composite because it extends to the many parts of the metropolis where the arts may be enjoyed in congenial surroundings, perhaps near " 'pear blossoms whiter than clouds' " or where pin-oak leaves "barely show / when other trees are making shade, beside small / fairy iris."

Into the poem go sensations of many earlier visits to Boston and to Cambridge, and some observations recorded in a notebook thirty years before. Then, she had seen in the window of a shop on Berkeley Street "a wooden model of a grasshopper vane by the man who made the one on Faneuil Hall"; later she proceeded by streetcar and subway to look at the original, the "gold grasshopper with antennae cocked forward."[33] On the same visit in 1937 she went to King's Chapel and copied inscriptions from a tombstone,[34] and heard an arrangement of a psalm by Virgil Thomson:

> . . . Despite secular bustle

> let me enter King's Chapel
> to hear them sing: "My work be praise while
> others go and come. No more a stranger
> or a guest but like a child
> at home."

Reading "In the Public Garden" with an awareness of its deep roots in Marianne Moore's life makes it evident that the poem was not so much fashioned for the occasion as brought alive by it. Poems exist in the mind and spirit—at least the best ones do—long before something compels them to be set down. "In the Public Garden" affirms this, answering the question "And what is freedom for?" with " 'freedom to toil' / with a feel for the tool." And this freedom transcends the public occasion in the three final stanzas leading to the reminder that "Art, admired in general / is always actually personal."

Other occasional poems indicate her pleasure in devising ever-changing rhymes and meters for the service of the arts. Her continuing interest in the dance (see her essay on Pavlova, for example) led to a tribute in verse to Arthur Mitchell, a dancer and choreographer of the American ballet. "Combat Cultural" cleverly contrasts the Cossack dancers in a Sol Hurok performance, "feet stepping as through harp strings in a scherzo," with the quadrille of old Russia, "aimlessly drooping handkerchief / snapped like the crack of a whip." Another poem, "Carnegie Hall: Rescued," will communicate to future readers the conviction that New York must not destroy the buildings, the traditions, that foster the life of music, of the theater, of all the arts. Slight as such poems are (they might all be thought of as variations on the theme of "Values in Use"), they exemplify new departures in form. For me, "Enough," written for the Jamestown Tercentenary (1607-1957), has particular attraction for the terse narrative in octosyllabic couplets—a meter not hitherto chosen by Marianne Moore, and one that delivers her pithy aphorisms in a new accent:

> Marriage, tobacco, and slavery
> initiated liberty,
>
> when the Deliverance brought seed
> of that now controversial weed—
>
> a blameless plant Red-Ridinghood.
> Blameless, but who knows what is good?

The answer to the final question, whether the settlers had done something that would endure, pertains to many such doubts: "It was enough; it is enough / if present faith mend partial proof." And in "Hometown Piece for Messrs. Alston and Reese," both the apt doggerel of the meter and the occasional aphorism are suited to the game: "A-squat in double-headers four hundred times a day, / he says that in a measure the pleasure is the pay."

Aside from tributes of an almost satiric kind like those to George Bernard Shaw or to Molière ("To the Peacock of France") Marianne Moore had written hardly any poems about individuals. There are a number of them in these later books, belonging to a genre that has been little discussed. For want of a better term I shall call it the portrait poem. Within this category one should make a distinction between those written about figures from the past and those devoted to people of the writer's generation. Suppose for a moment we consider Ben Jonson's "To Camden" or "An Epistle to Master John Selden;" then Hardy's "Lausanne, in Gibbon's Old Garden." The human traits that Jonson elects to engrave exemplify the "ethical ideas of great potency and grip"[35] that mark the writer himself. He builds his poem by declarative statements or questions and exclamations addressed to the subject. Camden is one "to whom my country owes / the great renowne and name wherewith she goes" because of his achievement in *Britannia*; Selden is asked, "Which Grace shall I make love to first? your skill, / Or faith in things? . . . your unweary'd paine / Of Gathering? Bountie in pouring out again?" To see the lineaments of either moral portrait clearly, we must know something of the man's work. We never glimpse his appearance or specific behavior, but the terms of praise ring true and bring before us an individual's capability.

But "Lausanne, in Gibbon's Old Garden" transports us to a real place, the garden where Gibbon had finished *The Decline and Fall* a century before. Hardy stood musing there, close to midnight, and saw the demeanour of the great historian when he had finished his task at the same hour.

199

A SPIRIT seems to pass,
Formal in pose, but grave withal and grand.
He contemplates a volume in his hand,
And far lamps fleck him through the thin acacias.

. . . .

And at the alley's end
He turns, and when on me his glances bend
As from the past comes speech—small, muted, yet composed.

How fares the truth now?—Ill?
Do pens but slily further her advance?
May one not speed her but in phrase askance? . . .

The subtly accented account of the scene and the time of the
imaginary dialogue reveal the temper of the historian and
portray the poet's own mind and spirit as well.

Marianne Moore's portrait poems include one of a con-
temporary, Yul Brynner, and from the past, the ones on
W. S. Landor, St. Jerome, and Leonardo da Vinci. "Yul
Brynner" does more than almost any similar poem to bring
a unique person before us. The first stanza quickly sets forth
the errand of mercy that sent a famous actor, whose mag-
netism and vitality have enchanted thousands, to refugee
camps in Europe and the Middle East. As consultant to the
United Nations, he was to offer hope to these "displaced
persons" of World War II—resettlement in the New World.
The poem skilfully seizes upon Yul's perception that the
older people in the camps would be reluctant to move again,
but might endure the uncertainty for the sake of their chil-
dren. Yul, "the reporter with guitar" encouraged them. He
said " 'You may feel strange; nothing matters less / No-
body notices; You'll find some happiness. . . .' "

But "Rescue with Yul Brynner" is not, like "Rigorists,"
simply a tribute to a deed well done and to the man who
performed it. A portrait of the actor who had performed in
circuses as acrobat and clown before he began his career in
the theater becomes the primary interest. "Mysterious Yul
did not come to dazzle" when he "flew among the damned."

200

>   Instead of feathering himself, he exemplified
>   the rule that, self-applied, omits the gold.
>
> . . . .
>
>   Yul can sing—twin of an enchantress—
> elephant-borne dancer in silver-spangled dress,
>   swirled aloft by trunk, with star-tipped wand. . . .

In the final stanza, his role in *The King and I* is magnified
and the reader has something to remember that is more
vivid than any of the splendid photographs in his own
book.[36]

>   "Have a home?" a boy asks. "Shall we live in a tent?"
>   "In a house," Yul answers. His neat cloth hat
> has nothing like the glitter reflected on the face
> of milkweed-witch seed-brown dominating a palace . . . .
>   . . . His deliberate pace
> is a king's, however, "You'll have plenty of space."
>   Yule—Yul log for the Christmas-fire tale-spinner—
> of fairy tales that can come true: Yul Brynner.

The progress from the slow rhythm of the boy's hesitant
questions to the spinning pace, the rapidly fired salute of
the last two lines is a study in itself. The portrait of a real
man becomes a character in a story.

In contrast, the succinct "W. S. Landor" sketches in a
few swift strokes one aspect of this complex man. Reading
an introduction to his work, Marianne Moore came upon a
(probably apocryphal) anecdote: that Landor in a fit of
anger could "throw / a man through the window, / yet,
'tender toward plants,' say, 'Good God, / the violets!' (be-
low)." However gentle herself, she was capable of soldierly
indignation, and, on things that matter most, reserved. The
final lines fuse Landor's portrait with qualities of her own:
"Considering meanwhile / infinity and eternity, / he could
only say, 'I'll / talk about them when I understand them.' "

The portraits of St. Jerome and of Leonardo da Vinci
share the moral strength of the poems by Ben Jonson and by

Hardy cited earlier, but differ in procedure from either—
although as in the Yul Brynner and Landor poems she fol-
lows Hardy's model in giving a sense of actual place and in
alternating narrative and dialogue. "Leonardo da Vinci's"
(the title that starts the first line)

> Saint Jerome and his lion
>   in that hermitage
> of walls half gone,
>   share sanctuary for a sage—
> joint-frame for impassioned ingenious
>   Jerome versed in language—
> and for a lion like one on the skin of which
>   Hercules' club made no impression.

Initially, this is a poem about a painting. Kenneth Clark
in his discussion of it calls St. Jerome's domicile a "dark
cave,"[37] but Marianne Moore saw the masonry that is un-
deniably visible in the background as a "hermitage of walls
half gone." This image intensifies the metaphor of "joint-
frame" for the skeleton of Jerome straining against his
muscles as he stares at whatever vision was commanding
him.

The poem now departs from the painting, making room
for the days when Jerome had befriended the lion—all re-
lated in a most amusing fashion. The climax unifies Jerome's
saintliness and his talent as a writer: "Pacific yet passion-
ate— / for if not both, how / could he be great? / Jerome—
reduced by what he'd been through— / with tapering waist
no matter what he ate, / left us the Vulgate." This pleas-
ingly unexpected end rhyme closes a sequence that offers
variations on the sounds a and i, both long and short (lion,
sanctuary, sage, hermitage, skin, ass, recognized, chagrined,
twinned, passionate, ate, Nile, famine, pale, paint, sover-
eignty—to notice only some).

"An Expedient—Leonardo da Vinci's—and a Query" con-
templates Leonardo not, primarily, as a painter, but as

universal man enduring man's ultimate limitations. The poem draws upon knowledge of his notebooks and reflects a profound agreement with the concept of man as a part of nature, subject to the same laws of growth as all other things. For Leonardo this belief stimulated his scientific researches, uniting them with his painting. "With a passion, / he drew flowers, acorns, rocks—intensively" and "saw as treachery / the all-in-one-mold." Yet art and science cannot be served equally by anyone, and Leonardo succumbed to dejection when his belief in the omnipotence of mathematics seemed to be refuted. Hence the sadness of his self-questioning, often set down on his drawings and mathematical notations, "Di mai si fu fatta alcuna cosa." Although Marianne Moore modifies this refrain by her own query, she lets Leonardo's words conclude the poem.

> Could not Leonardo
>   have said, "I agree; proof refutes me.
> If all is mobility,
>   mathematics won't do":
>   instead of, "Tell me if anything
>   at all has been done?"

To compare her "Leonardo da Vinci's" St. Jerome with "An Expedient—Leonardo da Vinci's—and a Query" makes evident how much more abstract the later poem is. Homely imagery such as that of the lion as guest in the hermitage would be inappropriate in this anatomical drawing of Leonardo's mind, a portrait tinged with his melancholy in old age.

One sees increasingly in the later Moore poems the free play afforded to her incidental moods and her quickness to seize upon any source—a quotation from a newspaper article, a photograph in a magazine, an overheard remark—that could accent or even catalyze the poem preexisting in her meditations. The later notebooks, unlike the earlier ones, include almost inadvertent recordings of her own feelings

side by side with trial lines and phrases. There is evidence
of her suffering after her mother's death ("Suffering you are
my friend")[38] and of the isolation she felt when paid unwel-
come attention or compliments. "It is depressing to be liked
for something other than one's self," she was driven to state,
at the same time noting her appreciation of "the magic of
unobtrusiveness."[39] These entries are of the same period as
trial lines of "Like a Bulwark" and of poems written be-
tween 1947 and 1951.

Because of its fidelity to the selected traits of its subject,
the Leonardo poem, like Hardy's "Lausanne: Gibbon's Old
Garden," casts a silhouette of the writer. Her imagination,
although smaller in scale than Leonardo's, did instinctively
embrace discoveries in the world of science and technology
as well as of the lively arts. She extracted and transformed
ideas and nuggets of information from the annual reports of
industry[40] as well as from magazines, newspapers, and tele-
vision programs. It may be hazarding too much to wonder
if she intended or desired to embody the unity shared by art
and science, mighty but incomplete routes of knowledge, in
a design larger than any she (as far as we know) had at-
tempted. I would not rule out the possibility. After one of
the most heart-rending entries made almost two years after
her mother's death, she added "I almost pray / To Dante
and to Bunyan / who made their visions real."[41] This clari-
fies a preceding note, "Dante looms before our eyes / 'But
we don't come in that large size.' "[42] (The second line is a
quotation from R. P. Blackmur.) And such entries occur
side by side with others about the positron or about the
photon theory of light, or the suggestion of "Measuring the
Meson" as the title for a future poem.[43]

The alternating impulses of the search for accuracy in
observing inalterable phenomena and of giving the fancy
unchecked rein did not escape her "speculating conscious-
ness."[44] In the spring of 1950 a reviewer's statement about
de la Mare's *Collected Tales* went into the notebook: "fan-

tasies and symbols have a higher truth for Mr. de la Mare than facts and probabilities."[45] Throughout the struggle to maintain inner equilibrium and integrity of spirit almost everything was susceptible to conversion into rhyming lines. Some were never used, never meant to be; others we recognize as drafts of famous poems; some passages and notations of remarkable beauty were never developed. But the constant practice freed her from almost obsessive doubts.

The process accounts for the exhilaration of some of the later poems, the seeming rapidity of execution and accomplished informality of tone, willingness to be herself the speaker without assuming any mask. But the expert meter and syllabic patterns offset the informality enough to protect the essential form. "These words, Mr. Davis, in lieu of the lyre" might serve for an ending of a brief message in rhyme—but it is a good line, all the same, in the little piece where Harvard rhymes with yard. An article written for the *Christian Science Monitor* at that time describes the stimulus: "It is for himself that the writer writes, charmed or exasperated to participate; eluded, arrested, enticed by felicities. The result? Consolation, rapture. . . . One may hang back or launch away. 'With sails flapping, one gets nowhere. With everything sheeted down, one can go round the world'—an analogy said to have been applied by Woodrow Wilson to freedom."[46]

And so it is that various minor poems ("Blue Bug," "My Crow Pluto," "Baseball and Writing," "Occasionem Cognosce," and others intentionally modest in aim) reveal the activity of an older poet's mind and may divert the reader by their melodic variations or linguistic surprises. The passage from uncommon fact to dream and fancy appears, for example, in "Saint Nicholas." The notebook of those years simply tells us that the moonlight was so bright one evening that she mistook it for a light she had failed to turn off, and getting up to do so discovered the real source.[47] The poem relays to Saint Nicholas ideas for gifts—a striped chameleon "with tail that curls like a watch spring" or perhaps a dress of *"qiviut,"* the fleece of the "Arctic Ox" or goat praised in another poem of that time.

> But don't give me, if I can't have the dress,
> a trip to Greenland, or grim
> trip to the moon. The moon should come here. Let him
> make the trip down, spread on my dark floor some dim
> marvel, and if a success
> that I stoop to pick up and wear,
> I could ask nothing more.

The change from appearance to reality and back occurs again in "The Magician's Retreat," her last published poem.[48]

"Accessibility to experience"—Henry James's phrase—denominated for her one meaning of New York. In this chapter I have tried to chart new bearings in her own accessibility to experience as it prompted poems differing in significant ways from those written before she was sixty years old (the year that her mother died). After that, she had written the "Hitherto Uncollected" section in *Collected Poems* (1951), finished the La Fontaine translation, then the thirty-nine new poems in her last three books and a few others.[49] This is a remarkable output for a writer in the last twenty years of her life. The poem that to me is a summation of the capacity to draw upon deeper sources of knowledge is "Granite and Steel." It should be read in the context of the book's title, *Tell Me, Tell Me, Granite, Steel, and Other Topics,* and in relationship to the other poem making up that title.

One of Marianne Moore's reading diaries has a few notes on a talk that Robert Frost gave in 1958. She quotes him as saying, "Every individual is in too much danger of the material. You must just do the best you can with this great difficulty." And later he said, "All poems are about the preservation of the spirit in the material."[50] This human conflict occupies the center of "Granite and Steel." Brooklyn

Bridge had entered into the thinking of other writers on this subject—especially Henry James and Hart Crane.[51] How her poem resembles and how it differs from the conception of James's essay "New York Revisited" and Crane's *The Bridge* reveals something about her place in the tradition of American writers, and about the nature of the poem "Granite and Steel."

When Henry James revisited America in 1906 after an absence of many years, he found New York greatly changed. The arrogance of the skyscrapers appalled him, and the "pitiless ferocity" he saw at work. But he looked upon the harbour with fascination; it was "as if, in the whole business and in the splendid light, nature and science joyously romping together, might have been taking on, for their symbol, some collective presence of great circling and plunging, hovering and perching seabirds, white-winged images of the spirit, of the reckless freedom of the Bay." As he looked from the harbour to the bridge linking Brooklyn to lower Manhattan, his view was that "the lacing together across the waters . . . does more than anything else to give the pitch of the vision of energy." The conflict, however, is not resolved, since the energy he could not help enjoying had its source in "the pursuit of inordinate gain."[52]

Hart Crane resumed the exploration of this American dilemma. He contrasted Brooklyn Bridge, and the seagull's wings "Shedding white rings of tumult, building high / Over the chained bay waters Liberty," with streets where "Down wall, from girder into street noon leaks," and with "Inventions that cobblestone the heart."[53] But he personified and mythologized the bridge, as able to pardon and reprieve, to "condense eternity."[54] As Alan Trachtenberg concludes, in his *Brooklyn Bridge, Fact and Symbol*, "Hart Crane completed the passage of Brooklyn Bridge from myth to symbol. . . . He refused to—or could not—acknowledge the social reality of his symbol, its concrete relations to its culture."[55]

The social reality of the bridge is precisely (but not

solely) what Marianne Moore does bring alive in "Granite and Steel"; and reading Trachtenberg's book gave her the means to do this. For he unfolds the debt of John Roebling, designer of the bridge, to transcendentalism, in his belief that matter represented an "evolution of the spiritual," or was "an expression of spirit."[56] We have taken account of Marianne Moore's affinity with transcendentalist writing, compressed in her line "the power of the visible is the invisible."[57] Belief of such a kind is no mere assumption. The conflict caused by what Frost called "this great difficulty," the "danger of the material" occupies the center of "Granite and Steel"; the poem recreates the "dream of spirit and matter"[58] and their union in actuality on the bridge. To Roebling the catenary curve was "the microcosmic unity"[59] of opposing forces; he knew that it would support the weight of the bridge. Equally significant was his invention of the woven steel cables that stretch diagonally from the towers and would support the roadway even if the catenary curve did not.

Marianne Moore of course knew Crane's *The Bridge*[60] and James's "New York Revisited." But she was not a self-conscious writer and would not have been likely to compare her poem as it was being set down to either of these parallels. She restates the contrast and varies the design, both the visual one and the fundamental theme. Like the proem of *The Bridge*, the vista in *Granite and Steel* extends to the Statue of Liberty. In Crane's proem the seagulls' wings "build" liberty over the "chained bay waters"; the image in "Granite and Steel" is different, and integral to the structure: the "Enfranchising cable, silvered by the sea ... / and "Liberty dominate the Bay— / her feet as one on shattered chains, / once whole links wrought by Tyranny." The challenge of this dynamic relationship announces the theme that is to be developed (and it should be read with her earlier poem "Light is Speech" in mind). The very term *enfranchising* refers to liberty of choice symbolized by the French

Bartholdi in his statue, and made an actual path to a better life for the German immigrant, John Roebling, designer of the bridge. That is why, later in the poem, the bridge becomes a "composite span"—uniting different cultures by their community of freedom in America.

The choric voice of the poem introduces the dissonance of "man's uncompunctious greed, his crass love of crass priority," as resolutely as James or Crane had. The difference lies in the fact that the "uncompunctious greed" represents an evil that cannot be projected upon any single group. Marianne Moore sees it in Robert Frost's terms, as something that every individual has to resist. "Profit is a Dead Weight," a prose piece in the same volume, confirms this interpretation of "Granite and Steel." An early draft of the poem contains the lines "Let me say with the poor / 'O my Lord . . . / if it endanger my soul / take it from me.' " This quotation, borrowed from the conversation of a diamond miner in *The Diary of Helena Morley*,[61] was not kept in "Granite and Steel"; but it appears in the essay "Profit is a Dead Weight." The catenary curve of the bridge is the "implacable enemy" of "the mind's deformity," greed and the desire for power.

The whole poem might be described as "compacted," a term Marianne Moore resorts to sometimes in her criticism. The virtually Platonic idea seen by the eye of the mind, John Roebling's, loses nothing by becoming an actuality. To convey the visual sensation of someone crossing the bridge at night, it seems wholly appropriate that Hart Crane's image of a "path amid the stars / crossed by the seagull's wing" should be incorporated, as well as a revised line from his proem. Her revision, "O radiance that doth inherit me," rather than Crane's "O thou whose radiance doth inherit me,"[62] avoids personification of the bridge and gives a different connotation to the radiance "affirming interacting harmony." The city, the discoveries of the modern mind, are not seen as intrinsically evil. What comes in question is the use man makes of them. The bridge, "sublime elliptic two-fold egg," symbolizes freedom—"romantic passage way, way out; way in" between cities, between nations old and new, between the spaces of individual lives. Instead of the grandiose vision of a voyage to Atlantis in Crane's poem, a modern sense of the interacting experience of individuals and a grasp of how an internal vision of the mind can be realized lends her poem historical veracity. The implicit symbolism, the awareness in the "climactic ornament" of something approaching Joseph Stella's apocalyptic painting[63] do not contradict the resolution of harmonies and discords in "Granite and Steel." "First seen by the eye of the mind, then by the eye," the bridge is not symbol alone but "composite span—an actuality."

"Granite and Steel," then, is one more example of fresh development in the later poems of Marianne Moore. It differs from the work in *Collected Poems* (1951) not only in the subject and the way the subject is handled, but technically as well. Instead of stanzas or verse paragraphs in which line length is governed by the syllabic pattern, and the rhymes correspond, here we find strophes of varying length. The rhyme initiated by the word *sea* is maintained, linking these strophes. The interpolated variation on Hart Crane is an unexpected use of apostrophe, resumed in "O steel! O stone!" in the last section. The only other example of it that I know is in the poem "Sun" that ends both this volume and *Complete Poems* (1967)—deceptively, for it is an early one, written in 1910.[64]

This willingness to vary form is noticeable in other poems of the later books, for example in "Blue Bug" and "Enough." "Blue Bug" repays attention in a number of ways. Like "Saint Valentine," or the funny "Dream," it could be regarded as light verse—and why shouldn't Marianne Moore write light verse if she wished to? But it would be a mistake to underestimate or disregard these improvisatory poems; for they have musical inventiveness and élan. The power of aphorism, too, takes on different functions, especially the last line in the allegory "Charity Overcoming Envy" ("One need not cut the Gordian knot").[65] A more general observation about the structure of the later poems might be that while, like the ones in her previous collections, they begin *in medias res*, it is in the middle of different things going on in the life of America.

Leonardo da Vinci's query, "Tell me if anything / at all has been done?" may have a reprise in "Tell Me, Tell Me," a more complex poem than it seems. To Leonardo's question, or her own, the only answer comes in the beautifully reversed rhyme that ends her poem on the Renaissance composer Melchior Vulpius,

> a contrapuntalist—
> > composer of chorales
>
> . . . .
>
> but best of all an anthem:
> > "God be praised for conquering faith
> > which feareth neither pain nor death."
>
> We have to trust this art—
> > this mastery which none
> can understand.
>
> . . . .
>
> > Almost
> > > utmost absolutist
> and fugue-ist, Amen; slowly building
> from miniature thunder,
> > crescendos antidoting death—
> > love's signature cementing faith.

"Melchior Vulpius" represents the increasing number of poems in her work that identify an indefinable sentience in human beings—all kinds of people—able to respond to something better than themselves. Sometimes by concise narrative with cinematic cutting, or by description bordering upon fantasy, or by sleight-of-hand rescue of the unexpected in the seemingly commonplace object or circumstance, these poems support a conviction expressed by William Faulkner. Asking himself and his audience (in his Nobel Prize acceptance speech) what writing should do, he replied, "It should help a man endure by lifting up his heart"—a statement that Marianne Moore fervently endorsed.[66]

8

The Reader's Response

PLACE Marianne Moore's books side by side upon the shelf, in what seems their chronological order. Glancing from the Cretan terra cotta pattern of the slight *Poems* of 1921 to the tall, green and blue and gray *Complete Poems* (really incomplete) of 1967, we note that the physical characteristics of the different volumes almost confirm our sense of the poet's advance. Now it is time to look for the continuity, the qualities belonging to all, or most, of these "exercises in composition," even when they differ in form or implication. "What distinguishes one artist from another is the characteristics that he does not share with others," Bernard Berenson said, adding that "to isolate the characteristics of an artist, we take all his works of undoubted authenticity and we proceed to discover those traits that invariably recur in them, but not in the works of other masters."[1]

When we need not doubt the authenticity of a writer's published work, or manuscripts, the constant problem and pleasure of recognizing elements of poems written over a long period is not so arduous. But to set them forth we must trust instinct rather than definition; for, as Coleridge declared, "Could a rule be given from without, poetry would cease to be poetry, and sink into a mechanical art."[2] And his caveat applies also to our conception of individuality in a writer. We seek, then, not to define it so much as to look for some clue that will bring examples of it simultaneously to our understanding. Marianne Moore's own statement that "art is but an expression of our needs; is feeling, modified by the writer's technical and moral insight,"[3] affords a good point of departure.

213

Moral insight cannot be imparted by poetry unless the writer's technical insight is appropriate to it. One of Marianne Moore's recognized technical resources, her syllabic patterns, has received undue attention. Auden made a considerable point of this, and acknowledged that it was one of the "inventions" that he borrowed from her;[4] others have stressed this device. But I believe that the importance of this ground pattern in her poetry has perhaps been overestimated and its probable origins misunderstood. Her earlist poems exemplify a way of rearranging the line breaks to disguise the highly traditional octosyllabic couplet. In *Tipyn O'Bob* of May 1909 one may read, for example,

Emotion	3
Cast upon the pot,	5
Will make it	3
Overflow, or not,	5
According	3
As you can refrain	5
From fingering	4
The leaves again.	4

The words could have been set down in more conventional lines: "Emotion, cast upon the pot, / Will make it overflow or not / According as you can refrain / From fingering the leaves again." So arranged, the rhythm seems a monotonous iambic, without the accented amphibrach (Emotion, According). The control of this economical stanza depends upon the typography as much as on the number of syllables. The relating of typography to sound, even to the theme of a poem, George Herbert understood very well.[5] Donne and other poets in the sixteenth and seventeenth centuries had written stanzas of differing line lengths corresponding to the number of syllables. Marianne Moore particularly admired Herbert; but the progress of thought in many of her poems demanded the weight of a verse paragraph similar to Donne's.[5]

The metrical pattern of hymns and of the translation of

psalms meant to be sung must from the beginning have suggested syllabic equivalences and variations to her ear, as they had to Sidney's and to Herbert's. In a major essay, Theodore Spencer pointed out the experimentation in verse forms in Sidney's translation of the psalms, and the development of these possibilities by Herbert. Sidney's example, as Spencer described it, taught that "words had to be broken up, each syllable had to be weighed and considered, and new rhythmical combinations had to be found which were as far as possible from 'the . . . prevalent iambic habit.' "[6] The departure from prevailing iambic norms, aided by greater sensitivity to the quantitative values of words, and syllables, has been one of the accomplishments of modern poetry, and Marianne Moore was as much an innovator in this respect as Pound.

Reviewers of her early work paid little attention to the relation of syllabic count and line length. She herself called attention to it in a note that she furnished for an anthology edited by William Rose Benét and Norman Holmes Pearson:

> I tend to write in a patterned arrangement, with rhymes; stanza as it follows stanza being identical in number of syllables and rhyme plan, with the first stanza. (Regarding the stanza as the unit, rather than the line, I sometimes divide a word at the end of a line, relying on a general straight-forwardness of treatment to counteract the mannered effect.)[7]

But later she rarely referred to this subject, because she considered it misleading, I believe. For when the treatment of syllables is a consistent one, it becomes an aspect of rhythm. All recurrences in equal or proportionate time manifest rhythm (even the blinking on and off of traffic lights). In poetry, not only the recurrence of numbers of syllables, but rhyme, as well as accent, affect rhythm favorably or adversely. When the number of syllables varies in length from line to line as markedly as in Marianne Moore's

poems, and the pattern is maintained through several stan-
zas, it has a function similar to that of continuo in music—
heard throughout, but not determining the tempo.

Syllabic pattern in her poems, then, constitutes a subor-
dinate feature of their markedly individual rhythm. T. S.
Eliot perceived in her first book "a quite new rhythm, which
I think is the most valuable thing." He added, rightly, that
rhythm is not determined by a verse form.

> It is always the real pattern in the carpet, the scheme
> of organization of thought, feeling and vocabulary, the
> way in which everything comes together. . . . What is
> certain is that Miss Moore's poems always read well
> aloud. [Rhythm] is not separable from the use of words,
> in Miss Moore's case the conscious and complete ap-
> preciation of every word, and in relation to every other
> word, as it goes by.[8]

Eliot's comment—his principle here—is more enlightening
than Auden's stimulating but not wholly accurate state-
ment that Marianne Moore's is "the opposite of sprung
rhythm."[9] Of course, her practice would not have permitted
the use of extra, "outriding" syllables, and does not exem-
plify "sprung rhythm" as Hopkins defined it. In other re-
spects, however, her verse fulfills some of his principles—
for example, his view that sprung rhythm "is the rhythm
of common speech and of written prose, when rhythm is
perceived in them," and that "the scanning runs on without
a break from the beginning, say, of a stanza to the end and
all the stanza is one long strain."[10]

In the few lectures she gave, or in statements about her
poetry in interviews, her emphasis was on rhythm and its
relation to speech. And one must not forget that one of her
first critical essays dealt with "The Accented Syllable."
Answering one of Donald Hall's well-directed questions,
she said, "I have a passion for rhythm and accent" (not
equating the two); and later in that interview she referred
to her poems as "observations, experiments in rhythm, ex-

ercises in composition,"[11] these elements being, really, inseparable. Her statement in the Voice of America broadcast quoted earlier should be recalled: she said that from the beginning rhythm was the "prime objective," adding, "if I succeeded in embodying a rhythm that preoccupied me, I was satisfied."[12] Here of course we are on mysterious ground. A number of poets could probably say that one sometimes hears the rhythm of a line before being conscious of the words. Paul Valéry suggests this in something Marianne Moore quoted, describing the origin of a poem as "a group of words around which other words demand to be written."[13] Her various notebooks contain such groups of words, from conversation, from reading, from her own inner life. These phrases or sentences she recopied and varied to uncover their inherent rhythmic possibilities. These she occasionally indicates by conventional marks of scansion for the new words needed to sustain the pattern of her trial lines.[14]

Yet words demanding others to accompany them in a rhythmic whole would not be there without the dynamism of feeling. Her comments on one question put to her by Howard Nemerov in the questionnaire for the Voice of America program unfold like a rocket in multiple stages. To the question, "Is there, or has there been, a 'revolution' in poetry, or is all that a matter of a few tricks?" she answered:

> I see no revolution in the springs of what results in poetry. No revolution in creativeness. Irrepressible emotion, joy, grief, desperation, triumph—inward forces which resulted in the Book of Job, Dante . . . Chaucer, Shakespeare, are the same forces which result in poetry today. "Endless curiosity, observation, research, and a great amount of joy in the thing," George Grosz, the caricaturist, said, explained his art. These account for many other forms of art, I would say. One's manner of objectifying feeling has many variants, of course. . . . Flaubert's "Describe a tree so no other tree

could be mistaken for it" is basic—exemplified by Leonardo da Vinci in his every sketch. Mannerism and pedantry have no place in art.[15]

The "variants" in "the manner of objectifying feeling" that she brings into this discussion call upon the reader, as well as the writer, to take an express interest in technique. Her essay "Idiosyncrasy and Technique" emphasizes the derivation of the latter term: "*teknikos* from the Greek, akin to tekto, to produce or bring forth—an art, especially the useful arts."[16] Using this etymology, Marianne Moore brings the *means* of objectifying feeling into the feeling itself. In the statement from Grosz that she quoted above, "observation and research and a great amount of joy in the thing" are the *source* of art, comparable, really, to Cézanne's speaking of his painting, the actual doing of it, as *mes recherches*.

The conceptual depth of her poetry, regarded at first by various editors and reviewers as a shortcoming, accounts for her now widely recognized originality. To illuminate its nature I must borrow a triadic concept from the American philosopher C. S. Peirce. He unfolds it by the terms Firstness, Secondness, and Thirdness. They conjoin the world within us and the world outside ourselves, both human and non-human.

I think it sound to recognize that what we experience, what we are confronted with, is not a finished product. The element of freshness, of pristine novelty in sense data, and of freedom in ourselves, Peirce calls Firstness.[17] But we cannot altogether do what we will; the "element of struggle,"[18] the persistence of events contrary to our purpose, gives Secondness a place. "There can be no resistance without effort; there can be no effort without resistance."[19] Secondness as Peirce conceives it is predominant in what we call reality, "for the real is that which forces its way to recognition as something *other* than the mind's creation."[20] Thirdness mediates between the unpredictable variety of Firstness and the stubbornness of fact. "The beginning is first, the end second, the middle third. The thread of life is a third; the fate that snips is second. . . . Continuity represents Third-ness almost to perfection. Moderation is a kind of Third-ness. . . . Sympathy, flesh and blood, that by which I feel my neighbour's feelings is third."[21]

What may be unique in Marianne Moore's poetry, com-pared with that of her contemporaries, is that Thirdness comes *first* in her observation of the concrete. This may ex-plain why I would distinguish her method from allegory. One can see the way that moral insight mediates between the first look of things and what they may be heading for (the element of struggle or loss). The relative value given to immediacy, to hard fact, and to the continuity of fellow-feeling varies a great deal when poems from different peri-ods are compared. But the poetry of all the different periods brings these possibilities into a live relationship. We can find it compressed in an early epigram like "To a Steam-roller," where the thread of life is suspended from the quixotic ending. "A Grave" and "The Fish" liberate first-ness in their images of sensory experience; but both have an underlying, almost defiant, grasp of destructive or ob-structive forces. Thirdness in such poems inheres in the vi-tality of the observer's consciousness, and the order of the composition, the arrangement of the piece as a whole.

As her poetry developed from the sharp impressions of human folly and recalcitrance, matched by the implacabil-ity of physical events, to the freer explorations of the serial poems, especially "An Octopus," and then to the equilib-rium of "Part of a Novel, Part of a Poem, Part of a Play," the themes more visibly spun what Peirce called "the thread of life." Decisiveness in setting aside the substitute thing never disappears—the hero is "not out / seeing a sight but the rock / crystal thing to see . . ." that "covets nothing that it has let go." Such poems, however, allow a larger scope for "that by which I feel my neighbour's feelings," Peirce's description of Thirdness. The pangolin "stepping in the moonlight / on the moonlight to escape danger" and the human journey from night to daylight in that poem place surprising encounters and first-hand sensations directly in relation to the "element of struggle." Then the triumph of renewal, of flesh and blood (Thirdness) ends the poem, truly mediating between basic contrasts.

The form of the poem transmits to the reader all these phenomena, and as the form changes so does the relative impact of each kind affect our impression of the whole. "Four Quartz Crystal Clocks" and "The Icosasphere" bring into poetry something like constructivism in painting or sculpture, freedom in the design of a resistant hard material. Kenneth Burke remarks, "I think there would be no use in looking for 'symbolist' or 'imagist' motives behind the reference to the fact that precisely *four* clocks are mentioned [in the first of these two poems]. It is an 'objectivist' observation. We read of four, not because the number corresponds, for instance, to the Horsemen of the Apocalypse, but simply because there actually are four of them in the time vault."[22] In the poem the pleasure of knowing a mere fact is induced by the coolness and precision of rhyme and tempo:

> There are four vibrators, the world's exactest clocks;
>   and these quartz time-pieces that tell
> time intervals to other clocks,
>   these workless clocks work well;
> and all four, independently the
>   same, are there in the cool Bell
>   Laboratory time
>
> vault.

But Mr. Burke considers that at another level the theme "[not] of clocks that tell the time, but of clocks that tell the time to clocks that tell the time" is "thoroughly symbolic," as, in his terms, signalizing the "withinness-of-withinness of motives, the motives behind motives."[23] I should prefer to

say that this more inclusive level of meaning enters the
poem after the satiric dance of references to comparative
timing heard by various signals ("The sea- / side burden
should not embarrass / the bell-boy with the buoy-ball / ...
nor could a / practiced ear confuse the glass / eyes for taxi-
dermists / with eye-glasses from the optometrist.") leads us
to the counter subject—one of her rare mythological solu-
tions. When you dial for the time, and hear the new data
in the same operator's voice,

> you realize that "when you
>   hear the signal," you'll be
>
> hearing Jupiter or jour pater, the day god—
>   the salvaged son of Father Time—
> telling the cannibal Chronos
>   (eater of his proxime
> newborn progeny) that punctuality
>   is not a crime.

The "stubborn facts," the novel data, their ultimate rec-
onciliation by the universal that generates them, need all
the devices that, obviously, gave the writer pleasure to in-
vent. A similar poem, "The Icosasphere," *begins* with the
counter subject rather than moving to it. The opening lines
quickly suggest the virtuosity of birds nesting in hedgerows
with "bits of string and moths and feathers and thistle-
down, / in parabolic concentric curves." Their "spherical
feats" rival "steel-cutting at its summit of economy,"
achieved by the ingenious icosasphere.

It holds true then of Marianne Moore's poetry at all times
that the form, the instrument designed, varies with the in-
tended point of view and the scope of experience looked
into or out upon. Naturally she did not always succeed in
these experiments; in some of her early poems (like
"Snakes, Mongooses") discursiveness may defeat the shape
of the whole. But she always obeyed a counsel that she of-
fered younger writers: "Be just to initial incentive."[24] If the

subject had attraction, she would not desert it; and some-
times the effort of execution sets up a tension with the in-
tended theme. The tension keeps even the lesser poems alive
because the subject of the poem is never sought for but
comes as an involuntary summons. The reader too becomes
aware of the interaction between the beckoning subject—
inhering not in any one theme or image, but in all the words
together—and the objectifying figure of spoken sound.[25]

Marianne Moore's poetry shares some technical qualities
with the three modern poets most closely associated with her
—T. S. Eliot, Ezra Pound, and William Carlos Williams.
All these poets developed new rhythmic patterns, freeing
verse from the over-use of iambic pentameter and the cul
de sac of elaborate post-Swinburne stanzaic forms. All of
them introduced a conversational tone, a greater proximity
of poetry to spoken language. They could all convert seem-
ingly "non-poetic" material into the substance of art.

At the same time, the differences among them are as
marked; otherwise none would have been a true writer. A
number of the qualities that differentiate Marianne Moore's
work from that of the others identify her in the way that
Berenson asked. She does not juxtapose motifs from the
past (of art, literature, history) with fragmentary present
scenes in the way that Pound and Eliot had. Instead, if she
uses past events or quotations from earlier writers, it is to
bring them directly within the range of her observation
(in poems as different as "The Jerboa," "Virginia Britan-
nia," or "Tippoo's Tiger"). Likewise, although she some-
times invokes myth for its suggestive power, she does not
rely upon it for unifying heterogeneous subjects. Dialogue
in her poems, when it occurs, sounds like people talking in
the present, not being overheard or remembered. As she
remarked, she never considered herself an "imagist," but
every page of her work presents images for which alone the
poem deserves to be remembered. But the imagery never
becomes isolated, left to do the work of the poem by itself,
and this corroborates Coleridge's statement that images

give promise only of "transitory flashes and meteoric power [without] depth and energy of thought."[26] The latter, the depth and energy of thought, although skilfully subordinated to the rhythmic and visual design, and often presented in humorous guise, particularly distinguishes her poetry and accounts for the fact that most of it rewards deliberate study. As Ezra Pound said, she had one of the best minds of her generation.[27]

H. D., in an early article (1916, in the *Egoist*), called attention to a characteristic of Marianne Moore's poetry that was to continue: "She is fighting in her country a battle against squalor and commercialism. We are all fighting the same battle."[28] Yes, this could be said of Eliot, of Pound, and of Williams, of Stevens, as well as of Marianne Moore—although none of them wrote poems for the purpose of fighting a battle. But in Marianne Moore and Williams alone, an unswerving respect for human equality becomes a poetic strength. Pound's *Cantos*, it need hardly be said, are seriously damaged by his anti-semitism and incorporation of meaningless but fervent tributes to fascism. Eliot's Christian belief overcame any similar leanings, and they do not mar his poetry. If all four of these poets directed the barbs of satire against the ignorance and insensitivity of the opulent, Marianne Moore affirmed the sense of human dignity as a possession of all races: . . . "one keeps on knowing / that the Negro is not brutal, / that the Jew is not greedy, / that the Oriental is not immoral, / that the German is not a Hun." Real people are at home in all her poems for their own sake, as when she expressed a hope to see

> that country's tiles, bedrooms,
> stone patios
>   and ancient wells: Rinaldo
> Caramonica's the cobbler's, Frank Sblendorio's
>   and Dominick Angelastro's country—
>   the grocer's, the iceman's, the dancer's—the
> beautiful Miss Damiano's; . . .[29]

after fascism had been conquered. She was conservative in her political views, almost to the point of naiveté; but her poetry gives imaginative life to the hewers of wood and the drawers of water, as well as to champions and heroic rigorists. She does not tend to circumscribe or to romanticize the experience of others, and as her work progressed found it natural to epitomize her own hopes and sensations with candor.

In the 1963 interview broadcast on the Voice of America program (quoted earlier) she said, "I find that we become more and more concise—take for granted more as not needing to be explained."[30] The poems written during and after the La Fontaine translation reflect this willingness to trust the reader for an imaginative leap. We may observe this in the quasi-allegory, "Charity Overcoming Envy." The beginning gently alerts the reader to unexpected implications: "Have you time for a story / (depicted in tapestry)?" and proceeds to make a seeming story out of the colorful figures on the millefleur ground. One need not doubt that Marianne Moore was stirred by Charity's appearance riding an *elephant.* Envy (equally fascinating because of his coat of mail), "crouching uneasily" on his dog, shows the wound inflicted upon him by Charity. He begs for reassurance, asking "pitiless Destiny" what will become of him, until the elephant "at no time borne down by self-pity," convinces him "that Destiny is not devising a plot."

There is a wide departure here from the design of the tapestry the poet had seen illustrated in the *Scottish Art Review.*[31] No sign there of the elephant's having any other function than to carry Charity. This divagation—the elephant's entry into the dialogue—allows for a suspended resolution. "Deliverance accounts for what sounds like an axiom. / The Gordian knot need not be cut." The climactic, anti-climactic last line delivers an instructive enigma in the balance of living faith and moral inconclusiveness. What is the Gordian knot that need not be cut? We may notice that

Charity's "overcoming" Envy is expressed in a continuing present tense. Envy is just about the only thing that Charity, that Love, can never wholly overcome, for Envy refuses love. Charity, however, knows that her offer has wounded envy; she has a care for him, and rejects no fault we suffer from, turning away the obdurate ones that kill vitality and meaning. "Emancipation comes from within," Marianne Moore's notebook records at the time this poem was being drafted.[32] Its design is new; and "the dramatic vigor of axiom"[33] has superseded aphorism (as it had in "Logic and the Magic Flute"). Nevertheless, "Charity Overcoming Envy" confirms a poetic principle that guided all her work, early or late, "One tries to keep the several parts of a poem in balance—all cryptic, all lucid."[34] This is an ethical insight as well as a principle of form.

Describing the criterion of growth he called "etherialization," Arnold Toynbee defined its essence as "a transfer or shift of emphasis from some lower sphere of being to a higher sphere."[35] His exploration of it in technology, in history, and in art demonstrates a change from elaboration to simplicity, resulting in "heightened perception and thought and imagination."[36] Something like this occurs in the work of writers, too, except that the *first* transfer of energy may be from the relatively simple to a richer manifold, an apparently greater complexity. The ultimate transfer, if it occurs, may be to an unanalyzable purity in the medium itself (Cézanne's late watercolors, for example). Marianne Moore's latest poems suggest a shift of emphasis like the one Toynbee describes. The phenomenon appears in "The Magician's Retreat."[37] It is affirmed to be

> of moderate height.
> (I have seen it)
> cloudy but bright inside
> like a moonstone,
> while a yellow glow
> from a shutter-crack shone,

225

Figure 4: Ezra Pound and Marianne Moore Say Farewell, 1969 (Olga Rudge beside Pound)

a cat's-eye yellow crack in the shutter,
and a blue glow from the lamppost
close to the front door.
It left nothing of which to complain,
nothing more to obtain,
consummately plain.

A black tree mass rose at the back
almost touching the eaves
with the definiteness of Magritte,
was above all discreet.

In Magritte's "Empire of Light, II," the house of moderate height, the blue glow from the lamppost, the cat's-eye yellow seen through the shutter of the two lighted rooms, the dark tree mass rising at the back, have a completeness and mystery comparable to the poem's. But in the upper half of his canvas white cumulus clouds float in a pure blue daylight sky. Infinitely haunting, the whole composition finds its match in the "consummately plain" words of the poem. The implications of "retreat" and of the black tree mass that is "discreet" prepare for the magician's future emergence, or metamorphosis. The image of a cat's-eye yellow *crack* in the shutter may be another example of Marianne Moore's association of Magritte's "Empire of Light, II," with another of his paintings, where the left-hand panel shows an interior with two hunters pressing hard against the plain wall of the room; the right half of the canvas is wholly filled by an intensely dark sky bisected by a thin horizontal line, a crack of sunlight.[38]

Although the picture in the poem would satisfy Flaubert ("describe a house so that it cannot be mistaken for any other house"), essentially the lines recreate a private experience. No single category suits all Marianne Moore's poetry, and this mysterious composition has no predecessor in her work. The theme of magic, however, appears early, and recurs. Merlin is present in the *Tipyn O'Bob* poems, for example, and Houdini in *Observations*. She answers her own question. "What is more precise than precision? Illusion."

Of her work, as of our best poets, the weave is harmonious throughout, from early to late; variations in form only make the imaginative continuity more apparent. "Enough" and "Mercifully" set free once more themes that gave a powerful momentum to "The Jerboa" and "Propriety," respectively, and may be sensed in many other pieces as well. The "celestial refrain" in "Mercifully" is David's ("Dirge-like David and Absolom. *That*. Let it be that.") In a very early poem she had searched for the verity of art in the psalms or hymns of David.[39] The jerboa's enjoyment of his simple habitat, and the sufficiency of present faith to mend partial proof in the Jamestown tercentenary poem "Enough," have their counterpart in a Bach cantata that no doubt she knew: "Es ist genug."[40] And in the last poem to be given the title "Enough," her affinity with Ben Jonson, musicianly poet, unites them both with Pythagorean Plato. Having expressed in the first stanza a desire to be sitting "under Plato's olive tree / or propped against its thick old trunk," to "be away from controversy," the writer looks out from there to answer her opening query, "where would I be?"

> If you would see stones set right, unthreatened
>> by mortar (masons say "mud"),
>> squared and smooth, let them rise as they should,
> Ben Jonson said, or he implied.
>> In "Discoveries" he then said,
>> "Stand for truth, and 'tis enough."[41]

Years before, a very young poet had written "Feed Me, Also, River God," and remembered "the Israelites who said in pride / And stoutness of heart; 'The bricks are fallen down, we will / Build with hewn stone.' " This austere meditation continues "I am not ambitious to dress stones . . . / I am not like them, indefatigable, but if you are a god you will / Not discriminate against me, Yet—if you may fulfill / None but prayers dressed / As gifts in return for your own gifts— disregard the request."[42] The form of "Enough," as of "Mercifully" and "The Magician's Retreat," says more swiftly that the pleasure of knowing needs no adornment, brings its own grace.

Looking again at the volumes side by side, and imagining the unpublished ones that someday will be added to them, we may be sure, on opening any book of hers, that a courageous act of self-exploration will be found, whether taking place in a scene from modern American life, or accomplished by observations on the book of the creatures. For this poet is not narcissistic or solipsistic, and if severe at times on the intruders or pretenders, is undeceived by her own finiteness and insubordination. They gave her, as she knew, the power to celebrate the gifts of others, in both her poetry and her prose. "That which is able to change the heart proves itself."[43]

Speaking to a group of students, Marianne Moore attributed to Pound a misquotation of Coleridge, saying that "poetry should have a continuous undercurrent of feeling without separate excitements." She then remarked that she believed a poem should have separate excitements as well. Coleridge, in fact, attributed these sensations to the reader: "Our genuine admiration of a great poet is a continuous *undercurrent* of feeling; it is everywhere present, but seldom anywhere as a separate excitement."[44] But I think this expectation can cut both ways; and that in reading her work from start to finish we discover a continuous undercurrent of feeling like that of the student in her poem with that name, and the separate excitements of rhythmic arrangement and idiom proper to herself, and to no one else.

Notes

NOTES

ABBREVIATIONS USED IN THE NOTES

MM : Marianne Craig Moore
JWM : John Warner Moore
MWM : Mary Warner Moore
EP : Ezra Pound
TSE : T. S. Eliot
LS : Laurence Stapleton
RD : Reading Diary
CN : Conversation Notebook
Canaday : Bryn Mawr College Library

1

Note to the title: "So this was how it all began" was Joseph Conrad's comment on Henry James' prefaces to the New York edition of his works (cited in the prospectus of the re-issue, ed. Leon Edel).

1. See Emily Wallace, "Penn's Poet Friends" in the *Pennsylvania Gazette* 71 (1973), pp. 33-36; also *Reader*, p. 255.

2. Mrs. John M. Moore, Marianne's mother, lived with her father in St. Louis, Missouri after her husband suffered a nervous breakdown and went back to his parents' house in Ohio. When her father died (in 1894), she moved to Carlisle, Pa., her early home, and became a teacher at the Metzger Institute.

3. MM to JWM, September 22, 1915.

4. See comment in MM to JWM, October 18, 1915, about going to Mercersburg "with ennui so far as the meetings are concerned."

5. MM to JWM, November 23, 1913.

6. MM to JWM, December 14, 1913.

7. MM to JWM, February 1, 1914.

8. MM to JWM, March 26, 1915.

9. MM to JWM, February 4, 1914.

10. The *Egoist* had referred to MM as an imagist, and William Rose Benét sent word advising her not to let herself be associated

with this group. "I'll have to tell Billy," she wrote, "or rather show him that it's like getting married; I'm sorry to disappoint him, but it is not possible to meet his views on the subject and please myself" (MM to JWM May 9, 1915). William Rose Benét was Warner Moore's classmate at Yale (1908) and had been Marianne's escort on several occasions when she visited New Haven. At the time when this letter was written, he was married. This letter is an exultant one, reporting the publication of three of her poems in *Poetry*.

11. Her second letter to Warner about the New York visit is headed "Sojourn in the Whale: part II" (December 19, 1915). She later used this phrase as the title of a poem.

12. Miss King's acquaintance with Gertrude Stein began in the 1890's. She visited the studio in the Rue de Fleurus where the Steins kept their paintings, and there would have seen Picasso's 1906 portrait of Gertrude Stein. See Charles Mitchell, "Mr. Cooper and Miss King," *Bryn Mawr Alumnae Bulletin* 61 (1961), 5-8.

13. MM to JWM, undated [December, 1915]. Marianne Moore continued to frequent Stieglitz's galleries after her move to New York. In her tribute to him after his death she wrote of "291" as "an American Acropolis so to speak, with a stove in it, a kind of eagle's perch of selectiveness, and like the ardor of fire, in its completeness. . . . [Stieglitz] was not exactly a theologian but a godly man; and he was right; a thing is remembered, not for its shadows but itself" (*Stieglitz Memorial Portfolio 1864-1946*), ed. Dorothy Norman (Twice a Year Press, New York, 1947).

14. MM to JWM, October 3, 1915.

15. Supra, n. 13.

16. Ibid.

17. The poems were "Apropos of Mice," "Holes Bored in a Workbag by the Scissors," and "In 'Designing a Cloak to Cloak his Designs,' You Wrested from Oblivion, A Coat of Immortality for Your Own Use" (uncollected). On Guido Bruno and his various publications, see *The Little Magazine* by Frederick J. Hoffman, Charles Allen, and Carolyn F. Ulrich (Princeton, 1946), pp. 27-28.

18. *The Marianne Moore Reader* (Viking, 1961), p. 255. Future references will cite this book as *Reader*.

19. She met Eliot at Edmund Wilson's apartment in New York

in 1933. He had come back to the United States to give lectures at Harvard and at the University of Virginia (published, respectively, as *The Use of Poetry and the Use of Criticism* and *After Strange Gods*). Pound, who returned to the United States in 1939 to promote his views of Mussolini, called upon MM in New York.

20. *New York Times Book Review*, October 4, 1959.

21. *The Letters of Ezra Pound*, ed. D. D. Paige (New York, 1950), pp. 142-144.

22. See T. S. Eliot, *Poems Written in Early Youth*, ed. John Hayward; early poems by Wallace Stevens in A. Walton Litz, *Introspective Voyager* (New York, 1972), Appendix.

23. T. S. Eliot quoted "The Talisman" in his introduction to her *Selected Poems* (1935), but MM did not include it in any of her books except *Observations*.

24. Pound, *Letters*, p. 40.

25. Statement in response to a questionnaire, quoted in *Little Review Anthology*, p. 372.

26. In a brief article in the *Christian Science Monitor* "The Author Speaks: Poetry" (Dec. 24, 1958), MM said, "I think books are chiefly responsible for my doggedly self-determined efforts to write; books and verisimilitude; I like to describe things."

27. Voice of America broadcast, 1963.

28. Ibid.

29. "Some of the Authors of 1951, Speaking for Themselves: Marianne Moore," *New York Herald Tribune Book Review*, October 7, 1951, pp. 14-16.

30. At least a dozen of the poems published in magazines before 1920 were not included in any of her books. In addition, there are many "unfinished" poems she never published. See *Unfinished Poems by Marianne Moore* (The Philip H. and A.S.W. Rosenbach Foundation, Philadelphia, 1972).

31. The *File End*, Aug. 20, 1916 (Rosenbach). Earlier issues were called the *File*.

32. John Warner Moore was commissioned Ensign in the U. S. Naval Militia on March 2, 1916. During his period of training he continued to search for a position as minister of a Presbyterian Church, but it is evident from his letters to "Mole" and "Rat" that he loved his work with the men of the Navy. When he left Chatham to report for duty at Norfolk, Mrs. Moore made every effort to insure his return to the Ogden Memorial Church after a

leave of absence. He wrote firmly, "As it is, *I couldn't* get back to *Chatham* for three years, if *I wanted* to come back, *if the war were over* and peace declared *tomorrow*. . . ." The strain in their relationship is evident in the fact that he addressed her in these letters as "Dear Mother" rather than "Mole," and signed himself "Warner" (JWM to MWM, December 7, 1917). Mrs. Moore's opposition to his engagement was as firmly rebuffed. "Badger" had come of age, and was ready to live an independent life. In the same letter (December 20, 1917) affirming his love and respect for his fiancée, he described his feelings on conducting his first funeral service—for a member of the Naval Brigade he had been in the year before. These are some of the circumstances underlying the poem "A Grave."

33. *Reader*, p. 256.

34. The late poem "Charity Overcoming Envy" is about an allegorical design in a tapestry; but the eye of the poet is upon the object seen in it, and the end of the poem is characteristically inscrutable.

35. *Predilections* (New York, 1955), p. 4.

36. Review of *Poems* (1921) in the *Dial*, 75 (1923), p. 595. In a letter to TSE about the pieces to be included in *Collected Poems* (1951), MM said that " 'Those Various Scalpels' seems to me to grow tired toward the end but if you think it would pass muster I am willing to include it" (August 4, 1950).

37. MM submitted this poem to *The Lantern* after it had been rejected by several magazines.

38. The metaphor is taken from a passage in the *Greek Anthology* that she had copied into her 1910-1921 RD (Rosenbach 1250/2), p. 56.

39. In the CN (Rosenbach 1250/23), p. 31, the following entry occurs: "Badger: I don't know. I suppose I'm stubborn—I feel sometimes as if the wave can go over me if it likes and I'll be there when it's gone by" (p. 31).

40. The painting is of a disguised St. Christopher carrying a child across a river.

41. The resemblance to Poe's "A City in the Sea" is more evident in the early draft of MM's "A Graveyard in the Middle of the Sea." That draft began "The cypresses of experience dead, yet indestructible by circumstances; shivering and strong in the water; not green," and the stanza (later omitted) ends "every-

thing everywhere / Yet nothing; because nowhere; infinity defined at last, still infinity because there / where nothing is." This may have been the version sent to Ezra Pound. Even the more experimental little magazines could hardly have printed it in that form because the extremely long lines would have required an exceptionally wide page. The draft has four stanzas of six lines each, and end-rhymes that are "nested" in the final version.

42. *The Letters of Ezra Pound*, ed. D. D. Paige (New York, 1950), pp. 141-143. He had acted for a time as poetry editor of the *New Freewoman*. When this was renamed the *Egoist* Richard Aldington as sub-editor had charge of the poetry selections. After Aldington volunteered for service in the war, T. S. Eliot (on Pound's suggestion) became assistant editor. Throughout, Pound maintained an informal relation with the editorial staff.

43. MM to EP, January 9, 1919, in *Marianne Moore*, ed. Charles Tomlinson (Englewood Cliffs, N. J., 1969), p. 16.

44. Ibid., p. 17.

45. Conversation with LS, February, 1953.

46. MM to EP, note 43, supra.

47. Gordon Craig's work was of interest to other modern poets, including Wallace Stevens. For his association with Stieglitz, see Dorothy Norman, *Alfred Stieglitz: An American Seer* (New York, 1973), pp. 107-109. Marianne Moore's poem to him, "To a Man Working his Way Through the Crowd," appeared in the *Egoist*, April 1, 1915.

48. Note 43, supra, p. 17.

49. The line in her poem stems from a statement about Duns Scotus that she copied into her notebook from Henry Osborn Taylor's *The Medieval Mind*: "if you enter his lists you are lost. The right way to attack him is to stand outside and laugh." RD 1916-1921 (Rosenbach 1250/2) p. 141. She did not include this reference in her notes to this poem.

50. After her first stay in New York with HD, Bryher accompanied her on a visit to California. From there she wrote MM offering to give her $5,000 so that she and her mother might spend some time in England, where MM could do some writing. The offer was refused. In letters to her brother about conversations with and letters from Bryher as well as HD, nothing is said about plans for the publication of a book, but this had been mentioned in earlier letters from HD to MM.

51. TSE to MM, April 3, 1921.

52. MM to TSE, April 19, 1921.

53. MM to Bryher. This extract is from a long letter to Bryher (July 7, 1921) that includes an account of MM's first impression of HD when they were students, as well as a description of an albino rattlesnake at the Bronx Zoo. It is amusing that she here refers to herself as a pterodactyl, one of the winged saurians thought of as flying dragons. Bryher had addressed her as "Dactyl" in the letter referred to in note 50, supra.

54. William Carlos Williams, *Autobiography* (New York, 1951), p. 146.

55. Ibid., p. 171.

56. Alfred Kreymborg, *Troubadour* (New York, 1957), p. 260. This description is perhaps not accurate in every detail. MM said that she did not meet Stevens until 1941 on the occasion of the "Entretiens de Pontigny" at Mt. Holyoke College.

57. Review in *Contact* no. 4 (Summer 1921), p. 6. A striking statement in this review refers to "the impersonal, inevitable attrition of life," reminding one of the phrase in "Black Earth," about the elephant's skin as "cut into checkers by rut upon rut of unpreventable experience."

2

1. Nicholas Joost, *Scofield Thayer and the Dial* (Carbondale, Illinois, 1964), pp. 26-27.

2. Ibid., pp. 102-103. See also William Wasserstrom, Introduction to *A Dial Miscellany* (Syracuse, N. Y., 1973) and Frederick J. Hoffman et al., *The Little Magazine* (Princeton, N. J., 1946), pp. 196-206.

3. Marianne Moore, "The Dial: Part I" in *Life and Letters Today*, 27 (1940), 175-183, and "The Dial: Part II" in *Life and Letters Today*, 28 (1941), 3-9.

4. Scofield Thayer to MM, July 11, 1921. All quotations from the correspondence of MM and Scofield Thayer are from the Scofield Thayer papers now on deposit in the Beinecke Library of Yale University.

5. MM to Scofield Thayer, July 27, 1921.

6. The painters Demuth, Sheeler, and Hartley were associated with the group of writers whose meetings are described in W. C.

CHAPTER 2

Williams, *I Wanted to Write a Poem*, and in Alfred Kreymborg's *Troubadour*. E. E. Cummings' paintings and drawings were of interest to MM. She formed a close friendship with Gaston Lachaise and his wife; the *Dial* published a number of his sculptures, and Thayer commissioned him to do a bust of himself. He also did a bust of Dr. Watson, and one of Marianne Moore that is now in the Metropolitan Museum.

7. Harold Rosenberg, "The Philosophy of Put-Togethers," the *New Yorker*, March 11, 1972, p. 117.

8. Ibid., p. 122.

9. Virginia Woolf, *Granite and Rainbow* (London, 1958), p. 22.

10. His daughter has been unable to locate the papers, and thinks they may have been accidentally destroyed.

11. Scofield Thayer to MM, August 19, 1924.

12. MM to Scofield Thayer, August 26, 1924.

13. Scofield Thayer to MM, August 28, 1924.

14. MM to Scofield Thayer, August 26, 1924.

15. MM to Scofield Thayer, September 2, 1924.

16. MM to Scofield Thayer, September 9, 1924.

17. MM to Scofield Thayer, September 15, 1924.

18. Ibid. The letter gives more sources for the quotations.

19. Scofield Thayer to MM, September 22, 1924.

20. MM to Scofield Thayer, September 22, 1924.

21. Scofield Thayer to MM, September 24, 1924.

22. MM to JWM, March 18, 1923.

23. Rosenbach 1251/7, p. 16.

24. Ibid., pp. 18-19 (crossed-out words are not included).

25. The hint for the opening begins on p. 12 of the *Poetry Workbook* (Rosenbach 1251/7), p. 12, where marriage is not only termed an "institution" and "enterprise" but referred to as "this piece of prevailing unapologized for prose." On the same page there are notes from Darwin's *The Expression of the Emotions in Man and Animals* (London, 1972).

Of the many extraordinary phrases dashed down in this workbook one that I find especially interesting is the reference to marriage as a crucible "exhaling the glassy essence of vitality," an obvious recollection of Shakespeare's lines "but man, proud man, / dressed in a little brief authority, / most ignorant of what he's most assured / His glassy essence . . ." (*Measure for Measure* II, 2, ll. 118-121).

26. *Manikin* Number Three (Monroe Wheeler, New York).

27. Rosenbach 1250/23, p. 59.

28. MM to JWM, February 20, 1921.

29. MM to JWM, April 4, 1921.

30. See William Carlos Williams, *Autobiography*.

31. "Marianne Moore," *Dial*, 78 (1925), 399.

32. Ibid.

33. The map of Mount Rainier showing the octopus pattern of its glaciers may be seen in the collection of Marianne Moore papers at the Rosenbach Museum as may a photograph of Marianne and her brother ascending the mountain. In the poem she uses the Indian name of the mountain, Tacoma.

34. In a letter to Scofield Thayer (September 15, 1924) MM had given an account of the many books from which she had culled statements about unicorns. He made a very interesting point in his reply: "Some times your quotations . . . suggest an opposite, or perhaps I should say converse, meaning to that intended by the author. . . . From your poem I had gathered that Sir John Hawkins had deduced the presence of lions from the existence of unicorns. But, come to think of it, I am not sure that one does not get an even more elaborately caressing overtone from deducting the natural historical from the mythological."

35. The authors of the unsigned Comment section of the *Dial*, usually one of the editors, are identified in Nicholas Joost and Alvin Sullivan, *The Dial: Two Author Indexes* (Carbondale, Illinois, 1971).

36. Both Pound and Eliot use quotations from actual conversations as well as from literary sources; often the reason is to suggest ironic contrasts. In *The Cantos*, however, Pound's introduction and later repetitions of certain quotations serve the purpose of "Subject-rhyme" (*Letters*, p. 210).

37. See D. R. Welland, "Half-Rhyme in Wilfred Owen," *Review of English Studies* N. S. 1 (1950), pp. 226ff.

38. *Predilections*, pp. 44-45.

39. Basil Lann, "Bach Defended against the Second Viennese School," the *Listener*, 26 August, 1971.

40. "Poetry watches life with affection" is part of her statement to the National Book Association in 1952. For the "impersonal, inevitable attrition of life" see chap. 1, note 42, supra.

3

1. MM to JWM, undated [January, 1916].

2. MM to JWM, January 14, 1916.

3. MM to JWM, September 19, 1920 refers to this.

4. MM to JWM. Thayer had already asked her to review *The Sacred Wood*.

5. The *Dial*, 76 (1924), 343-346.

6. "Virginia Woolf," *Horizon*, 3 (1941), 313.

7. "It is Not Forbidden to Think," the *Nation*, 142 (1936), 680.

8. "Sweeney Agonistes," *Poetry*, 42 (1933), 106-107.

9. "Comment," the *Dial*, 84 (1928), 179.

10. See "Unanimity and Fortitude," *Poetry*, 49 (1937).

11. "Comment," the *Dial*, 83 (1927), 540.

12. "Comment," the *Dial*, 85 (1928), 89.

13. "Comment," the *Dial*, 81 (1926), 535.

14. Rosenbach, 1251/27. Cf. "Comment," the *Dial*, 80 (1926), 44.

15. Cf. the *Dial*, 76 (1924), 343-346 with *Predilections*, pp. 115-118.

16. The *Dial*, supra, n. 5, 344.

17. Ibid., 343.

18. See *Tell Me, Tell Me*, p. 5, p. 47; *Reader*, Foreword.

19. The first two are reprinted in *Predilections*; the third in *Reader*.

20. "Announcement," the *Dial*, 86 (1929), 90.

21. Voice of America broadcast, p. 2.

22. Ibid.

23. See "The Ways Our Poets Have Taken Since the War," *Reader*, pp. 241-242.

24. "Comment," the *Dial*, 85 (1928), 89.

25. "Emily Dickinson," *Poetry*, 41 (1924), 87.

26. "Unanimity and Fortitude," *Poetry*, 48 (1936), 270.

27. Review of *A Draft of Thirty Cantos*, the *Criterion*, 13 (1933-34), 484.

28. Ibid., p. 482.

29. Supra, n. 1, p. 49.

30. Supra, n. 10, p. 272.

31. Supra, n. 19, p. 482.

32. "Well Moused, Lion," the *Dial*, 76 (1924), 87.

33. "The Cantos," *Poetry*, 39 (1931).

34. Review of Charlotte Brontë, the *Criterion*, 11 (1931-32), 717.

35. Supra, n. 32, p. 89.

36. Ibid., p. 84.

37. "The Man Who Died Twice," the *Dial*, 77 (1924), 169.

38. Supra, n. 10, p. 272.

39. Ibid., p. 271.

40. "Comment," the *Dial*, 86 (1929), 269.

41. "A Modest Expert," the *Nation*, 163 (1936), 354.

42. Supra, n. 32, p. 86.

43. Ibid., p. 90.

44. "A Draft of XXX Cantos" [review], the *Criterion*, 13 (1933-34), 483.

45. Supra, n. 32, p. 90.

46. "An Eagle in the Ring," the *Dial*, 75 (1923), 504.

47. "Announcement," the *Dial*, 86 (1929), 90.

48. Comment on a student's manuscript, March 1953 (Canaday).

49. "Thistles Dipped in Frost," the *Dial*, 77 (1924), 252.

50. Ibid.

51. "Comment," the *Dial*, 81 (1926), 536.

52. Supra, n. 29, p. 169.

53. "Memory's Immortal Gear," the *Dial*, 80 (1926), 417.

54. In *Tell Me, Tell Me, Granite, Steel, and Other Topics* (New York, 1965), pp. 5-7 and pp. 20-25.

55. *Complete Poems* (New York, 1967), p. 240.

56. Interview with Donald Hall, *Reader*, p. 273.

4

1. See RD 1916-21 (Rosenbach 1250/2), pp. 48ff. for notes on luxury, preceded by a reference to ibis and ichneumon. The set of Gibbon had belonged to MM's grandfather.

2. Her letter to Dr. Ditmars and his reply may be read in the Rosenbach collection: her query concerned the sustenance of the jerboa, what served for food and drink in the African desert.

3. RD 1924-30 (Rosenbach 1250/5), p. 172 has a drawing of an Egyptian toy, ichneumon with snake, from the book *Children's Toys of Bygone Days*; the entry was made in 1928. R.D. 1930-43 (Rosenbach 1250/6), p. 48 has a drawing of a box "in the form of a duck with reverted head and the lid formed of wings pivoting on a nob," copied from *Illustrated London News* 21 Nov. 1936. In the same notebook, p. 4, we find the stone locust for the keeping of locust oil, from *Illustrated London News* of 26 May 1930.

4. My use of these terms (subject, countersubject, etc.) is validated by MM. See, for example, her notes on the structure of fugue in a Music Notebook (Rosenbach 1251/16).

5. With characteristic quickness of mind, MM had singled out the jerboa from a number of desert rodents described in an article in the *National Geographic Magazine*, May 1918, "Smaller Mammals of North America." Her celebration of its elegance as equalling that of the finest artisans results from her ability to observe the intricacies of both expert craftsmanship and natural phenomena. See, for example, notes in RD 1916-21 (Rosenbach, 1250/2), *Variation of Plants and Animals under Domestication*, followed immediately by notes on the design of a piece of velvet in an exhibition of Persian objects at the Bush Terminal. She particularly noted floral pattern "on a field of light brown ivory so that the whole bears the likeness of the leopard's spots" and, in another piece, "shapes of blue and eggplant colors" (pp. 101-102).

The flageolet on the other hand was a family tradition. MM must often have heard her mother's account of its being played by her grandfather in Carlisle. After the instrument had been given to MWM in 1938, her vivid recollections of dancing to it in her childhood were recorded by MM: "First upon my heel then upon my toe—and round my body will go. Round and round *my body will go!!!*" CN 1935-69 (Rosenbach 1251/1), pp. 60, 62.

6. From the context it appears that they had all seen "the Californian's photograph" probably during the time MM and MWM visited JWM when he was stationed in Bremerton. The maternal mouse in the photograph would obviously have amused them all, given the fact that MWM was called Mouse by her children.

7. MM to JWM, August 6, 1932, has a draft of the poem with a different fourth line ("ambidextrous legs"). The candelabrum

tree belonged to Lord Balfour, whom JWM had apparently met on Lord Balfour's visit to America.

8. These clippings are in the collection at the Rosenbach Museum.

9. MM to JWM, September 3, 1933 and undated subsequent letter of October 1933.

10. After the poem had been accepted MM saw a movie, "Wild Cargo" and wrote in a letter to JWM, "For me personally it was a great moment when I perceived the white water buffalo for I have been worrying about my BUFFALO and wondering if I could have dreamed. . . . As I would have had to throw away the whole description of it if I couldn't use the word albino as a rhyme. No other word would do" (April 23, 1934). Cf. also her early poem in *Tipyn O'Bob*, "Beasts of Burden."

11. MM to JWM, October 1933.

12. In an interview with a reporter for the Philadelphia *Inquirer*.

13. MM to JWM, June 1, 1934.

14. See RD, 1930-1943, pp. 98ff.

15. See M. Oldfield Howey, *The Encircled Serpent* (Philadelphia, 1926), pp. 256, 321 and *passim*, and L. Newton Hayes, *The Chinese Dragon* (Shanghai, 1922).

16. TSE to MM, June 20, 1934.

17. That is to say, I intend something like Aristotle's distinction between simple and complex plots as described in *Poetics*.

18. At the time when MM was studying biology at Bryn Mawr there was greater emphasis on vertebrate paleontology than is common today. See for example H. G. Seeley, *Dragons of the Air, An Account of Extinct Flying Reptiles* (London, 1901).

19. MM to JWM, July 19, 1932. This letter is of major interest for its detailed and amusing account of a "big day" at the Museum of Natural History in which she observed a number of creatures that appear in her poems, and some that do not. She described tortoises of Burma and Ceylon "ivory white and seal brown, the under side . . . with a central pattern and two side-paths of marking, like wall-paper put on without reference to matching the figure. I stood and blinked at the turtle and finally made a drawing for I knew I would want later to look at it again."

20. The film showing the tuatera is described in the letter from MM to JWM, December 3, 1932. Her conversation about the

plumet basilisks diving is related in the next letter to JWM, December 19, 1932.

21. The letter containing Mrs. Moore's tribute to "Rat" lacks the first page and cannot be dated precisely. It belongs to a group sent to reach Warner Moore and his family in Samoa before Christmas, and probably is close in time to another in which Mrs. Moore had also inserted a few handwritten lines, saying that "Rat's basilisk is beautiful. But he didn't grow fast. I think he is almost finished." This letter is internally dated as of December 8, 1932.

22. In RD 1916-21 (Rosenbach 1250/2), p. 127.

23. Notes on lizards and dragons appear in RD 1916-21 (Rosenbach 1250/2) and 1921-22 (Rosenbach 1250/3), but the drawing in RD 1924-30 (Rosenbach 1250/5) has a direct bearing on lines in the poem. The notes on books consulted for this poem are in RD 1930-43 (Rosenbach 1250/6).

24. RD 1924-30 (Rosenbach 1250/5), p. 172.

25. Cf. MM to JWM, July 9, 1933: "But now I am on my *story*, after a recess of one year. . . . I am not discarding the essential content but I doubt if I can ever get it fluent and natural as it has to be if it comes out. It is plausible enough for any poor gudgeon needing novels, to publish, but I would rather perish than let it be seen as it is." The whole subject of her continuing interest in her story-novel needs separate study and will be illuminated when the manuscript versions of it and related manuscripts are published. At a Bryn Mawr party, the young James Flexner said to MM, "I guess you wouldn't stoop to write a novel, would you?" and she replied, "I would if I could; I'd call it reach up. It's the most fascinating form of literature there is, I think" (MM to JWM, October 29, 1933).

26. She told me this in a telephone conversation, which reflected her eagerness to have the play performed. See also her correspondence with Lincoln Kirstein.

27. The earlier version of "The Student" incorporates more specific contemporary references, naming Einstein, for example.

28. See MWM to JWM, June 5, 1932 and June 26, 1932, in which she copied this passage from Williams' letter to her.

29. After the appearance of *Collected Poems* in 1951, I expressed regret that MM had deleted the lines about "the college student named Ambrose." She said that a number of other readers

had felt the same way, including R. P. Blackmur, who was "quite fierce on the subject."

30. MWM to JWM, January 29, 1933.

31. MM to JWM, June 11 and June 18, 1933.

32. Eliot had returned to America to give the Norton lectures at Harvard which became his *The Use of Poetry and the Use of Criticism*. MM met him at a cocktail party at Edmund Wilson's apartment in New York.

33. TSE to MM, January 31, 1934.

34. MM to JWM, March 1, 1934.

35. Undated letter of 1934, written after JWM's return from Samoa and move to Norfolk, Va.

36. MCM to JWM, June 7, 1934.

37. George Plank to MM, September 8, 1935.

38. For example, Donald Hall in *Marianne Moore: The Cage and the Animal* (New York, 1970) or Geoffrey Hartman in his excellent commentary on her Spoken Arts recording made at Yale.

39. MM to JWM, October 25, 1934 describes an event that underlies the myth of Psyche in this poem. She asked a girl in a bookstore in New York to "get a large book out of the window that was fastened open with elastics—copied something out of it . . . about Aristophanes and his version of the fable of Cupid and Psyche. . . ."

The genesis of this poem was earlier. She wrote to JWM on December 11, 1932, "It also came to me after my journey to the Museum, that I should write something on the tiger swallow-tail, the tiger-salamander, and the tiger horse, and I said so to Mouse, and she said, 'Don't be bizarre.' Now I *hate* that, for it is more serious than leverets for me. I wish you would speak to Mouse about damping me." This notation of her original concept accounts for the imagery in the poem describing the butterfly as "*trampling* the air and having *drover*-like tenacity" and other equine virtues or traits (italics added). Was "Half-Deity" omitted from later editions because of Mouse's lack of enthusiasm for it?

40. "To explain grace requires a curious hand" is one of her mother's saying that MM adapted for a liberating effect in her poem. "One may be a blameless / bachelor and it is but a step / to Congreve" rephrases another of Mrs. Moore's wry remarks.

5

1. The quotations from the poems in this chapter will follow the text of *What Are Years* (New York, 1941) and *Nevertheless* (New York, 1944).

2. TSE to MM, August 29, 1941.

3. MM to JWM, April 29, 1941.

4. H. S. Latham (Vice-President of Macmillan) to MM, October 23, 1943.

5. H. S. Latham to MM, January 5, 1944.

6. MM to Miss Katherine King (Latham's secretary), January 19, 1944.

7. The drafts are in the Moore collection at the Rosenbach Museum.

8. Conversation with LS, March 1953.

9. "What Are Years?" broadcast, April 5, 1940.

10. See also MM to JWM, January 16, 1941.

11. The first published version is in the text of "Part of a Novel" as it was printed in *Poetry*, June 1932. It is considerably longer than the version printed in *What Are Years*.

12. See RD 1916-1921 (Rosenbach 1250/2) where MM entered this quotation.

13. MM was thoroughly professional in her desire to have her books reviewed by her peers rather than the predictable person usually chosen by periodical editors. Before and after her work at the *Dial*, she went out of her way to do justice in her own reviewing of poets.

14. *New York Times Book Review*, October 15, 1944. Among other things that pleased her in a later Auden review was that "he defends my funny prosody" (MM to JWM, October 15, 1944).

15. The prose that MM thought might accompany the poems in *Nevertheless* included "certain reviews of E. E. Cummings, Gertrude Stein, William Carlos Williams, T. S. Eliot, Conrad Aiken, John Stewart Curry, and an essay on Henry James; possibly one on Sir Francis Bacon, a short comment on Dürer, and one on, Oliver Goldmith," as well as an article on documentary films (MM to Harold Latham, February 18, 1944). Some of these pieces were included in *Predilections*.

16. For example, she reported that *Poetry* had paid $5 for a

review of Williams and the *Hound and Horn* paid $25 for the
Henry James article (MM to JWM [April] 1934). In 1943 her
combined income from royalties on her books and for reading
manuscripts for the Macmillan Co. totaled $310, supplemented by
less than a thousand dollars from other sources. This was less
than she had earned as editor of the *Dial* (MM to JWM, January
26 [1944]).

17. MM attended a reading of poetry by Alfred Kreymborg
and Harriet Monroe at the Pratt Institute. In spite of Miss Monroe's inability to admire poems of MM, great courtesy was shown
to her on this visit to New York including roast duck for dinner at
the Moore apartment. "We agree about nothing intellectual but
admire one another's humanity."

At the end of the poetry-reading Harriet Monroe and Alfred
Kreymborg were unable to tell a naive questioner what poetry
is. MM wrote to Warner, "I wanted to get up and say what
poetry might be . . . and how poetry and other forms of art manifest . . . transfiguration experienced and communicated" (MM to
JWM, November 6, 1932).

18. A comical letter (MM to JWM, May 21, 1943) describes
collecting elephant hairs at a performance of the circus—
equipped with food for the elephants and a small pair of scissors
blunted with a cork. Helped by one elephant-tender but refused
by another, "from the small herd away from the benevolent tender
I got three for myself by administering peanuts the children had
dropped . . . the theft was not a matter of any great subtlety."

19. MM to JWM, May 20, 1944.

20. MM to JWM, April 23, 1934, refers to elephants in the
movie "Wild Cargo" and to an article she had saved on "temple
of the tooth" and another on "white elephants."

21. In his Essay on Dramatic Poetry, Dryden says of Ben Jonson, "I admire him, but I love Shakespeare."

22. A few of these phrases have been noted earlier, but there
are other important examples, especially "the power of the visible
is the invisible" in the poem "Light is Speech," as well as the
title itself. But there is no poem in which the sayings of Mary
Warner Moore are so powerfully incorporated as "In Distrust of
Merits."

23. CN 1935-69 (Rosenbach 1251/1).

24. Ibid., pp. 57, 59, 81, 101. Mrs. Moore was recalling a verse

in 1 John 2: "he that hateth his brother is in darkness"; and probably also 2 Corinthians 3, 4.

25. Vera Brittain, *England's Hour* (New York, 1941), p. 145.

26. CN 1935-69 (Rosenbach 1251/1), p. 97.

27. Ibid.

28. Ibid., p. 105.

29. Conversation with LS, March 1953.

30. Haile Selassie's resistance to Mussolini, the first real challenge to fascism, evoked the Moores' admiration. See RD 1930-43, p. 120.

31. Cf. Erwin Panofsky, *The Life and Art of Albrecht Dürer* (Princeton, N. J., 1971), p. 196.

32. MM to JWM, September 8 [1944].

33. The quotations are her notes on John F. Genung, *The Epic of the Inner Life* (Boston, 1900).

34. CN 1935-69 (Rosenbach 1251/1), p. 104. Mrs. Moore's statement that "All are suffering from the disease, myself" (p. 104) obviously stems from Pope's "this long disease, my life" in the "Epistle to Dr. Arbuthnot."

35. MM wrote of Wallace Stevens that "like Handel in the patterned correspondences of Sonata 1, he has not been rivalled" (*Predilections*, p. 32).

36. The phrase "heart heard" in an early draft of "What Are Years?" is one of the rare echoes of another poet—from Gerard Manley Hopkins, "What heart heard of, ghost guessed," l. 13 in "Spring and Fall." MM owned a copy of the 2nd ed. (1931) of Hopkins' poems and made some entries on his notebooks in RD 1930-43 (Rosenbach 1250/6). When asked to review them for *Poetry*, she suggested Elizabeth Bishop instead of herself.

37. Quoted in Panofsky, p. 171.

38. "Still Falls the Rain," in Edith Sitwell, *Street Songs* (London, 1942).

39. Although too skilful an artist to make any oversimplified use of it, MM was acquainted with the psychology of Freud, as some entries in the Reading Diaries indicate.

40. These drafts are in the Moore collection at the Rosenbach Museum. We are indebted to Marianne Moore's niece and namesake, who spent the summer of 1965 with her aunt in Brooklyn helping to prepare for the move to New York, for persuading her aunt not to destroy early drafts of some of her poems.

41. MM to Mrs. John Warner Moore (née Constance Eustis) September 19 [1932]. MM and her mother were staying at the house of Constance Moore's sister. Manuscripts to complete were taken along; but as MM wrote at a later time from a camp on Black Lake, New York, near Utica, that also belonged to Constance Moore's family, "I would rather observe the wild animals and the herbage than do my work" (MM to JWM, September 9, 1933).

42. MM to JWM, July 19, 1932.

43. MM to JWM, November 6, 1932.

44. Cf. Sidney, the Psalms have "an unspeakable and everlasting beauty to be seene by the eyes of the minde" (*Defence of Poetry* in *Elizabethan Critical Essays*, ed. G. Gregory Smith, Oxford, 1904, I, p. 182). The metaphor stems from Plato, *Republic* VII, 533 d. 2: "the eye of the Soul," lifted upward by dialectic. The whole passage is relevant to MM's poem.

45. MM to JWM, January 15, 1941.

46. Her nieces have confirmed this. A very different example is her writing "Hometown Piece for Messrs. Alston and Reese" to the tune of "Li'l baby, baby, don't say a word: Mama goin' to buy you a mocking bird."

47. MM to JWM, January 4, 1945.

48. MM to JWM, January 11, 29, and 31, 1945.

49. MM to JWM, January 4, 1945.

50. MM to JWM, January 12, 1945.

51. MM to JWM, January 14, 1945.

52. MM wrote JWM on April 3, 1945, that "Henry Allen Moe came over. . . . And he said that the Guggenheim Foundation aims to give me a Fellowship! . . . That extra funds were available that ought to be used." He overcame her scruples about accepting the money and approved the work she had already begun on the Stifter translation as a suitable project.

53. A characteristic example is given in MM to JWM, November 27, 1934: "We are having a *terrible* time with a poem on three mocking birds that I am writing. . . . Mouse blinks and . . . reflects and bleats and then . . . returns it for improvement! And the pattern is such as not to admit of *any* change!!"

The necessary economies observed by MM and her mother were often fiercely administered by the latter. "Mouse makes me stand there abjectly milking out the pennies after I have been on an errand and usually takes away a 5 bill and gives me a dollar or takes away a dollar and gives me change. . . ." (MM to JWM, undated but clearly of June 1934.)

54. TSE to MM, July 16, 1947.

55. Her comment on this poem is enlightening: " 'A Face' sounds to me like conversation. I do not limit its implication by saying what face; it is not so long that it overtaxes the attention; it is positive, an affirmation—not a revenge" (*Poet's Choice*, ed. by Paul Engle and Joseph Langland, New York, 1962, p. 11).

56. TSE to MM, September 7, 1950.

57. J. M. Keynes, *Essays in Biography* (New York, 1963), pp. 312-313.

58. Quoted in the *Listener*, June 6, 1974, p. 727.

6

1. W. H. Auden to MM, undated [probably January 1945].

2. MM to W. H. Auden, January 16, 1945.

3. MM to W. H. Auden, February 13, 1945.

4. MM to JWM, February 2, 1945.

5. MM to JWM, April 26 [1945].

6. Ibid. The contract for *What Are Years* included an option on her next two books of poetry. *Nevertheless* having been published, and Macmillan having foregone the right to publish the *Fables*, the option covered *Collected Poems* (1951) and from then on MM was free to give her later books to Viking.

7. A change in the staff at Reynal and Hitchcock took place at the end of 1947, and the firm informed MM that the *Fables* might be a loss. Monroe Engel, who had moved from Reynal and Hitchcock to Viking, then asked her to plan with him for the publication of this book. See MM to Harry Levin, January 4, 1948; Monroe Engel to MM, March 16, 1948; MM to Monroe Engel, June 4, 1948.

8. Work on the *Fables* was necessarily interrupted by the preparation of the text for her *Collected Poems*. Although in her contract she had set a 1951 date for the completion of the *Fables* translation, she did not finish it until 1953.

9. This is the chief point of his article "Translation and Tradition," *Encounter* 1 (1953). Some statements in this article are in-

accurate; but Auden's insight compensates for the questionable judgments.

10. *The Fables of La Fontaine*, trans. by Marianne Moore (New York, 1954), p. x. The examples from Pound are taken from "The Seafarer" and from "Planh for the Young English King" (translated from Bertrand de Born).

11. There probably was a man named Aesop who composed fables, since Herodotus refers to him as if he were an acknowledged writer, of perhaps the sixth-century B.C. Although a few earlier fables exist (in Hesiod and Archilochus) in the fifth and later centuries fables were traditionally attributed to Aesop. The "morals" attached to the fables in the versions we know may have been added at a later time. See E. Chambry, *Aesopi Fabulae* (Paris, 1925-26) and B. E. Perry, *Aesopica* (Urbana, Illinois, 1952). An excellent selection with a helpful introduction may be found in the Penguin edition *Fables of Aesop*, trans. by S. S. Handford (1954).

12. Pierre Clarac, *La Fontaine, L'Homme et L'Oeuvre* (Paris, 1947), p. 73.

13. Excerpt from letter of Harry Levin [probably to Walter Pistole], April 14, 1945 (Rosenbach).

14. Ibid.

15. MM to Harry Levin, August 6, 1949. Pound's suggestions for revision were made in 1948-49. These and later suggestions were copied in notes by MM and may be seen at Rosenbach. They show his extraordinary attentiveness to all the aspects of language. He queried words that were "literary" or "dead," and gave more colloquial renderings, of which MM adopted many.

16. MM to Harry Levin, April 2, 1951.

17. MM to Harry Levin, May 5, 1951.

18. "Ce La Fontaine, qui a su faire, un peu plus tard, de si admirable vers variés, ne les saura faire qu'au bout de vingt ans qu'il aura dediés au vers symmétrique; exercises d'entre lesquels *Adonis* est le plus beau." Paul Valéry, "Au Sujet d'Adonis," Introduction to *Adonis par Jean de La Fontaine*, Paris, n. d. (Le Florilège Français, publié sous la direction de J.-L. Vaudoyer), p. xiii. Later in the introduction Valéry notes a line from *Adonis* which to him is worthy of "le grand art et la puissance abstraite de Corneille" (p. xx). A less well-known but equally valuable discussion of La Fontaine by Valéry appears in *Dictionnaire des*

Lettres Françaises: Le Dix-Septième Siècle (Paris, 1954), pp. 556-559. At the end of this article Valéry says of La Fontaine, "Il y a du Molière en lui, par le sens du comique assez amer . . . et il y a du Racine avant Racine, préfiguré dans les vers d'*Adonis*."

19. La Fontaine, *Oeuvres Complètes* (Bibliothèque de la Pléiade, Paris, 1954), I, p. 343.

20. "Enfin, l'invention du 'vers varié' témoigne de la variété même des modes de la vie intérieure de notre poète." Paul Valéry, "La Fontaine," in *Dictionnaire des Lettres Françaises* (n. 14, supra), p. 559.

21. These two fables were among those submitted to Monroe Engel of the Viking Press when the possibility of the publication of her translation was being considered. See MM to Monroe Engel, June 4, 1948.

22. Since the complete edition of *The Fables of La Fontaine Translated by Marianne Moore* has an excellent index of titles, I have not given the numbers of the books and the fables except when quoting passages.

23. Her characteristically individual relish of growing things comes out in a note thanking Miss Frances Steloff (of the Gotham Book Mart) for a present: "I am very fond of herbs and grasses. And apart from the health value . . . the look of it all! The little yellow balls, violet petals, black seeds, rages of yellow and green would charm the most dogged drudge. . . . Herbs are a tonic, Galen, Hippocrates, the Egyptians certainly verified it" (Letter to Frances Steloff, quoted in *Journal of Modern Literature*, Special Gotham Book Mart Issue, April 1975, p. 875).

24. Between the 1668 collection and the "deuxième recueil" of 1678-79, a few fables had been separately published. For details, see "Note Bibliographique" in La Fontaine, *Oeuvres Complètes* I, pp. 853-854 (ed. cit., n. 15 supra).

25. La Fontaine's "Preface" in *Fables trans. Marianne Moore*, pp. 6, 7.

26. Pierre Clarac, *La Fontaine*, p. 127. Chapter XI of Clarac's book is a succinct presentation of the new material and La Fontaine's other innovations in the 1678-79 collection. On his greater independence in drawing upon his older sources and in adapting the new material to his own purposes, see Ferdinand Gohin, *L'Art de La Fontaine* (Paris, 1929), pp. 55-60. See also Noël Richard, *La Fontaine et les "Fables" du Deuxième Recueil* (Paris, 1972).

27. Margaret Guiton, *La Fontaine, Poet and Counterpoet* (New Brunswick, N. J., 1961), p. 183. Professor Guiton stresses the fact that "the later fables . . . fit into a certain tradition of poetry: the great Latin tradition of the first century B.C." (p. 171). Marianne Moore, who had studied Latin at Bryn Mawr with Tenney Frank and Arthur Wheeler, was no novice in her knowledge of Latin poetry, although she had probably not then read Lucretius.

28. Her major poems about animals never set the animal before the reader as primarily a symbol of a virtue or vice. Contrast the panther or the phoenix in the Old English bestiary *Physiologus* with, say, the tiger in her "Elephants" or the horse in "Tom Fool." She does see a moral significance in all she observes; but the look, the movement and behavior of animals are not subordinated to a traditional meaning. The two poems in which traditional symbols appear are "To Statecraft Embalmed" and "Charity Overcometh Envy."

29. "Peut-on trouver aujourd'hui un véritable plaisir à lire les Fables [of La Fontaine], comme si elles fussent tout franchement composées? . . . Quel profit pour son art peut aujourd'hui tirer de cette lecture l'artiste en matière de vers?" Valéry's answer is a positive one. Quoted from his article on La Fontaine in *Dictionnaire des Lettres Françaises* (supra, n. 14), p. 557.

30. Cf. her poem "To the Peacock of France," included in *Observations* (1924) and retained in *Complete Poems* (1968). There are many references to Molière in her early reading diaries.

31. "Ce ne fut jamais un jeu d'oisif que de soustraire un peu de grâce, un peu de durée, a la mobilité des choses de l'esprit; et que de changer ce qui passe en ce qui subsiste." Paul Valéry, "Au Sujet d'Adonis," p. iv (note 18, supra). MM's translation, or the one she quoted, differed from my freer version; but I have no copy of the one she read, probably her own.

7

1. This statement occurs in a draft of a letter, MM to Margaret Marshall, March 23, 1950 (Rosenbach). The sentence was omitted from the retyped copy.

2. See C. Abbot, *Marianne Moore: A Descriptive Bibliography* (unpub. Ph.D. dissertation, Univ. of Texas, 1971).

3. Poetry Workbook, Rosenbach 1251/8, p. 112.

CHAPTER 7

4. Ibid., p. 114.

5. Ibid., p. 114, p. 122.

6. Written in margin from bottom of left-hand side of page 114.

7. Ibid., p. 114; followed by the question, "And on the contrary are scruples always attractive?"

8. Ibid., p. 115.

9. The entry "violets by Dürer even darker" is dated February 16, 1952. A note about implosion is set down on the left hand side of p. 119; an entry on the right hand side is dated April 5, 1952.

10. Bettina Linn, "The Fiction of the Future," *The Yale Review*, 34 (1945), p. 251.

11. The one image reinforces the other, since a jack-in-the-green is a man or boy enclosed in a framework covered with leaves, hence virtually blinded. Probably a figure in Bryn Mawr May Day ceremonies.

12. CN, Rosenbach 1251/1.

13. Rosenbach 1251/8, p. 61.

14. Rosenbach 1251/8, p. 69.

15. Ibid.

16. Ibid., p. 86.

17. Ibid., p. 72.

18. Ibid., p. 71.

19. See for example a note on one of Dr. McGarry's sermons on p. 73 of this notebook. There are others that indicate the help she derived from meditating on his interpretation of Biblical texts.

20. Rosenbach 1251/8, p. 89.

21. Conversation with LS, February, 1953.

22. A reference to the death of Fats Waller with his "feather touch" occurs in the Poetry Workbook, Rosenbach 1251/8, p. 117.

23. Howard Moss to MM, May 15, 1953.

24. MM to Howard Moss, May 17, 1953.

25. Her notes to the poem refer to articles in the *New York Times* about Ted Atkinson and about "Signor Caposella." Reading them abundantly verifies her talent for singling out the detail or the quotation that seem inevitable in the poem.

26. "If I am Worthy, There is no Danger," *Poetry*, 47 (1936), 280.

27. The Moores sometimes referred to themselves as field mice;

Mrs. Moore was sometimes called "Mouse" or "Micey" by MM or JWM.

28. W. H. Auden and Chester Kallman, *The Magic Flute* (New York, 1956). See the introduction for Auden's interpretation of Papageno.

29. Gray Linen Travel Notebook, Rosenbach 1251/19, p. 30. The image of the winding staircase refers to the NBC Opera Theatre for Color Television Viewing where she had watched the performance. See MM to Hildegarde Watson, January 14, 1956, in University of Rochester Library Bulletin, 29 (1976), 138-139.

30. CN, Rosenbach 1250/25, pp. 167-168.

31. Ibid., p. 168.

32. Henrietta Holland, "Marianne Moore's New England," *Yankee*, November 1963, pp. 106, 107.

33. Gray Linen Travel Notebook, Rosenbach 1251/19, p. 13. These notes were made in 1937.

34. Ibid., p. 19. The tombstone was John Lowell's, and the phrase "occasionem cognosce" is part of the inscription. It was used in her much later poem "Occasionem Cognoscere" read at Lowell House, Harvard, in 1963.

35. C. H. Herford, P. and E. M. Simpson, eds., *Bon Jonson* (11 vols., 1925-52) II, p. 370.

36. "Rescue with Yul Brynner."

37. Kenneth Clark, *Leonardo da Vinci* (Cambridge, 1939), p. 42.

38. Poetry Workbook, Rosenbach 1251/8, p. 67.

39. Ibid.

40. The phrase "like flying Old Glory full mast" is copied from the Annual Report of the John Deere Co. (ibid., p. 56). It was used in the poem "Bulwarked Against Fate." Material for part of "An Icosasphere" was taken from "Steel Facts."

41. Ibid., p. 74.

42. Ibid., p. 72.

43. Notes on this begin on p. 86, ibid. Title is given on p. 102.

44. Ibid., p. 67.

45. Ibid., p. 96.

46. "Subject, Predicate, Object," reprinted in *Reader*.

47. Poetry Workbook, Rosenbach 1251/8, p. 168.

48. Published in the *New Yorker*, February 21, 1970, p. 40.

49. Other uncollected late poems include "Enough," "Merci-

fully," and "Like a Wave at the Curl," all published by the *New Yorker*, and others in the Rosenbach archive.

50. RD, Rosenbach 1251/10, p. 15.

51. See Alan Trachtenberg, *Brooklyn Bridge, Fact and Symbol* (New York, 1965).

52. "New York Revisited" in *The American Scene* (New York and London, 1908), p. 72, p. 73, p. 74.

53. Hart Crane, *Collected Poems*, ed. Waldo Frank (New York, 1940), p. 3, p. 4, p. 58.

54. Ibid., p. 4.

55. Trachtenberg, p. 167.

56. Ibid., p. 60.

57. In "He Digesteth 'Harde Yron'."

58. This concept is central in Marianne Moore's view of science as actively related to religion.

59. Trachtenberg, p. 70.

60. See *Reader*, p. 269.

61. See "Senhora Helena," review of Elizabeth Bishop's translation of *The Diary of Helena Morley* in *Poetry*, 94 (1959), 247-249.

62. Crane, *The Bridge*, p. 58.

63. His paintings emphasize the flashing colours as well as the phenomenal structural pattern of the bridge. See the one in Yale University Art Gallery, for example. In an early draft of the poem, MM referred to the bridge as a "Magritte-like thing."

64. MM said it was written in 1910.

65. Cf. the lines in Poe's "Valentine": "And yet there is in this no Gordian knot / Which one might not undo without a sabre, / If one could merely comprehend the plot."

66. *Tell Me, Tell Me*, p. 6.

8

1. Quoted in the *New York Times*, October 8, 1959, p. 3.

2. *Biographia Literaria*, 2 vols., ed. J. Shawcross (Oxford, 1907) II, p. 65.

3. "Feeling and Precision," in *Predilections*, p. 11.

4. As quoted on the jacket of *Collected Poems* (1951).

5. On this subject see "The Poem in the Eye" in John Hol-

lander's *Vision and Resonance* (New York, 1975), pp. 245-287. I cannot, however, agree with his description of her verse form as "pure syllabics from the French" (p. 259).

6. Theodore Spencer, "The Poetry of Sir Philip Sidney" *ELH*, XII (1945), 528. See also Hallett Smith, "English Metrical Psalms in the Sixteenth Century and Their Literary Significance" *HLQ*, IX (1946), 249-271; William Ringler, ed., *The Poems of Sir Philip Sidney* (Oxford, 1962), pp. 505-508; Coburn Freer, *Music for a King* (Baltimore and London, 1972). A letter from MM to W. H. Auden, March 3, 1958, answering his query about the source of her syllabic patterns would be of great significance, but her carbon copy of it has unfortunately been lost and a year's search by the staff at Rosenbach has failed to locate it. Nor is the original among the Auden correspondence acquired by the British Museum to date. The shelf list of her library shows that Auden's letter and her reply were laid in her copy of *The Shield of Achilles*.

7. *Oxford Anthology of American Literature, ed.* William Rose Benét and Norman Holmes Pearson (New York, 1941), p. 1319.

8. T. S. Eliot, review of *Poems* (1921) in *Dial*, LXXV (1923), p. 595.

9. W. H. Auden, review of *Nevertheless, New York Times Book Review*, October 15, 1944, p. 7, p. 20.

10. *Poems of Gerard Manley Hopkins*, ed. Robert Bridges (London, 1930), Author's Preface, p. 4. A letter from MM to her niece Marianne C. Moore, May 5, 1942, refers to Hopkins' discussion of rhythmic patterns in relation to the number of syllables in successive lines, and compares his principle with her practice. MM was well acquainted with Hopkins' thinking on this subject. In this important letter to "Craig II," she explained why she preferred to make the title an indivisible part of the poem, and continued: "Nor do I object to having the line begin weak, or to having what would naturally be the end of the line, come in the middle . . . because I think of the stanza . . . as the unit. . . . In Gerard Hopkins' correspondence with, I think, Robert Bridges, it was brought out that when one follows a ten syllable line with a 9 syllable line, or in any alternation of odd with even, the main pause comes in the middle of the line . . . ; and the long pauses usually between stanzas, come in the middle (of each stanza). I do not try to make this kind of pattern, it is instinctive, and usually I would prefer not to divide words at the

end of the lines but am willing to, for the sake of the larger and more inclusive symmetry." (MM to Marianne Craig Moore, May 5, 1942, quoted by the latter's permission).

11. *Reader*, p. 259, 258.

12. Voice of America Broadcast.

13. As quoted by MM in a talk to students, Bryn Mawr College, February 1952. Cf. her statement that "words cluster like chromosomes and determine the procedure" (*Reader*, p. 263).

14. See, for example, Poetry Workbook, Rosenbach 1251/8, p. 21.

15. Voice of America Broadcast.

16. *Reader*, p. 73 (from *Idiosyncrasy and Technique*, the Ewing Lectures at the University of California, October 3 and 5, 1956).

17. Charles Sanders Peirce, *Collected Papers*, 6 vols., ed. Charles Hartshorne and Paul Weiss, 2nd ed. (Cambridge, Mass., 1960), l. 302, pp. 148-149.

18. Ibid., l. 322, p. 161.

19. Ibid.

20. Ibid., l. 326, p. 170.

21. Ibid., l. 337, pp. 170-171.

22. *A Grammar of Motives* (New York, 1945), p. 487.

23. Ibid.

24. From resumé of "The Poetic Principle Unscientifically Approximated," inaugurating her series of commentaries on contemporary poets at Bryn Mawr College, February 3, 1953 (carbon of TS, Canaday).

25. *Journals and Papers of G. M. Hopkins*, ed. Humphrey House, 2nd ed. (London, 1959), p. 290; "Verse then is speech wholly or partially repeating the same figure of sound."

26. *Biographia Literaria* II, p. 19.

27. *The Letters of Ezra Pound*, ed. D. D. Paige (New York, 1950), p. 236.

28. "Marianne Moore" in *The Egoist*, August 1916, p. 119.

29. "'Keeping Their World Large,'" in *Complete Poems*, p. 145.

30. Supra, n. 12.

31. *Scottish Art Review* VI, 3, cover and pp. 7-8. The treatment of the theme of charity overcoming envy in MM's poem differs considerably from that of the traditional war of the virtues with

the vices as it is described in William Wells' article, "Two Tapes-
tries in the Burrell Collection." Cf. the title of Purcell's Compo-
sition, *The Gordian Knot Untied* (rather than *cut* by the sword
of Alexander), as a gloss on the ending of this poem.

32. Poetry Workbook, Rosenbach 1251/10, p. 29.

33. From comment on a student's MS, February 17, 1953. (Car-
bon of MM's TS, Canaday.)

34. From comment on a student's MS, 1953 [undated]. Carbon
of TS, Canaday.

35. *A Study of History* (London, 1934), III, p. 183.

36. Ibid., III, p. 288.

37. The *New Yorker*, XLVI (February 21, 1970), p. 40.

38. *Marianne Moore Newsletter* I, number 2 (Fall, 1977), re-
produces the drawing by Jean-Jacques Lequeu from which MM
took the title "The Magician's Retreat." The accompanying note
explains that she wrote this above "a small color reproduction of
René Magritte's painting 'Domain of Lights'" that she had
clipped from the *New York Times Magazine* of January 19, 1969,
a painting lent to the Guggenheim Museum by the Peggy Gug-
genheim Foundation.

Magritte gave the title *l'Empire des Lumières* to a number of
his paintings—ten are reproduced in *Magritte: Ideas and Images*
by Harry Torczyner (New York, 1977). *L'Empire des Lumières
II*, Plate 382, was acquired by the Museum of Modern Art in
1951. MM would surely have seen it on her frequent visits. The
imagery of the poem, especially the black tree mass *at the back*
"almost touching the eves" and the "blue glow from the lamp-
post" suggest this painting more than the one lent to the Gug-
genheim Museum. There are other instances where a clipping or
postcard available to MM at a particular time evoked deeper
layers of experience.

Magritte's interest in magic and enchantment deserves men-
tion. In her monograph on Magritte, Suzi Gablik quotes his state-
ment that "it is the power of enchantment which matters." (*Ma-
gritte*, Greenwich, Conn., 1970, p. 170.) The resemblance to the
line in "The Mind is an Enchanting Thing" is striking. See also
his comment on *L'Empire des Lumières* in Torczyner, p. 177.

39. "That Harp You Play So Well" in *Poetry*, VI (1915), p. 70.

40. "Es ist genug" in Henry S. Drinker, *The Bach Chorale
Texts* (New York, n.d.), p. 18.

41. Ben Jonson, *Timber or Discoveries* (London, 1898), Temple Classics ed. xxii, p. 10.

42. "Feed Me, Also, River God," in *Egoist*, August 1916, p. 118.

43. From "Anna Pavlova," in *Predilections*, p. 159.

44. *Biographia Literaria*, I, pp. 14-15. Pound's misquotation appears on p. 77 of *Predilections*.

Bibliography

SELECTED BIBLIOGRAPHY

Bibliographical Note

THREE books on Marianne Moore's poetry are primarily intended to serve as an introduction: those of Donald Hall, Bernard Engel, and George Nitchie. Mr. Engel's book is a chronological survey supplemented by some information about her life. Mr. Nitchie's book takes account of Moore's revisions and is sensitive to the relationship between earlier and later poems. Donald Hall is wise in his understanding of the undogmatic nature of ethical values and belief in the poetry.

Two collections present the ideas of major contemporary writers and critics. The "Marianne Moore Issue" of the *Quarterly Review of Literature* (1948) is notable for the contributions of Elizabeth Bishop, Wallace Stevens, John Crowe Ransom, George Dillon, and Cleanth Brooks. Charles Tomlinson's *Marianne Moore: A Collection of Critical Essays*, contains early articles and reviews by Pound, Eliot, Williams, Kenneth Burke, and significant recent ones by Hugh Kenner, Denis Donoghue, and Henry Gifford.

Grace Schulman's unpublished Ph.D. dissertation, "Marianne Moore: The Poetry of Engagement," has an excellent analysis of Moore criticism and in general is more thorough and more accurate than Engel's and Nitchie's books.

No complete Moore bibliography exists. The two listed below are useful, although Abbot is inaccurate in describing some items.

Abbot, C. *Marianne Moore: A Descriptive Bibliography*. (Ph.D. Diss. University of Texas, 1971).

Sheehy, Eugene P. and K. A. Lohf, comps. *The Achievement of Marianne Moore: A Bibliography, 1907-1957*. New York: New York Public Library, 1958.

Books by Marianne Moore

POETRY

Moore, Marianne. *Poems*. London: The Egoist Press, 1921.
———. *Observations*. New York: The Dial Press, 1924.
———. *Selected Poems. With an Introduction by T. S. Eliot*. New York: Macmillan, 1935. London: Faber and Faber, 1935.
———. *The Pangolin and Other Verse*. London: The Brendin Publishing Company, 1936.
———. *What Are Years*. New York: Macmillan, 1941.
———. *Nevertheless*. New York: Macmillan, 1944.
———. *Collected Poems*. New York: Macmillan, 1951. London: Faber and Faber, 1951.
———, tr. *The Fables of La Fontaine*. New York: Viking, 1954.
———. *Like a Bulwark*. New York: Viking, 1956.
———. *O to Be a Dragon*. New York: Viking, 1959.
———. *The Arctic Ox*. London: Faber and Faber, 1964.
———. *Tell Me, Tell Me: Granite, Steel, and Other Topics*. New York: Viking, 1967.
———. *Complete Poems*. New York: Macmillan and Viking, 1967. London: Faber and Faber, 1968.
———. *Unfinished Poems by Marianne Moore*. Philadelphia: The Philip H. and A.S.W. Rosenbach Foundation, 1972.

PROSE

———. *Predilections*. New York: Viking, 1955.

MISCELLANEOUS

———. *Adelbert Stifter, Rock Crystal, A Christmas Tale*. Rendered into English by Elizabeth Mayer and Marianne Moore. New York: Pantheon Books, 1945.
———. *A Marianne Moore Reader*. New York: Viking, 1959.

————, tr. *Puss in Boots, the Sleeping Beauty and Cinderella: A Retelling of Three Classic Fairy Tales Based on the French of Charles Perrault.* New York: Macmillan, 1963.

————. *Omaggio a Marianne Moore.* Prepared by Vanni Scheiwiller. Milan: All' insegna del Pesce d'Oro, 1964. Ltd. 1000 copies.

RECORDINGS

————. *Marianne Moore Reading Her Own Poems.* Harvard Vocarium Records (P-1064), 1944.

————. *Marianne Moore Reading Her Poems and Fables From La Fontaine.* Caedmon (TC 1025), 1955.

Relevant Studies

Aesop, *Fables of*, trans. by S. S. Handford. Penguin ed., London, 1954.

Auden, W. H. and Chester Kallman. *The Magic Flute.* New York: Random House, 1956.

Beloof, Robert. "Prosody and Tone: The 'Mathematics' of Marianne Moore." *Kenyon Review,* 10, No. 1 (Winter, 1958), 116-123.

Blackmur, R. P. *The Double Agent: Essays in Craft and Elucidation.* New York: Arrow Editions, 1935.

Bogan, Louise. *Achievement in American Poetry, 1900-1957.* Chicago: Henry Regnery, 1951.

Burke, Kenneth. "Motives and Motifs in the Poetry of Marianne Moore." *Accent,* 2 (Spring 1942), 157-169.

Clarac, Pierre. *La Fontaine, L'Homme et L'Oeuvre.* Paris: Boivin, 1947.

Clark, Kenneth. *Leonardo da Vinci.* New York: Macmillan, 1939.

Crane, Hart. *Collected Poems.* New York: Liveright Inc., 1940.

Darwin, Charles. *The Expression of the Emotions in Man and Animals.* New York: D. Appleton and Company, 1873.

Dijkstra, Bram. *The Hieroglyphics of a New Speech: Cubism, Stieglitz and the Early Poetry of William Carlos Williams.* Princeton, N. J.: Princeton University Press, 1969.

Engel, Bernard F. *Marianne Moore.* New York: Twayne Publishers, 1964.

Frankenberg, Lloyd. *Pleasure Dome.* Boston: Houghton-Mifflin, 1949.

Gablik, Suzi. *Magritte.* Greenwich, Conn.: New York Graphic Society, 1970.

Garrigue, Jean. *Marianne Moore.* University of Minnesota Pamphlets on American Writers, No. 50. Minneapolis: Univ. of Minnesota Press, 1965.

Gohin, Ferdinand. *L'Art de la Fontaine.* Paris: Garnier, 1929.

Guiton, Margaret. *La Fontaine, Poet and Counterpoet.* New Brunswick, N. J.: Rutgers University Press, 1961.

Hall, Donald. *Marianne Moore: The Cage and the Animal.* Pegasus American Authors. New York: Western Publishing Company, 1970.

———. "Interview with Marianne Moore." *McCall's,* xciii (Dec., 1965), 74 ff.

Hoffman, Frederick J. et al. *The Little Magazine.* Princeton: Princeton University Press, 1946.

Holland, Henrietta. "Marianne Moore's New England." *Yankee* (Nov., 1963).

Hollander, John. *Vision and Resonance.* Oxford: Oxford University Press, 1975.

Hopkins, Gerard Manley. *Poems of Gerard Manley Hopkins.* Ed. Robert Bridges, rev. ed., 1930; ed. W. H. Gardner, enlarged ed., London: Oxford University Press, 1948.

Jarrell, Randall. "Two Essays on Marianne Moore: The Humble Animal; Her Shield." *Poetry and the Age.* New York: Vintage-Knopf, 1953, pp. 162-166; 167-187.

Jonson, Ben. *Timber or Discoveries.* Temple Classics ed. xxii, London, 1891.

Joost, Nicholas. *Scofield Thayer and the* Dial: *An Illus-*

trated History. Carbondale: Southern Illinois University Press, 1964.

Kenner, Hugh. "Meditation and Enactment." *Poetry: A Magazine of Verse,* CII (May, 1963), 109-115.

———. "Supreme in Her Abnormality." *Poetry: A Magazine of Verse,* LXXXIV (Sept., 1954), 356-363.

———. *The Pound Era.* Berkeley: University of California Press, 1971.

Kreymborg, Alfred. *Troubadour.* New York: Sagamour Press, 1957.

La Fontaine, Jean de. *Oeuvres Complètes.* Bibliothèque de la Pléiade, Paris, 1954.

Levin, Harry. *Grounds for Comparison.* Cambridge, Mass.: Harvard University Press, 1972.

Linn, Bettina. "The Fiction of the Future." *The Yale Review,* XXXIV (Winter, 1945).

Nichols, Lewis. "Talk with Marianne Moore." *The New York Times Book Review,* May 16, 1954, p. 30.

Pearce, Roy Harvey. *The Continuity of American Poetry.* Princeton, N. J.: Princeton University Press, 1961.

Peirce, Charles Sanders. *Collected Papers.* 6 vols., ed. by Charles Hartshorne and Paul Weiss, 2nd. ed. Cambridge, Mass.: Belknap Press of Harvard University Press, 1960– .

Plimpton, George. "The World Series with Marianne Moore: Letter from an October Afternoon." *Harper's,* CCXXIX (Oct., 1964), 50-58.

Porter, David T. *The Art of Emily Dickinson's Poetry.* Cambridge, Mass.: Harvard University Press, 1966. Chapter IV.

Pound, Ezra. *The Letters of Ezra Pound.* Ed. D. D. Paige. New York: Harcourt, Brace, 1950.

———. *Literary Essays of Ezra Pound. Edited with an Introduction by* T. S. Eliot. Norfolk, Conn.: New Directions, 1954.

Richard, Noel. *La Fontaine et les "Fables" du Deuxième Recueil.* Paris: Nizet, 1972.

Rosenberg, Harold. "The Philosophy of Put-Togethers." *The New Yorker* (March 11, 1972), 117.

Sargeant, Winthrop. "Humility, Concentration, and Gusto." *The New Yorker*, XXXII (Feb. 16, 1957), 38-73.

Schulman, Grace Jan. *Marianne Moore: The Poetry of Engagement*. Ph.D. Diss. New York University, 1971.

————, ed. "Conversation with Marianne Moore." *Quarterly Review of Literature*, 16, Nos. 1-2 (1969), 154-171.

Smith, Hallett. "English Metrical Psalms in the sixteenth Century and their Literary Significance." *Huntington Library Quarterly*, IX (May 1946).

Soby, James Thrall. *René Magritte*. Museum of Art, New York: Distributed by Doubleday, Garden City, New York, 1965.

Stieglitz Memorial Portfolio 1864-1946. Ed. Dorothy Norman. New York: Twice a Year Press, 1947.

Tomlinson, Charles, ed. *Marianne Moore: A Collection of Critical Essays*. Englewood Cliffs, N. J.: Prentice-Hall, 1969.

Trachtenberg, Alan. *Brooklyn Bridge, Fact and Symbol*. New York: Oxford University Press, 1965.

Valéry, Paul. "Au Sujet d'Adonis." Introduction to *Adonis Par Jean de La Fontaine*. Paris: Le Florilège Français, publié sur la direction de J.-L. Vaudoyer, 1921.

————. "La Fontaine, in the *Dictionnaire des Lettres Françaises*: *Le Dix-Septième Siècle*. *Paris*: A. Fayard, 1954.

Villa, José Garcia, guest ed. "Marianne Moore Issue." *Quarterly Review of Literature* IV, No. 2 (1948). Essays by William Carlos Williams, Elizabeth Bishop, John Crowe Ransom, Wallace Stevens, Louise Bogan, Vivienne Koch, John L. Sweeney, Wallace Fowlie, Cleanth Brooks, Lloyd Frankenberg, T. C. Wilson, George Dillon.

Wasserstrom, William, ed. *A Dial Miscellany*. Syracuse, N.Y.: Syracuse University Press, 1973.

Welland, D. R. "Half-Rhyme in Wilfred Owen." *Review of English Studies* N.S.I. (1950), 226 ff.

Williams, William Carlos. *Autobiography*. New York: Random House, 1951.

———. *Kora in Hell and Spring and All*. Rpt. in *Imaginations*, ed. with introduction by Webster Schott. New York: New Directions Publishing Corporation, 1970.

———. *I Wanted to Write a Poem*. Reported and edited by Edith Heal. Boston: Beacon Press, 1958.

Winters, Yvor. *In Defense of Reason*. New York: The Swallow Press & W. Marrow and Company, 1947.

Woolf, Virginia. *Granite and Rainbow*. London: Hogarth Press, 1958.

ɩ

INDEXES

I. Works by Marianne Moore

273

II. General Index

LIBRARY OF CONGRESS CATALOGING IN PUBLICATION DATA

Stapleton, Laurence.
  Marianne Moore, the poet's advance.

  Bibliography: p.
  Includes index.
     1. Moore, Marianne, 1887-1972—Criticism and
interpretation.   I. Title.
PS3525.05616Z83   811'.5'2   78-51193
  ISBN 0-691-06373-7